THE GOLDEN YEARS...

The Florida Legislature, '70s and '80s
Reflections on Campaigns and Public Service

by

Florida State Senator Robert W. McKnight

Copyright 2007 by Robert W. McKnight

All rights reserved
Manufactured in the United States of America

Designer: Karen Towson Wells
Editor: Caroline Claiborne
Typeface: Broadway and Palatino Linotype
Printing and binding: Durraprint

Library of Congress Control Number: 2007938632

ISBN 978-1-889574-28-8

Sentry Press
424 East Call Street
Tallahassee, Florida 32301
(850) 224-7423

TABLE OF CONTENTS

Dedication   iv

Acknowledgments   v

Foreword   vii
By the Honorable John Phelps, Former Clerk
   of the Florida House of Representatives

Chapter 1 – The First Campaigns   1
Chapter 2 – Go Seminoles and Uijongbu or Bust…   13
Chapter 3 – Taking on the Incumbent   27
Chapter 4 – Unopposed…Almost   37
Chapter 5 – The Gentleman from the 116th   47
Chapter 6 – "The Plan"   63
Chapter 7 – The Campaign Against Two Senators   83
Chapter 8 – The Junior Senator from the 38th   89
Chapter 9 – The McKnight Commission and the 1986   133
   Gubernatorial Election
Chapter 10 - Reflections on Campaigns and Public Service   155

Appendices   161

Appendix A: Robert W. McKnight Biography   161

Appendix B: Major Legislative Achievements and Selected   163
   Legislation sponsored by Senator McKnight,
   1974-1982

Appendix C: Selected Legislation sponsored by Senator   167
   McKnight, 1974-1982

Appendix D: Members of the Florida House of   211
   Representatives and Senate, 1974-1982

Index   235

DEDICATION

This book is dedicated to my supportive family: Susan, my wife; Michelle, our daughter and her family: Von, her husband, and Riley, Bailey, and Andrew, their children; Bob, our son and his family: Heather, his wife, and Miles and Norah, their children; and my brother Jim. Thank you all for your unfailing help and love.

ACKNOWLEDGMENTS

This is my first attempt at writing a book. I have always enjoyed reading, but now have a far greater appreciation for authors and what goes into helping them create such important vehicles for communication. I have wrestled for a number of years whether to undertake this project, and I guess I was prompted to do so by the admonitions of former Clerk of the Florida House of Representatives John Phelps and former Florida attorney general Bob Butterworth. In his foreword John reminds us of the importance of capturing valuable history from the baby boomers before they are gone. And General Butterworth reminds us all of our obligations to our fellow citizens with the statement, "If not us, then who?"

Let me thank and acknowledge the people who were directly involved with the creation of *The Golden Years*. I start by thanking my publisher and the director of Sentry Press, Dr. William W. Rogers. Bill is an extraordinary academician and has taught me so much about his craft in a relatively short time. A talented and gregarious graphic artist, Karen Towson Wells, ably assisted him. Thank so you much, Bill and Karen.

Other than me, the person who spent more time on this project was my editor, Caroline Claiborne. Caroline has an extensive background in writing and editing, and her sophistication took this writing to the highest level possible. She was willing to tell me no even when I did not want to hear it.

Two more professionals of this industry were invaluable—Dianne Nagle of Lithohaus Printers, Tallahassee, Florida, and Rhett Devane, an accomplished author, also from Tallahassee. Both sat with me for hours to explain the intricate workings of writing a book and gave me numerous suggestions and tips for whatever success we may have with this publication. I am confident you will see their names in one form or another in future outstanding publications.

Lastly, thanks to you, the most important people in this equation. As an old marketing man, I consider you the market, and you are what makes this thing called commerce work. After deliberation, you have decided to purchase this book and for that I thank you so much. I hope that you enjoy reading it as much as I enjoyed writing it.

FOREWORD

Many long-standing observers of Florida politics look upon the 1970s and early 80s as a Golden Age of political and administrative reform. The U.S. Supreme Court ruling that mandated legislative redistricting set the stage for a realignment of legislative power toward urban, more moderate population centers. The cadre of legislators arriving from these newly reapportioned districts sought to modernize Florida Government. What they found in Tallahassee was a Legislative Branch starved of the resources necessary to accomplish that goal and a system that made them dependent upon the Executive Branch and lobbyists for information and policy advice.

In search of more balanced professional advice, the Legislature aggressively pursued the hiring of a staff accountable only to itself. This staff became the eyes and ears of the Legislature; being present in Tallahassee even when the Representatives and Senators were in their home districts. This added capacity allowed the Legislature more effectively to keep track of the performance of executive agencies. More importantly, it enabled the Legislature to produce a General Appropriations Bill based on its own priorities rather than those of the Governor.

About the same time the movement for legislative reform was getting started, a revision of the State Constitution was ratified by the people of Florida. Among other important changes, the revision called for the Legislature to meet in regular session every year rather than biennially as previously provided in the old Constitution. Annual sessions along with professional staff meant that Legislators would now be in Tallahassee virtually year-round and, in so doing, became much more knowledgeable of the day-to-day workings of State Government.

The foundation was now in place for a Legislature that was to play a much more direct role in the governance of Florida. A second generation of reformers reached Tallahassee in 1974, on the heels of the Watergate Scandal. Ethics in government was very much on their minds. Thanks to the efforts of their predecessors, these new legislators had the tools in place to allow the assembly to aggressively pursue its policy objectives. Bob McKnight was to become one of the leaders of this second generation.

Through a chronology of his own experiences and observations, Senator Bob McKnight describes his early years and his introduction to the dynamic world of Florida politics. He candidly writes about learning to be a legislator, including the mistakes he made and successes he enjoyed. The men and women who became his partners in leadership during this period transformed Florida Government, making it more transparent and accountable than at any time in its history.

This book is not an analytical discourse. Those may be found in a variety of scholarly articles and textbooks. Instead it describes the workings of the Legislature from the point of view of an insider, a perspective rarely documented in political literature.

Legislatures are poorly equipped to write their own histories, a problem that term limits has only served to compound. Additionally, political scientists generally have shown little interest in writing about the performance of state lawmaking bodies, perhaps because they are amorphous and their power is distributed so widely and variously depending upon each issue.

It is, therefore, exceedingly important that memoirs such as Senator McKnight's be preserved. The stories legislators tell about their work enriches the record of events in a way that cannot be conveyed in customary publications or in the working media. The human side of political negotiations with all its imperfections, affronts and acts of courage says more about how our democracy works than is revealed in the bare bones of a final lawmaking agreement.

This is the face of legislative public service that Senator McKnight shares with us.

John B. Phelps
Tallahassee, FL
September 2007

CHAPTER 1

The First Campaigns

It was the wrap-up of the Lake Worth, Florida, Student City Council election in 1962. The students from the local high school were invited to assume the role of city council members through an actual election. By most accounts, I should have been the favorite for District 1 because after all, I was an All-Conference End on the varsity football team, was selected as "Best Personality" in the senior class and was selected the Homecoming "Heart Throb." Talk about the lack of qualifications!! When I made my speech, I was very nervous and my presentation was rather flat, but the audience did give me a polite ovation.

I had a feeling that the election would be close because the audience had received my opponent's speech favorably. There is just something about public sentiment and support for the underdog in America. *The lesson here is not new, but still very important—assume nothing and recognize that the unrecognizable is what can hurt you. In other words, be very careful of the underdog or "longshot."*

I won this, my first election, by a margin of about 20 votes. I was sworn into office along with a number of my closest high school friends: Mayor Ben Tallman (my future roommate my freshman year at Florida Southern College); Commissioner Bill O'Connor (my lifelong friend and the quarterback on the varsity football team); Commissioner Sherry Fincher (a wonderful friend then and today); and Commissioner Lanny Fox (again, a lifelong friend and excellent student athlete, who would later earn a law degree at the University of Florida). The issues confronting the newly elected body were not significant, but we did discuss the future of the city and how we could integrate the vitality of the high school students into a rather sleepy retirement community. Perhaps the most important thing I took from this experience, other that the election itself, was the adherence by the Council to Roberts Rules of Order.

I recall other political experiences from that time in Lake Worth. I often talked politics with my boss, Don McCoy, an elected member of the Delray Beach Inlet Board, while working summers as a car washer at McCoy Motors. I had an opportunity to meet and discuss politics with Palm Beach County's premier public servant, the late congressman Paul Rodgers (D., West Palm Beach), after his address at Lake Worth High School. I also recall the engaging public service of Lake Worth mayors Carl Leverentz and Andy Andrews, and Palm Beach county commissioner Lake Lytal. Although they probably do not remember it, their taking the time to have an interest in me, made a positive and lasting impression. All of these elected officials demonstrated another important political lesson: *communicate often with your constituents whether it be in person, or in writing. People appreciate being remembered. Perhaps more important than formal correspondence are handwritten personal notes or phone calls, which are often remembered for a lifetime. The best I ever saw at staying in touch with his constituents was Alabama-born and later U.S. Senator and member of the U.S. House of Representatives Claude Pepper of Miami. The senator always remembered me and my wife, Susan, and something personal about us. To this day, I think it was because he genuinely cared about us.*

One of my teachers in grade school who stood out and provided an early political connection was Mrs. Catherine Lewis. She demonstrated a genuine interest in me and my applying good work habits in school. The political connection was her son, Harold. Harold Lewis was a star football player at Lake Worth High, and earned his law degree at the University of Florida. As will be seen later in this book, I mention having worked with a number of influential lobbyists—well, Harold was one of them. He had a particularly close relationship with Senate presidents W.D. Childers and Dempsey Barron and Governor Lawton Chiles. He and his wife, Susan, have remained good friends of Susan's and mine.

One event I still remember, although it was not political in nature, was the opportunity to meet and have a discussion with Herb Score of the Cleveland Indians. Herb, who was a star baseball player at Lake Worth High, was kind enough to autograph a baseball for me that I still have today. Readers who remember the late '50s and early '60s may recall that Herb was probably the best pitcher in baseball at that time. Many felt he was even better than Sandy Koufax of the Los Angeles Dodgers. Herb's career was cut short when he was hit by a line drive in the face during a game against the New York Yankees. Later, I became friends with his brother-in-law, Carroll Webb, who served in the Florida House of Representatives just before my election. For many years Carroll was the executive director and general counsel of the important Joint Legislative Committee on the Administrative Procedures Act in Tallahassee.

    Although this was early in my political experience, I did have exposure to a real political player during that time. My mother and father had a successful children's clothing business in Lake Worth called Kiddy Fair, and they were active in community affairs. Dad sensed that I might have an interest in politics, so he took the initiative to meet with our state senator Jerry Thomas (D., Riviera Beach) to discuss his suggestions for planning to seek public office. Later, after he set up a meeting with the senator for me, I had an opportunity to research his path to political office. He was from West Palm Beach, and had studied finance at Florida State University, where he served in student government. One of his best friends in student government there was future state representative, senator, and governor Reubin O'Donovan Askew from Pensacola. Jerry served in the Palm Beach County Legislative Delegation with state senator Fred Dickinson (D., West Palm Beach), who, after running for governor unsuccessfully, was appointed by then-Governor Farris Bryant as State Comptroller. Thomas was a young state representative at the time who assembled a group of local businesspeople to open a new bank in Palm Beach County. With the support of financial tycoon John D. McArthur, the Thomas group received a bank charter from Comptroller Dickinson. The bank grew into a holding company known as First Marine Banks, and was ultimately acquired by Barnett Bank and then the Bank of America.

The lesson I learned here was that serving in public office afforded me the opportunity to meet influential people I might otherwise not meet. However, it is important that one be very careful to avoid not only conflicts of interest but even the appearance of such. Do not cross the line of using your office to benefit financially in any way. Today, most governmental bodies allow elected officials to seek legal opinions, along with full disclosure, to avoid the potential conflicts.

In any event, I was very impressed with Senator Thomas, and followed his career (from state representative, senator, and senate president; to Assistant Secretary of the Treasury under President Ford) closely. He was nominated by the Republican Party in 1974 to oppose his old friend Reubin Askew for governor, but lost by a sizable margin of votes. I found myself using the senator's political career as a mentoring experience. Few people are aware that the current Florida Senate seal was created at the direction of Thomas, while he was Senate President in 1970-72. As will be mentioned later, I was particularly proud to be sworn in as a new senator in 1978 with Senator Thomas present with Susan and me on the floor of the Florida Senate.

Although politics were beginning to surface on my "radar screen" in high school, I remained somewhat obsessed with competitive sports—especially football and basketball. After my senior year on the varsity football team, I had hoped to receive inquiries about scholarships. Although I would describe myself as an overachiever in high school football, I did not think I had the natural attributes, like speed and agility, to succeed at the college level. Dick Coffman was my coach, and I believe his confidence in my potential helped spur me on to success that I otherwise would not have achieved. I was told that Princeton University, which had recruited a number of athletes from Palm Beach County schools at that time, had asked for film of my games. However, due to a lifelong phobia of taking standardized tests, which usually resulted in mediocre outcomes, I did not qualify academically for the prestigious Ivy League school.

Around this time, my brother, Jim, who was four years my senior, had returned from a volunteer stint in the Marine Corps, and was attending Florida Southern College (FSC) in Lakeland as a freshman. Our family had a chance to visit him on several occasions, and we were impressed with the school and the campus, which I later found out, boasted the largest collection of Frank Lloyd Wright academic institutional architecture in the world.

I applied for admission to Florida Southern that year and upon my acceptance, I worked hard to convert my intense competitive juices from sports to my studies. I managed to obtain a 3.1 (B+) grade point average during my first semester. Although FSC was a relatively small college (approximately 2,000 students), Greek fraternities and sororities were popular on campus. The college prohibited membership in them in the first semester to encourage freshmen to put good study habits ahead of the social activities of the Greeks. My brother had joined Pi Kappa Alpha fraternity (the "Pikes") and during the second semester I decided to pledge his fraternity. I was told that fraternity membership might result in contacts to further one's political ambitions, and I later found that to be true.

At the end of my first year at FSC, I decided to seek election to student government as vice president of my sophomore class. Although I recall the campaign as rather uneventful (probably due to a combination of my lackluster candidacy and a general apathy on campus toward student politics), I did manage to win this, my second election. Over the summer, I was advised that the person elected president of the class would not be returning to school, so I was elevated to president of the sophomore class. Little did I know then that I would not relinquish the class presidency during my remaining years at Florida Southern.

Although there were relatively few issues confronting student government at that time, the simmering issue of the Vietnam War was emerging into a raging controversy across most college campuses and FSC was no exception. ROTC was a requirement for men during their freshman and sophomore years, and since at that time military service was mandatory (unless excused), I decided to seek a commission in the Army while in college. I began feeling the conflict of my military training while sympathizing with the growing discontent with the United States' position in the war. I can recall my mother, whose judgment I always valued, feeling adamant that our political leaders in Washington were not telling the truth about the war.

It is important to seek the advice of people you respect, even if you disagree with their position. Later in politics, I adopted a policy of always seeking contrarian views on controversial positions. If persuaded that a position other than the one you hold is correct, have the courage to admit it, and adapt to the correct position.

Even though I went on to serve loyally in the military, I acknowledged that my mother was correct on Vietnam.

Politics in 1964 were not just confined to the national scene; Florida was in the middle of an exciting campaign for governor. Since the Republican Party had not yet achieved political parity with the Democrats, most of the campaign activity centered on the candidates in the Democratic Primary. The major candidates were Farris Bryant (D., Ocala); and state senators Jack Matthews (D., Jacksonville), Scott Kelly (D., Lakeland) and Fred Dickinson (D., West Palm Beach). I understood that the pundit consensus was that Senator Matthews was the best qualified to serve as governor, as a result of his outstanding service as President of the Florida Senate.

Even so, Senator Kelly, who came from a relatively small community, ran a very aggressive campaign. I had met him on several occasions, and found him very bright and personable. Since FSC was in Lakeland, the senator sought support among the college students at FSC, including me. Although I was not yet old enough to vote, I volunteered to work in his campaign, and began observing campaigning in "the big leagues." I was given grunt jobs like stuffing envelopes, dropping off campaign literature, and answering the phone. But I also paid very close attention to the campaign strategy sessions of the senator and his staff, when allowed to attend. It was a good experience that only fueled my political juices more. Kelly lost the primary and Farris Bryant went on to serve a two-year term as governor, being replaced in 1966 by

Republican Claude Kirk. Needless to say, Kirk figures prominently later in this book.

As I approached graduation at FSC, I developed close friendships with individuals who would later become part of my future campaign political brain trust—Gary and Lee Gregory from Coral Gables; Larry Boecklen from New Jersey; Don Hall, a future lawyer from North Miami; and Wiley Clayton from Deland (whose father served as a state senator from that area). Others were Tom Jones, a future insurance executive from Homestead, and Fred Lewis from West Virginia, who was an All-American basketball player at FSC. After getting his law degree with honors at the University of Miami, Fred went on to become and is, as of this writing, Chief Justice of the Florida Supreme Court.

As previously indicated, I was committed at that time, notwithstanding my reservations about our country's involvement in Vietnam, to obtaining my commission in the U.S. Army, and fulfilling my two-year military service obligation. At the same time, I felt that I would greatly benefit from an advanced education. I did not have an interest in studying the law or medicine, but believed that I needed to get a Masters of Business Administration degree, since my undergraduate degree was to be in that field. Having made that decision, I decided to continue my education without a break in studies, so I filed for a deferment. I applied to several universities, primarily in the South, and received an early acceptance from the University of Kentucky.

Meanwhile at home, Dad was continuing periodic visits with Senator Thomas, keeping him up-to-date on my activities in college. When I was accepted to the University of Kentucky, Senator Thomas advised him that I would be well served to obtain a degree from a university in the state where I intended to seek political office. I had heard that alumni of major universities formed cliques of sorts to ensure their alma maters benefited from the political (and financial) process in state capitals. Senator Thomas was proud of his education at Florida State and urged Dad to discuss FSU with me. I visited the campus and decided to apply for admission. I received acceptance from FSU's School of

Business shortly before the deferment deadline, and made plans to become a Seminole.

My college experience at Florida Southern proved beneficial. I successfully transferred my energies from athletics to academics and then politics, and I gained the maturing experience of living away from home and my family, in a relatively small school setting. I was fortunate to receive a number of awards from the college and my classmates, including the class presidency for three straight years. I was also president of Omicron Delta Kappa, the national leadership society; *Who's Who in American Colleges and Universities*; *ROTC Distinguished Military Graduate*; membership in Pi Kappa Alpha Social Fraternity and Delta Sigma Pi Business Fraternity; and appointment by the dean of students as a Justice of the college Supreme Court. I guess that it was a bit unusual to be a member of both the legislative and judicial branches of government at the same time. In 1995, I was selected by FSC to receive their Outstanding Alumni Award and served on their Board of Trustees for approximately ten years. The leadership of the college has been in great hands through these years having been led by former Speaker of the Florida House of Representatives, Terrell Sessums (D., Tampa), Presidents Dr. Tom Reuschling, and Dr. Ann Kerr, and Vice President for Development, Dr. Rob Tate. Both Kerr and Tate obtained their PhD degrees at FSU.

While at FSC, I got a telephone call from my mother advising me that during my dad's routine physical, cancer was discovered in his colon. In those years, routine exams for colon cancer were the exception and the most common remedy when cancer was discovered in the colon was radical surgery called a colostomy. That was the rerouting of the colon for bowel discharge purposes through the stomach. Dad had the surgery, and although successful, it was difficult for him to adjust to the change and associated discomfort. It was so hard watching him, a former football and baseball letterman at the University of Texas, appear so weak and handicapped. I tried to improve his spirits with my work at college—I loved him so much, and knew how proud he was of me.

After graduation from FSC and before starting graduate school at FSU, I accepted an invitation to spend the summer with a fraternity brother, Bill Lam, in Elkton, Virginia. Elkton is located in the center of the Shenandoah Valley of Virginia, as picturesque an area as any I had seen in the country. Even with my new college degree, the best summer employment I could secure was as a day laborer on a federal highway construction project in Central Virginia. As an aside, on my trip to Virginia for the summer, I stopped in Tallahassee to introduce myself to the dean of the graduate school of business administration at FSU, Dr. Jack Dobson. As I walked to my appointment with Dr. Dobson, I glanced at a newsstand at the Student Union and noticed a large headline stating that a sniper at the University of Texas, Charles Whitman, had just killed a number of students on that campus. I felt a chill down my back—Charlie Whitman was from Lake Worth, and I had played baseball on his dad's team, Whitman Plumbing. I could not help but recall the many times I played sports with Charlie at South Grade in Lake Worth.

After arriving in Virginia, and having some idle time, I reverted to my interest in politics. I read, and nearly memorized the political section of the *Washington Post* each day, upon return from work. That year, 1966, was a major election year in Virginia as their longtime senator A. Willis Robertson (a fraternity brother, I discovered) faced a strong challenge from a respected lawyer, William Spong. Although I did not know it at the time, Senator Robertson's son was none other than TV evangelist Pat Robertson, who went on to run for president. I did not get involved in the campaign, but paid close attention to how Spong successfully unseated the veteran incumbent. I also had an opportunity to visit the U.S. Capitol as a guest of Virginia's senior senator, Harry Byrd, Jr. After that visit, watching the debates on the floor of the Senate, I knew that I wanted to serve in public office. I was determined to achieve that goal, and vowed to pursue it with the same determination that I had developed in high school. With four successful elections under my belt, I felt it was time to begin planning a possible legislative campaign for public service.

Bob McKnight, 7th grade, 1957.

Herb Score, Cleveland Indians, 1957.

Bob McKnight, varsity football and basketball player at Lake Worth High School, 1961-62.

The Golden Years ...   10   *Robert McKnight*

Late Senate President, Jerry Thomas (R., Riviera Beach).

McKnight family (left to right) Bob, Jim, Gwendolyn, Joel, 1956.

The Golden Years ...   11   *Robert McKnight*

Letter from Senator Thomas to McKnight, 1972.

CHAPTER 2

Go Seminoles and Uijongbu or Bust...

The academic atmosphere of graduate school at FSU differed sharply from that of undergraduate studies at FSC. While at Florida Southern, I had time for extracurricular activities, including fraternity functions. That was not the case at Florida State. The competition in the classroom was greater, made more so because a number of my classmates were mature Air Force officers on leave to obtain their MBA's. Although my emerging interest in politics waned somewhat due to my academic studies, I followed with interest student politics at FSU. Three of the student leaders later became prominent lobbyists in Tallahassee, and close friends of Susan's and mine—Gene Stearns, past president of the student body and future assistant to Florida Speaker of the House of Representatives, Dick Pettigrew (D., Miami); Larry Gonzalez, president of the student body and a future attorney; and Steve Winn, attorney general and son of one of my favorite colleagues, Senator Sherman Winn (D., North Miami).

One of the most meaningful political experiences while at FSU was the opportunity I had to meet with Republican governor Claude Kirk in his office in Tallahassee. First, a little background: while at FSU, I had sought job interviews even though I had my two-year military service pending after my graduation from FSC. I figured if a company would give me a job offer after graduation and agree to rehire me upon return from my military service, they must really want me. To my surprise, I received company-paid site visits and job offers from IBM, Shell Chemical, and Westinghouse Corporations. I chose IBM because of its renowned sales training program, and planned to start work with them after graduation at their Federal Systems Division (working on the computers used in the U.S. space program) in Huntsville, Alabama.

At that time, a Greek freighter, the *Amaryllis*, encountered inclement weather in the Atlantic Ocean off the Florida coast and was forced to beach itself on the pristine beach at Singer Island in Palm Beach County. That is where my parents had moved after retiring from their children's store business in Lake Worth. The beached freighter was a novelty at first to the residents there but quickly became a nuisance due to the alleged drug activity and crime associated with the freighter. The residents were helpless to do anything, especially since they did not speak the language of the Greek sailors. It was apparent to me that someone with political clout was needed to step into the situation—enter from the right, Claude Kirk.

Governor Kirk had recently won an upset election over Miami mayor Robert King High, and quickly fashioned himself as an "action" chief executive for the state. I thought that I would try to take advantage of his self-proclaimed reputation and called the governor's office for an appointment. When asked by his office assistant of my employment, I said I was with IBM, which I guess was true since I had accepted their job offer. You need to know that IBM was particularly important to the governor's office at that time because they had just recently agreed to a major plant location of research scientists in Boca Raton, and basically anything they wanted, they got from the state (like Disney in Orlando, a few years before). Well, no surprise, his assistant said, "The governor will be glad to meet with you, Mr. McKnight." Needless to say, my parents and their fellow residents on Singer Island were quite impressed.

I arrived at the governor's office in my best business suit, but probably not of IBM quality, and was told that I would first meet with his environmental assistant, Nat Reed. Nat was a resident of Hobe Sound, just north of Singer Island, and was familiar with the *Amaryllis* situation. He was from a wealthy family and had agreed to join the Kirk administration for pay of $1 per year. Of course, he was expecting a corporate big shot from IBM, but after introductions and pleasantries, I managed to hold my own with him because I had done my research on the issue.

The lesson here is that there is no such thing as too much research in pursuing a political issue. It is also very important to thoroughly understand your opponent's position. Always understand the pros and cons of the issue and leave some room for your opponent to maneuver if you are winning the issue. Former attorney general Robert Kennedy wrote a great book about counseling President John F. Kennedy during negotiations with the Russians during the Cuban Missile Crisis in the early 60s. The attorney general emphasized the need to craft a "face-saving" position for your opponent in negotiations. The basis for that design is research, research, and more research.

After about a half an hour with Nat, an assistant interrupted us to say that the governor would meet with us. Governor Kirk was taller than I expected, although shorter than me (I am 6'2"). Like Reed, he appeared surprised that this "IBM executive," was just a college kid. Reed began by briefing Governor Kirk on the status of the ship and the governor responded by saying, "Let's get it out of there." Just as billed—an action guy who takes no hostages (he would say they cost too much to feed). Although I had forgotten it at the time, the governor pointed out that he had a personal residence in Palm Beach, which he called the "Duck's Nest," and planned to be there over the weekend. Reed recommended that the governor visit the *Amaryllis* site while there, and commented that I might want to join him. He gave me Kirk's personal telephone line at the residence and told me to call over the weekend to coordinate the visit. I assumed that the visit would be structured as a big media play since the governor was not shy about seeking publicity. He later sought the vice presidency under Governor Nelson Rockefeller (R., New York) who considered running for the Republican nomination for president in 1968, so Kirk was accustomed to press angles and eye-catching photos. The picture of the governor snorkeling around the ship appeared in all of the major print publications across the country the following week.

After leaving the governor's office, I called my parents to brief them, and then made plans for the ten-hour drive down to Singer Island from Tallahassee. As it turned out, the governor jumped the gun and visited the ship a day early, avoiding any unexpected questions from the residents of the island. Shortly after his visit, state and federal officials joined the ship's owner to announce that barges would finally remove the eyesore. The governor certainly scored points on that one.

Speaking of Governor Kirk, I have been with him a number of times over the years. First, while in his office regarding the *Amaryllis* issue, he volunteered to me that he was about to leave on his jet for Jacksonville to confront racial militant H. Rap Brown. Brown was expected to address a potentially tense situation in Jacksonville's inner city. The governor's visit caught Brown by surprise, and Kirk scored points again with the public. One of my colleagues in the Florida House of Representatives was his son-in-law, now Congressman Ander Crenshaw (R., Jacksonville). Ander and his terrific wife, Kitty, became very good friends of Susan's and mine, and we enjoyed boating together off of Elliott Key in Miami, often talking about the governor. Also, while later campaigning for the state senate in 1978, I sat next to Governor Kirk at the Miami Springs Villas while he was campaigning for the U.S. Senate. I was surprised that he remembered my meeting with him to discuss the *Amaryllis* years before. Claude Kirk had his faults I guess, but he certainly was a memorable chief executive for Florida.

Other elected officials I met while in graduate school at FSU were legislators attending the annual session of the legislature including senators Ralph Clayton (R., Deland), Elmer Friday (D., Fort Myers) and Lee Weissenborn (D., Miami). Weissenborn caught the attention of North Florida politicos (known as "Pork Choppers", described later) by suggesting that the state capital be moved to Orlando, as a more central location for Florida's citizens. North Florida businesses quickly responded to that threat by successfully obtaining funds to build a new Capitol in Tallahassee. A supporter of Senator Weissenborn's effort, Senator Ken Plante (R., Oviedo), placed a bronze marker on the first floor of the new 22-story Capitol honoring Senator Weissenborn for being the impetus for its construction. It has been said that Weissenborn has been seen trying to remove the plaque.

The lesson here is to have a sense of humor in politics. As Senator Louis de la Parte (D., Tampa) once declared on the floor of the senate, while being slaughtered in debate by the Dean of the Senate, Dempsey Barron (D., Panama City), "Curse You Red Barron." That quip resulted in the debate reverting to civil discourse and served both senators with honor. Perhaps the legislator with the best sense of humor during my service in the legislature was Senator Warren Henderson (R., Venice). Injecting humor into acrimonious debates can be difficult, but my experience was that it could pay big dividends in the long run.

After my initial adjustment to graduate school, I began to achieve excellent grades, and was elected into the scholarship honorary, Beta Gamma Sigma. I was also selected for a graduate assistantship to work on a new managerial textbook, written by FSU associate professors Dan Voich and Daniel Wren. I was now almost 24 years old, and, upon graduation, was going to step out into the real world of corporate business with the IBM Corporation.

Shortly after arriving in Huntsville to start work with IBM, I received orders to report for active duty in the U.S. Army in nine months. Since I was a *ROTC Distinguished Military Graduate*, I was given the military location of my choice for my first assignment. My parents had first met in New York City and since I had always heard exciting stories about the Big Apple, I decided to request that location of my first tour of service (never thinking there was a U.S. Army post in the city or its boroughs). As it turned out, I was posted outside New York City, at the U.S. Army Chaplain School at Fort Hamilton in Brooklyn. Another irony perhaps, was that my commanding officer, Colonel and Reverend James Harvester, was a graduate of Florida Southern.

My stay in Huntsville was obviously brief, and other than following the history and experiences of Alabama's senior senator, John Sparkman, most of my political experiences were put on hold. Still, I will say that upon researching Senator Sparkman's career, I began to understand the growing political clout of members of Congress from the South as a result of their seniority: Senators Sparkman, Richard Russell, Russell Long, Spessard Holland, Harry Byrd of Virginia, Robert Byrd of West Virginia, Strom Thurmond, Lyndon Johnson, Sam Ervin and Albert Gore. In the House of Representatives were Wilbur Mills, Bob Sykes, Mendall Rivers, Dante Fascell, Claude Pepper, and Sam Rayborn, among others. When the Civil Rights Act passed in 1964 with the push of southern President Johnson, these southern congressmen learned very quickly to move to the center of the political spectrum to embrace the millions of new African American voters. Most did so successfully.

One of the saddest days of my life was the day after Christmas in 1967. Dad's cancer had resurfaced and he was hospitalized for yet more surgery. While at the hospital I heard my dad say to Mom that they were proud of their two sons and felt they had done everything they could to prepare us for a productive life. Dad passed away later that day at the age of 67. It struck me that he would not be present to enjoy my political experiences, my marriage or my children. *The lesson here is to live every day as if it is your last, as it could be. I went on to a successful political and business career and have had a blessed family life. I know my dad would be proud.*

Back to my Army experience. At Fort Hamilton, my official assignment was as Personnel Officer at the Chaplain School, but I had additional duties such as escorting VIP guests around New York when they were visiting the post. With the Vietnam War in high gear, the Pentagon had an exchange program with South Vietnam, bringing their chaplains into the U.S. Chaplain school for training. Shortly after arriving in New York, I was asked to escort a dozen Vietnamese army chaplains around Fort Hamilton, New York City, West Point, and Philadelphia. Since this was my first exposure to most of those locations, I had to bone up quickly on their significance. As I previously mentioned, I am 6'2" tall and most of the visitors were barely 5' tall. It was almost comical to see me leading our guests on this tour, especially with the language barrier. We got to West Point the day Army played Columbia in football, and it was a real challenge to explain to our Vietnamese guests the single wing offense of Army Coach Red Blaik. They understandably became homesick, but I did become friends with them, and I remain in correspondence with some of them today.

The year was 1968, and Vietnam protests were everywhere, certainly including New York City. I was committed to completing my military service with honor, but it was hard when I read of Lt. William Calley at My Lai and other alleged atrocities of the war. I was now old enough to vote and I was determined to vote for Senator Eugene McCarthy (D., Minnesota) for president. My friends said it was a wasted vote, and I guess they may have been right, but I could not bring myself to vote for a proponent of the war. Out of the blue, I decided to ask for a meeting with former vice president Richard Nixon, who was running for the Republican nomination for president, and who lived on Central Park in Manhattan at the time. He had said he had a secret solution to bring the war to a peaceful conclusion, and as a good American, I wanted to know the solution. As I approached his building, the secret service quickly addressed me and interrogated me for about an hour. I was told Nixon was out of town, and I guess that my personal information was put under heavy scrutiny for the next few years.

As I was nearing completion of my first year of military service at Fort Hamilton, I received orders for my second and final year of service—to Uijongbu, South Korea. An explanation would be of help here. Many Americans (and others) saw the heralded Tom Hank's movie, *Saving Private Ryan*. It was based on the Pentagon policy that if a widow or widower had a child serving in a combat zone, no remaining children could be assigned to one. My brother, after getting his degree at Florida Southern, was commissioned in the Marine Corps and volunteered for his second tour of duty in Vietnam. Accordingly, I could not be sent to Vietnam, so I was sent to Korea, supposedly a non-combat assignment.

Coming from Florida, I was exposed to a different kind of winter weather. I finally knew what subzero temperatures felt like, being only a few miles from the potentially volatile demilitarized zone (DMZ), *the 38th parallel*. I remember, as a kid in the '50s seeing pictures of the Korean War being fought in the dead of winter and now I studied the history of that war in light of my location in that country. For *M*A*S*H* television and movie fans, the setting of the series was I Corps Headquarters at Camp Red Cloud in Uijongbu, about an hour north of Seoul. That was my post, and I was responsible for all U.S. officer assignments in South Korea. Due to officer vacancies in Vietnam, I, as a first lieutenant, reported to a three star general, Patrick Cassidy. I made many helicopter trips near the demilitarized zone (DMZ), receiving attack fire periodically.

    At about the time of my arrival in that country, in late 1968, the North Koreans off the coast of South Korea successfully attacked a U.S. battleship, the *Pueblo*, and the U.S. crew was taken hostage. The provocation put America on war alert. The commander of the vessel, Lloyd Bucher, was tortured as were members of his crew. Since I was an officer, I was exposed to the top-secret intelligence at the time, and I was aware of how serious the situation had become. It was the scariest time of my life.

    I guess the Pentagon never heard of the *Pueblo* and the 38,000 American troops on war alert over there. Fortunately, American negotiators were able to secure the release of Commander Bucher and his men after almost two years in captivity.

    One interesting individual I met while at Camp Red Cloud was Colonel Arthur "Bull" Simons, the Corp's chief of staff. As the name implies, Colonel Simons was one tough hombre and all of us who worked with him remembered it. Later, in the spring of 1970, he was assigned by no less than President Nixon to lead a clandestine group to attempt to rescue 450 known American prisoners of war (POWs) in North Vietnam and another 970 American servicemen who were missing in action. The mission was known as the "Son Tay Raid," and for his service on it, the colonel earned the nation's second highest military award, the *Distinguished Service Cross*. Even after his retirement, Bull Simons was not finished serving his country. In 1979 businessman and former candidate for president of the United States Ross Perot hired Simons to plan and conduct a rescue operation to free two of

Perot's employees taken hostage by the Iranian government. He not only succeeded in freeing the two employees, but also freed *11,000 Iranian prisoners.* A book and NBC-TV miniseries, *On Wings of Eagles* were produced on their escape. The Bull was then and always will be the prototype military fighter to me.

One perk offered by IBM to its employees in military service was a free subscription to the local newspaper of his or her choice. Although I was from Lake Worth in Palm Beach County and our daily newspaper was the *Palm Beach Post*, I selected the *Miami Herald* because of the breadth of its coverage. For the entire year in Korea, I read from cover to cover each issue of the paper, and became intimately familiar with the Dade County political scene. Larry King, of *CNN* fame, had a popular local radio program on *WIOD* at that time and a regular political column in the *Miami Herald* that I nearly memorized. In 1969, former vice president Humphrey visited Camp Red Cloud for a briefing on the situation in Korea. I had the privilege of attending the briefing, and wondered to myself if I hadn't made a mistake by not voting for him for president in 1968. He struck me as a good American, and he would later be successful in winning back his seat in the United States Senate.

During the heavy winters, I sequestered myself in my hooch (billet) and read as many political books as possible—one I particularly enjoyed was *The Senator*, by Drew Pearson, a controversial but informed journalist. Although fictional, it provided great insight into the inner workings of the world's most exclusive club. In my idle time, I thought about what my campaign theme might be if I were to run for office upon my return to Florida. I knew from reading the *Herald*, that there was almost universal disdain for the Vietnam War, but support for the individual soldiers and their sacrifices. I decided to frame a theme of supporting employment for the veterans. Upon my return, it was obvious that others felt the same way.

To gain further exposure to that part of the world, I took my Rest and Recuperation (R&R) in Tokyo, Hong Kong, Taiwan, Thailand, and Cambodia. Visiting Cambodia and particularly the ancient ruins of Angor Watt was a rare opportunity because America was bombing parts of the country to stave off the Viet Cong using it for a safe haven. My new experiences while overseas in the service included visiting Mount Fuji, the tallest mountain in Japan; shopping among the floating markets in Thailand; being a pedestrian among millions of residents in Hong Kong; and eating kimchi as a house guest in Korea. You will see a picture of me in Korea in this book, with Sergeant Kim of the Republic of Korea army. Kim-shi (the proper way to address a friend in Korean) went on to earn his Ph.D. degree at UCLA and is a distinguished professor in the United States today. My R&R served as a great education about the countries and culture of Southeast Asia.

As I was wrapping up my tour in Korea, General Cassidy told me that I would receive the *Army Commendation Medal* for my service over there. I was honored to receive the ARCOM since it was unusual to be awarded to a non-career officer.

From my reading of the *Miami Herald*, I knew that the upcoming governor's election in Florida was going to be extraordinary. Incumbent governor Kirk had drawn multiple Democrat opponents as well as a prominent Republican opponent, drugstore magnate Jack Eckerd. I did not know where I would be assigned by IBM upon my return to the U.S., but I hoped it would be somewhere in Florida so I could get involved in the campaign.

I can recall today sitting on the tarmac at Kimpo Airport in Seoul awaiting my departure for the United States. A stewardess approached me and asked if I was Lieutenant McKnight. I told her I was and accepted a package from her. In the package were orders for me to be reassigned from America to Vietnam. It was a joke, albeit a sick one, by my dear friend and fellow officer Russ Maxwell, who handled Vietnam assignments from Korea. Russ had a great sense of humor, and I will always be appreciative that he was in my wedding party. I still remember the thunderous applause of all 200 of us on the U.S. government air transport when its wheels touched the ground on the good old US of A runway in Washington State in 1970.

Sergeant Kim and Lieutenant McKnight, Uijongbu, Korea, 1969.

U.S. Army Commendation Medal awarded to Lieutenant McKnight for service in Korea, 1970.

Colonel Arthur D. "Bull" Simons

Colonel Arthur D. "Bull" Simons, answers questions about the Son Tay POW Rescue Raid from the Pentagon Press Corps. Also in the picture are (left to right): Melvin R. Laird, Secretary of Defense; Admiral Thomas H. Moorer, Chairman of the Joint Chiefs of Staff; and Air Force Brigadier General Leroy J. Manor, who commanded the overall operation.

Colonel Arthur D. "Bull" Simons, 1970.

Florida Governor, Claude Kirk (R.), 1966-70.

First Lieutenant Robert W. McKnight at Fort Hamilton, Brooklyn, New York, 1968-69.

Bob and Susan McKnight wedding: (left to right) Elizabeth and Herb Williams, Susan and Bob McKnight, Gwendolyn and Jim McKnight, Huntsville, Alabama, 1970.

CHAPTER 3

Taking on the Incumbent

Upon my arrival back in the States, IBM notified me that I was to report back to Huntsville to resume my career with the company. However, since my dad's passing my mother had suffered from several illnesses and was at the time particularly despondent with my brother being in Vietnam and me having been recently in Korea. Luckily for me, IBM had a great reputation for being employee sensitive and they offered to reassign me temporarily to their Boca Raton facility so that I could be closer to her.

Before leaving for Florida however, I met the person who would become the most important individual in my life, Susan Williams. Susan was a bright, striking woman who had recently graduated with a degree in home economics from Auburn University. She was originally from Huntsville, and had returned home to work with the Head Start Program. We lived in the same apartment complex and I managed to get what was almost a blind date with her, since we had barely met. She later told her mother that after that date, she knew she was going to marry me—can't help but question her judgment! We spent many hours discussing wide-ranging issues from the war to religion, to our families, and our hopes and aspirations. The more I was with Susan, the more I knew I could never leave her. The clincher was the sage input from my primary counselor, Mom. She loved Susan. We were married at the Mayfair Church of Christ in Huntsville on October 3, 1970.

My temporary assignment with IBM in Boca Raton turned out to be a permanent reassignment to Miami within their sales operation. After completing their acclaimed sales training program in Dallas, I looked forward to my new sales career with the company. All of this was marred by my second great loss—Mom died of a heart attack. Unlike my dad, Mom did get to see me marry, but she never knew my children nor really enjoyed the fruits of my career. I continue to miss them both.

Florida's 1970 election was in full swing, with most of the attention directed to the Democratic primary for governor. The favorite was Attorney General Earl Faircloth. A little known state senator from Pensacola, Reubin Askew, also announced his candidacy. He became a serious contender when he convinced Secretary of State Tom Adams to run with him as lieutenant governor. Adams actually had a much more experienced campaign staff than did Askew, and the names of Jim Apthorp, Jim Smith, Jim Krog, and Guy Spearman became legendary in the halls of the state Capitol for the next 35 years. I had the pleasure of working with each of them, and I am still grateful for their support. As previously indicated, incumbent governor Kirk faced a serious threat from Jack Eckerd in the Republican primary, but Kirk eked out a victory. After beating Faircloth in a run-off, Senator Askew went on to defeat Governor Kirk in the general election by a wide margin. So, in 1970, Florida had a new but untested governor. At the same time, another unknown state senator, Lawton Chiles, decided to walk the state to "meet the people," in his campaign for the U.S. Senate. The result: Walking Lawton became Florida's new junior United States senator. Those were good days to be a Democrat.

My first sales manager at IBM was Bob Ryalls, who was also a member of Miami's Young Democrats. When I mentioned to him my interest in politics, he suggested I meet with his good friend in YD's, Miami city commissioner Arden Siegendorff. The commissioner and I had a good discussion over lunch, and he suggested I consider hiring a political consultant, if I planned to seek office myself. He recommended Steve Fisher or Ron Levitt. He also mentioned Steve Ross, Bob Hurwitz, George DePontis, Stu Rose and Dick Troxel. I met with Levitt and decided to retain him to explore a race for the state legislature in 1972. Almost concurrently, IBM changed its corporate policy prohibiting its employees from seeking public office. The first IBMer to seek office successfully was U.S. Senator Don Reigle (D., Michigan). I discussed my possible candidacy with our branch manager in Miami, Vern Bue, and he approved provided it did not conflict with my company responsibilities. In 1971 my interests ran on parallel tracks—generating IBM sales and community involvement that would position me to run for the legislature. I exceeded my sales expectations by being selected to the IBM 100% Club and *Rookie of the Year* in the Eastern United States. In the community, I participated in the popular Jaycee "Speak Up" program, which was excellent training for campaign speaking. I also began to meet the movers and shakers in Miami through my involvement with the Mental Health Association and the Young Democrats.

The Dade Delegation was the state's largest, with eight senators and twenty-two house members. Under Florida's constitution, the members served in multi-member districts, which included three senators and five house members in my South Dade County district. I studied carefully the background, history and voting records of all of the incumbents and made a trip to Tallahassee with Levitt to conduct some research at the Capitol. If I were to run, it would obviously be best to run for an open seat, without an incumbent. This was especially true since I was so new to Miami. Yet, Miami was one of the few areas in the state where a newcomer could win election because of the rapid migration in and out of the community. Also, an open seat would certainly draw a number of challengers, where running against an incumbent might be a more direct head to head campaign.

In early 1972 I announced my candidacy for the Democratic nomination for state representative in District 119. The incumbent was Jeff D. Gautier (D., Miami), a member of a pioneer Miami family and an acknowledged expert on parliamentary procedure in the House of Representatives. Although Jeff was an attorney, he did not have an active practice. Many observers and some supporters thought I had lost my mind challenging such a well-known Miami name, but I had uncovered some startling information in my research into Jeff's business dealings. He and some associates had been charged by the state with dredging waterways in the Florida Keys without a permit. Frankly, I had hoped that since he had served in the House since 1966 that he might not seek reelection, but he did elect to run. My only strategy, by virtue of the circumstances I was dealt, was to take him on over the dredging issue. The strategy would be very controversial, and could backfire on me if he found an issue on which to challenge me.

  We began the long hard campaign of meetings, coffees, interviews, door-to-door canvassing, phone banks, direct mailing, and the all-important fund raising. I found out quickly that running against an incumbent with substantial name recognition made it that much harder. The initial endorsements began circulating and to my surprise they were favorable toward our campaign. I knew Jeff did not enjoy an overly positive reputation, but I found he had a number of constituents that did not like him at all for a number of reasons. To be sure, it was still an uphill battle.

  Perhaps the low point of that and maybe any campaign of mine was when we invited the distinguished rules chairman of the Florida House of Representatives, Murray Dubbin (D., Miami), to join us at a coffee being held in our honor in Kendale Lakes. Murray had served with Jeff and faced a tough reelection himself, but I guess he felt it could not hurt to simply stop by our event. A number of our supporters were present and we invited representatives of the local press to attend. As the time for the event to start approached, Representative Dubbin drove up to the house with his campaign aide. I began getting nervous that we might have a low turnout. An hour later it was a disaster—almost no one attended. One of our campaigner supporters present quipped, "I've seen more people on a motorcycle." I was embarrassed and apologized to Representative Dubbin.

  The lesson here is to plan every detail, and include a contingency plan. In this case we not only should have confirmed the attendees, but provided rides for them to the event as well. Some candidates even rely on "Rent a Supporter" to give their event every appearance of success. Also, I recommend never scheduling a function in a location that looks empty—if necessary move the function to a smaller location so it has the appearance of "SRO"—Standing Room Only.

Probably my best hope to win the election would be if the race were just between Gautier and me. Even that possibility went against me—community activist and gadfly Clark Merrill joined the race at the last minute. He had surprising name recognition in District 119, so, by most accounts, I fell to third place in the race. That did not help our fund-raising. Susan and I had decided that if it became necessary, we would draw from our savings to make the race competitive. It became necessary.

You can meet wonderful people during a political campaign and it was certainly true in our case. Five individuals quickly come to mind. Mike Sheridan was an insurance salesman active in the pro-environment movement. He was very impressed with our campaign against Gautier and made the first financial contribution to our race. Labor unions had varying degrees of influence in elections, and in my district the most influential was the teacher's union, headed by the fiery Pat Tornillo. Although Pat did not know me then, he was strongly opposed to Gautier's reelection and the United Teachers of Dade became my first organizational endorsement. Tom Gallagher was one of the few Republican candidates running for a House seat in our area, and we went on to sit side by side on the floor of the House of Representatives from 1974-1978. I personally believe Tom persuaded a number of his Republican colleagues not to run against me even though we had different voting records in the legislature. Mike, Pat, Tom and I have maintained our close friendship over all of these years. Unfortunately Pat passed away in 2007. Janet Reno was also running for the House of Representatives in a different district at that time and she later served eight years as U.S. Attorney General in the Clinton Administration. Susan and I became very good friends with her during that 1972 campaign. The fifth special person I met in the 1972 race was Charlie Papy, a successful attorney in Coral Gables and a fraternity brother. He was also running against an incumbent and we often ran into each other at campaign events. He was successful in his first race with a catchy campaign slogan, "Put Your Papy in the House."

The granddaddy of all endorsements for legislative candidates at that time was the *Miami Herald*. The editorial board of the *Herald* conducted an in-depth interview with me, and luckily for me, my research on the issues made a big difference to the campaign. I recall getting a telephone call from the Bahamas in the middle of the night from my campaign chairman, Gary Gregory, telling me that he had just seen an early edition of the *Herald* with its endorsements for the 1972 legislative races. The *Herald* was endorsing a newcomer—Bob McKnight for District 119 in the Florida House of Representatives. The next day our phone rang off the hook. All of a sudden, we went from dead last to a dead heat against a well-known incumbent legislator.

One tactical mistake we made in that campaign was to concentrate on the incorporated areas of my district. Although there were few, they were most visible because they had their own media outlets and newspapers. What I did not appreciate until after I saw the primary voting results was that a great majority of the voters in District 119 lived in the unincorporated areas. The best way to reach those individuals was by direct contact or mail, which we tried exhaustively to do. We did not have enough money to buy TV advertising. Gautier gambled that he would at least be in a run-off, and smartly, held his financial war chest for a run-off, if one occurred.

On Election Day, we sweated out the results. We had been going a mile a minute every day for over a year and then all of a sudden we had nothing to do but wait. The results were announced election night on the Miami television stations—there would be a run-off between incumbent Jeff D. Gautier and newcomer Bob McKnight in South Dade District 119. Gautier held a small lead, but if I could get Merrill's endorsement and the majority of his votes, I could win, albeit by a small number of votes. In the run-off Gautier unleashed his pent-up campaign war chest, and I struggled to even get an ad in the weekend issues of the *Miami Herald* and the *Miami News*. I met with Merrill and got his endorsement, so I had false hope that we might just pull that first election off. Gautier fought back hard, and, to my knowledge, fairly. I found individuals previously committed to me withdrawing their support and canceling our campaign functions. It was a grueling life experience for a 28-year-old. Susan was a trooper and a great campaigner during that time—her southern charm, personality, and good looks were magic ingredients during our campaign.

With Election Day came another unexpected surprise—rain. Run-off elections generally have low turnouts and bad weather reduces the turnout even further. Levitt told me that low turnouts almost always favored the incumbent. *The lesson here is get out your vote. Analyze where you got your votes in the primary and unleash all of your resources to get out those votes. Best of all, if you canvass those votes door to door or by phone, your opponent will never know. This is how many of the major upsets in political campaigns occur. It was a painful and expensive lesson for the McKnight campaign to learn in 1972. The old cliché "experience may not be the best, but it is the surest teacher" turned out to be true.*

Gautier won the run-off by less than 1,000 votes. Although his Republican opponent was not a serious threat, the Democratic Party asked me to endorse Gautier. It was hard for our supporters to understand, and difficult for me to do, but I did endorse Jeff and he easily won reelection to District 119 in Florida House of Representatives. I had a lot to think about over the next two years.

McKnight Campaign Brochure, 1972.

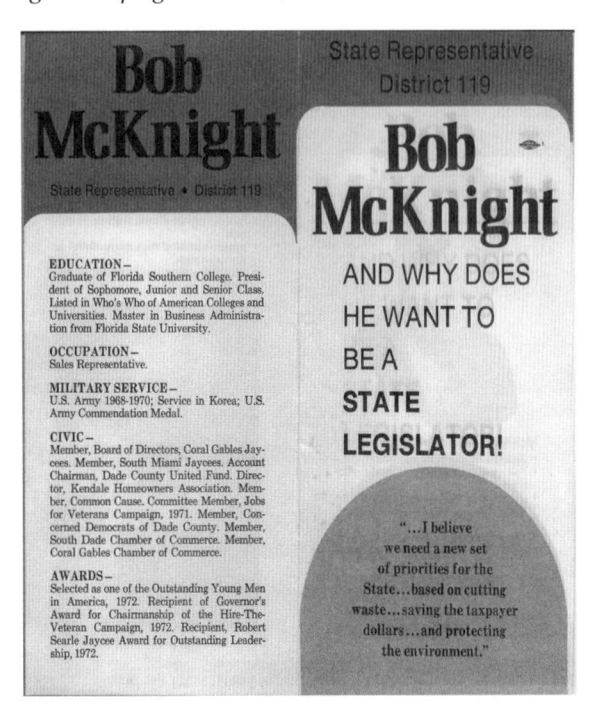

Bob McKnight
State Representative • District 119

EDUCATION –
Graduate of Florida Southern College. President of Sophomore, Junior and Senior Class. Listed in Who's Who of American Colleges and Universities. Master in Business Administration from Florida State University.

OCCUPATION –
Sales Representative.

MILITARY SERVICE –
U.S. Army 1968-1970; Service in Korea; U.S. Army Commendation Medal.

CIVIC –
Member, Board of Directors, Coral Gables Jaycees. Member, South Miami Jaycees. Account Chairman, Dade County United Fund. Director, Kendale Homeowners Association. Member, Common Cause. Committee Member, Jobs for Veterans Campaign, 1971. Member, Concerned Democrats of Dade County. Member, South Dade Chamber of Commerce. Member, Coral Gables Chamber of Commerce.

AWARDS –
Selected as one of the Outstanding Young Men in America, 1972. Recipient of Governor's Award for Chairmanship of the Hire-The-Veteran Campaign, 1972. Recipient, Robert Searle Jaycee Award for Outstanding Leadership, 1972.

State Representative District 119
Bob McKnight

AND WHY DOES HE WANT TO BE A STATE LEGISLATOR!

"...I believe we need a new set of priorities for the State...based on cutting waste...saving the taxpayer dollars...and protecting the environment."

Bob McKnight
State Representative • District 119 • Democrat

- Elimination of the sales tax on federal excise tax for tires.
- Require per unit labeling in food markets.
- Increase pay for Florida Highway Patrolmen.
- Implementation of mass transportation in populated areas.
- Establish safety standards for mobile homes.

McKNIGHT Stands For
- Reducing the size of the legislature.
- Full income disclosure for public office holders.
- Greater utilization of school plants by a 12-month school session.
- Stronger conflict of interest legislation.
- Reform of the Public Service Commission.
- Higher standards for repair of automobiles.
- More stringent controls on land and dredging to protect the environment.
- Reduction of requirements for qualified non-citizens to practice their profession.
- Realignment of the legislature calendar to work on appropriations and general legislation in alternate years.

Bob McKnight and his wife Susan

"...I believe we need a new set of priorities for the State..."

The Golden Years ...   *Robert McKnight*

McKnight campaign bumper sticker, 1972.

Campaign brochure for State Representative Jeff D. Gautier, 1972.

The Golden Years ...   35   *Robert McKnight*

Campaign endorsements for Robert W. McKnight, State House District 119, 1972.

CHAPTER 4

Unopposed...Almost

I returned to work at IBM after the election, but found it difficult to get my head back into my work. I found myself reviewing almost every element of the campaign, spending most of my time dissecting the many mistakes we had made. My colleagues at IBM understood, but my sales performance was beginning to suffer from my lack of energy and concentration. One important acquaintance I made during the campaign was former Florida Speaker of the House of Representatives, Dick Pettigrew (D., Miami). Dick was planning to run for the U.S. Senate in 1974, and decided to run for the state senate to show he could continue to win important elections. He defeated the Senate President-Designate George Hollahan (D., Miami) in a major upset. Dick had provided some excellent counsel for me during the campaign, and after the election introduced me to two young real estate executives, Seth Werner, Alan Levan, and Dick Wollack, who were starting a publicly traded real estate limited partnership program. After a period of time, I was invited to join them as director of marketing for their first real estate offering. Susan was pregnant at the time, and Seth and Dick allowed her to join me on my many sales calls around the country. Although I was new to the real estate industry, Seth and Dick mentored me, and I obtained my real estate brokers and securities license for selling limited partnership investments. We were successful, raising over $21 million in equity capital and purchasing approximately $100 million in existing improved real estate around the country.

On the political front, I continued to seek the counsel of Senator Thomas, as I had done in the '72 campaign. I was convinced that if I were to run again in 1974, I had to have a grassroots, precinct-by-precinct organization. I continued my activities in the Jaycees and the Mental Health Association, and was asked to join Ron Lieberman as his running mate on the Dade County Young Democrat ticket. We won without opposition.

Representative Randy Avon (R., Ft. Lauderdale), a past president of the Florida Jaycees, was elected to the legislature in 1972, and assisted me in moving up the political ladder in the Jaycees. Although I had not made up my mind to run, I tried to broaden my base by meeting with people who had not previously supported me.

As indicated earlier, Senator Pettigrew was expected to announce his candidacy for the democratic nomination for the U.S. Senate in late 1973. When he did, Representative Vernon Holloway (D, Miami) announced his candidacy for the vacant senate seat. I immediately announced my candidacy for Holloway's vacant seat and was surprised that no one jumped into the race to challenge me. I became better acquainted with the role and responsibilities of a legislator as a result of developing friendships with a number of people elected to the House in 1972: Representatives Barry Kutun, Paul Steinberg, Tom Gallagher, Alan Becker, Charlie Papy, Dick Clark, Randy Avon, Bill Nelson, Eric Smith, and Elaine Gordon, among others. Those relationships resulted in a continuing outreach to potentially new political supporters.

In September 1973, Susan and I welcomed the first of the two greatest blessings of our marriage—our daughter, Michelle Elizabeth McKnight (our second greatest blessing was the birth of our son, Robert Joel, in June 1978). The delivery, at Baptist Hospital in Kendall, took over 17 hours, but afterward, Susan and Michelle were doing just fine. As will be seen later, Michelle became a media personality in her own right in our future campaigns and press conferences.

During that time Susan and I met the famous peanut farmer Georgia governor Jimmy Carter, who was campaigning in South Miami for the democratic nomination for president. We found him to be extremely energetic and a very polished campaigner. His populist theme resonated with residents in South Dade County.

As the time of election qualification approached, I made the decision to work the campaign full time and resigned my real estate position with Werner and Wollack. I formed a real estate firm with a friend and supporter Karl Noonan, a former Miami Dolphins football star. I was successful in recruiting a number of recognized and respected community leaders from South Dade County to join our new campaign for District 116. Among them were state representatives Marshall Harris, Maxine Baker, and Bob Hartnett, grower George Cooper, investor Karl Noonan, businessman and future state representative and senator Larry Plummer, realtor George Cadman, attorney Bud Stack, and Miami mayor Maurice Ferre. Although not involved officially in our campaign, my good friend and former Dade County Democratic Party chairman and former state representative Mike Abrams (D., Miami), provided meaningful counsel. Two loyal supporters of both my '72 and '74 campaigns, Gary Gregory and Larry Boecklen, dated back to my college days at Florida Southern. Their wives, Shelia Gregory and Connie Boecklen, joined them in this campaign. Two couples from the Coral Gables Jaycees, Peter and Ronni Bermont, and Mike and Lynn Fitzgerald, in turn, joined also. The ten of us met at a different dining venue each month to discuss our campaign, and it became a wonderful regular social get together of our families for over 20 years. We named our group First Friday. As in 1972, the endorsements were solid behind our campaign, and unlike today, spelled a difference then of probably five percentage points in the outcome of the election.

It would have been extraordinary if no one had filed to run against me, since I was not in public office nor ever had been. On the last day of qualifying, Connie Baker, the wife of a circuit court judge, filed her Democratic Party paperwork in Tallahassee. Connie was young, bright, and a former beauty queen. Her husband, Judge Paul Baker, was a well-known public figure, so it looked like I would have a difficult race again. The good news was that no Republican filed in our District 116 race, so whoever won the primary would be going to Tallahassee as a new state representative.

Compared to my race against Gautier in 1972, this campaign was indeed tame. The only controversy I can recall was

Connie calling me at home and asking me to take down a yard sign of mine on highly trafficked Sunset Road in South Miami. Someone had thrown paint against it and although Connie insisted that her campaign did not do it, it looked that way to passersby. I told her I accepted that her campaign had nothing to do with the incident, but could not bring myself to help her by removing the sign. The sign stayed, and we won the election by a margin of 56 percent to 44 percent. In seeing the results on election night, I said to Susan, "Well I guess you, Michelle and I are off to Tallahassee for the next two years." Letters, telegrams, phone calls, and personal visits came in from all over the state. I must admit, it was an odd feeling to see all the communication addressed to me as, "The Honorable Robert W. McKnight."

As indicated above, because the campaign had not been a general election, I was effectively voted into office that night. In the general election I made one mistake. My good friend Representative Tom Gallagher (R. Coconut Grove) had a general election opponent, Bob Marlin. Bob was a wealthy businessman who had contributed to my race, and the Democratic Party had asked me to support his election. I thought that endorsing Marlin would do no harm, and that my endorsement would probably be rather meaningless. Tom, however, thought otherwise. He was hurt by my action and I deeply apologized to him afterward.

After the primary election, the new Speaker of the House, Don Tucker (D., Tallahassee), called a House Democratic caucus, to be held in the Florida House Chamber. Representative Charlie Papy, now my new colleague, invited my family to stay at his vacation home in Cedar Key en route to Tallahassee. It is a ten-hour trip from Miami to Tallahassee, so Susan, Michelle, and I appreciated a chance to stop and spend the night at Charlie's home. We arrived in Tallahassee the next day, and upon entering the House Chamber for the first time, I got goose bumps. I thought of all the great Floridians who had served in that venerable chamber, and felt somewhat in awe of it all. I looked around and saw members who had served for years in that body. One lobbyist told me that I was now a member of the second most exclusive club in Florida, the 120-member House of Representatives (the smaller State Senate, with 40 members, was the most exclusive). Speaking of lobbyists, all of us on the floor were joined by probably a hundred lobbyists, many of whom I knew by their names appearing on campaign contributions. One I well recall was a hero of mine when we were growing up in Palm Beach County. Our main football rival was the larger high school, Palm Beach High, whose star player was a halfback named Hugh MacMillan. Hugh, who went on to star as a single wing tailback at Princeton, had gotten both a divinity and a law degree, and was a lobbyist for Governor Askew. We sat in his office and got acquainted. He was chagrined to find out that I was a member of the Lake Worth Trojan football team that broke the Palm Beach High Wildcat winning streak in 1961. Hugh's father was a distinguished judge in West Palm Beach, and Hugh later followed him in public office by serving on the Palm Beach County School Board.

During the caucus, most of the discussion was about who would receive which committee assignments. *The lesson here is that the real heart of the legislative process occurs in the committees and subcommittees. That is where legislation is first heard and is subject to the apparent never-ending amendatory process. It is in committee that the staff influence is greatest on law-making and it is also the place where lobbyists have their best chance to influence legislation. The veteran legislators work the committees and leave the flowery speeches on the floor to the less effective lawmakers.*

Since the Democrats were the majority party in both the Senate and House in 1974, it could be argued that I might have had a chance to chair a subcommittee, even though I was a lowly freshman. Even so, I was told not to expect a chairmanship, since there were over 50 new members of the house. To my complete surprise, Speaker Tucker and House Health and Rehabilitative Services Committee chairman Kutun selected me to chair the important House Subcommittee on Corrections. Only one other freshman, Representative Lee Moffitt (D., Tampa), was granted the privilege of chairing a subcommittee. Even though it was certainly premature, word was starting to spread to keep an eye on that new House member from South Dade, Bob McKnight.

The Ledger - Bankers Club

Shop Talk

Politics was the main course when Aileen Lotz, who is seeking nomination for the House of Representatives, District 119, lunched with Robert McKnight. Mr. McKnight seeks the House seat in District 116.

Bob McKnight and Aileen Lotz, candidates for The Florida House of Representatives, 1974.

Susan, Michelle, and Bob McKnight, campaigning, 1974.

First Friday: (left to right) Sheila and Gary Gregory, Susan McKnight, Larry Boecklen, Ronni Bermont, Bob McKnight and Peter Bermont. Not pictured: Mike and Lynn Fitzgerald. (Photo by Connie Boecklen, 1974).

Campaign brochure for Connie Baker, State House District 116, 1974.

BAKER BELIEVES IN YOU

AND YOU CAN BELIEVE IN BAKER ELECT CONNIE BAKER FOR LEGISLATURE DEMOCRAT DIST. 116 LEVER 14-A

The Golden Years ...   44   *Robert McKnight*

Campaign endorsements for Robert W. McKnight, State House District 116, 1974.

The Golden Years ...   45   Robert McKnight

STATE OF FLORIDA

OFFICE OF GOVERNOR REUBIN O'D. ASKEW

September 13, 1974

Mr. Bob McKnight
1000 Kendale Boulevard
Miami, Florida 33156

Dear Mr. McKnight:

    Congratulations on your election to the Florida Legislature. The 1975-76 Legislature will be asked to solve some of the most difficult problems ever faced in Florida. With the leadership of Speaker Don Tucker and President Dempsey Barron, I am confident that solutions will be found.

    Looking forward to working with you on behalf of the citizens of Florida and with kind regards,

Sincerely,

Governor

ROA/mdm

Congratulations letter on election to the Florida House of Representatives From Governor Reubin Askew, 1974.

CHAPTER 5

The Gentleman from the 116th

Pursuant to the Florida Constitution, I was sworn into office on the first Tuesday, two weeks after the election. The state was apportioned at that time in multi-member districts in the urban areas, like Miami. Accordingly, District 116 was identical to districts 115-119, extending from the Tamiami Trail to the Florida Keys. Florida Chief Justice B.K. Roberts administered the oath of office to representatives Jim Eckhart, Charlie Papy, Dick Clark, Bill Flynn and myself at the same time. It was obviously important that the five of us work closely together as a team, to leverage our political clout. With some few exceptions, we did so, and generally had a good working relationship.

The House of Representatives authorized each representative one full-time legislative aide, and I selected a campaign supporter, Ellison Shapiro, for that position. He was only able to complete a portion of my first session, so for the remainder of my first term, my legislative aide was a former political writer for the *Palm Beach Post*, Bud Newman. Since I was honored to chair a subcommittee, I was given three full-time staff members: Susan Mabe, John Phelps, and Peter Mitchell. All three went on to spectacular political careers—Susan as one of the premier lobbyists in Washington, John as the clerk of the Florida House of Representatives, and Peter as the staff director of the House Appropriations Committee and chief of staff to Florida's Senior U.S. Senator, Bill Nelson. *The lesson here is that with few exceptions, the staff is there to assist the members. In most cases they have knowledge and experience with the legislation being considered, so use them. They are supposed to be nonpartisan and as indicated above, they also have political ambitions. As stated in the legislative golden rule, treat the staff with respect and they will return the respect to you.*

Shortly after I was sworn into office, the House convened for its monthly committee meetings. These occurred prior to the legislative regular session, which met for sixty days starting in

April 1975. My first Corrections Subcommittee meeting was a hearing on the Parole and Probation Commission's failure to collect a restitution fee from the prisoners to offset its costs of inmate supervision. An important member of the committee, Republican representative Don Hazelton (R., West Palm Beach), wrote the bill calling for the fee collection. Don became angry during the meeting when Commission chairman Ray Howard failed to respond to Don's questions regarding the agency's failure to collect the fee. It was everything I could do to keep order, especially when I had to rule on points of order. In addition to Don, a key member of the subcommittee was Representative Sam Bell (D., Ormond Beach). Sam was also a freshman, and obviously very bright, having obtained his undergraduate degree from Dartmouth and his law degree from Duke. Although it took several committee meetings to master chairing such important discussions on the corrections issues, I finally did so with the help of representatives Hazelton and Bell, and we passed some meaningful legislation that first year.

My Natural Resources Committee also met that first week for a hearing on an environmental reorganization bill that was controversial and strongly opposed by Governor Askew. The chairman of the committee, Representative Bill Fulford (D., Orlando), had indicated that the Speaker wanted to get the bill out of committee and on to the floor for consideration by the full House. The Majority Leader of the House, and my fellow representative from South Dade, Dick Clark, pulled me aside and suggested I vote for the bill in committee as a courtesy to the Speaker. He said that I could still vote against it on the floor if I were so inclined. Wanting to make a good early impression on my colleagues, I did vote for the bill, without noticing the glaring stare I was getting from the governor's chief of staff, Jim Apthorp, sitting on the front row in the committee. After my vote, Representative Clark said he and the Speaker appreciated my vote that day, and that they would remember it. Unfortunately for me the governor also remembered it. Later that day, I got a handwritten note from him saying he wanted to meet with me in his office. I was excited because I had never met Askew. At this time he was enjoying a 60 percent approval rating with the public, and it was even higher in my district.

I arrived for my appointment with Governor Askew in the Old Capitol. His office was dark and decorated quite differently from that of his predecessor, Governor Kirk. After about a 15-minute wait, his assistant said that the governor was ready to meet with me. After we shook hands, I started to sit down and then heard a thunderous bang—the governor had slammed his fist on his desk. He then shouted at me, *"You should be ashamed of yourself getting tricked into voting that bill out of committee today!!!"* I was more than stunned, and stammered, "Why, Governor?" He then proceeded to tell me all the things wrong with the bill and closed by pointing out that I had fallen into an old trap, as had many freshmen before me, by voting to appease a colleague, rather than voting my conscience. He told me how his (and, I hoped, still my) good friend, former representative Marshall Harris (D., Miami) had spoken so highly of me and how the governor was hoping I could carry some of his important legislation that year. It is unusual for a freshman to be given that privilege by a governor. I thought to myself, "I have blown this golden opportunity and this was just my first committee meeting." *When I left Askew's office, my clothes were dripping wet from nervous perspiration.*

As a sidebar on Governor Askew—he was known for keeping members' voting records on old envelopes in his coat pocket. I recall once when Susan and I were in the receiving line at the governor's mansion and as we approached him, he pulled out his tattered envelope. He looked at it, and said, "Nice to see you today, Susan." I can't say the same for your husband after his awful vote this afternoon on House Bill 804." I ended up shaking hands with myself and can tell you, it doesn't take too many of those "reminders" to begin checking with the governor's staff before casting votes in the House of Representatives. I will have more to say about the Askews' lobbying skills later in this book.

Another bill to come before the Natural Resources Committee dealt with attempting to clean up Lake Okeechobee. Potentially, it affected the quality of drinking water in South Florida. When the bill hit the floor, I drew an amendment to prohibit back pumping of waste into the lake, allegedly done by the politically powerful sugar industry. Their lobbyists ignored my amendment because they had enlisted the support of the powerful (and colorful) Chairman of the Rules Committee, Gus Craig, of St. Augustine. I offered my amendment and began debating its merits, but to my dismay, there were very few members on the floor at that time. *A lesson here is to not only learn, but also memorize the rules of the chamber in which you are serving.* I knew that I could call a point of order and ask the Speaker to call for a quorum of the House. I did that and the chamber quickly filled with potential voters. Another rule I used to my advantage was to request a roll call vote. After my debate on the amendment with the rules chairman, the Speaker called for a vote, and ruled that a voice vote went in favor of the rules chairman and against my amendment. I then invoked the rule of the House calling for a roll call vote. Since so many South Florida members could not afford to vote against what might be interrupted as a vote against clean water, my amendment passed, but by a slim margin. The distinguished rules chairman was stunned and quickly came to me on the floor to negotiate a compromise. That success would not have been possible had it not been for the adroit use of the rules.

The subject matter of my amendment to the Lake Okeechobee cleanup legislation was complex and really understood by only a few people in Tallahassee. I was fortunate to have the excellent counsel and advice of two of those people—Dr. Pat McCaffery and Chuck Littlejohn. Both gentlemen worked for the state and not only knew the environmental issues involved in the debate, but also understood the bare knuckles political implications involved. Were it not for Pat and Chuck's suggestions and even patience with my understanding of their advice, we certainly would not have had the success we had on the floor that day.

Another person who had substantial knowledge of Lake Okeechobee and the state's water management system was former representative, Jack Shreve (D., Merritt Island). Jack was elected in 1972 and only served one term, but packed a lot of political influence in those two years. He was the author of the landmark Water Resources Act legislation and was widely respected in the state's environmental community. Jack is best known for his outstanding service to the state as the Public Counsel to the Public Service Commission. In my opinion, he deserves even more credit for his great contributions to Florida's environment.

In the House of Representatives, the Speaker assigned all members their seats in the chamber. Historically, the most important members were assigned the seats closest to the center aisle, so they were in his or her direct eyesight. The less powerful members and almost the entire freshmen class were given seats near the two outside aisles. No surprise, my chair was two chairs from the outside aisle. Other than Majority Leader Clark and representatives Barry Kutun and Bob Hector, all from Dade County, most of the rest of the Dade Delegation had seats close to the outside aisle.

The following disclosure may be troubling to read about, but it was considered a non-objectionable practice. A member would often place a vote for another member, provided the absent member was somewhere else on the floor when the voting occurred (the assumption was that the absent member could not get back to his or her seat to vote). In any event, a number of the members sitting around me were often not present for votes, so in accordance with the accepted practice, I would vote for them if I knew their voting preference. As a result, although I was a lowly freshman and starting to fall out of favor with the Speaker, I began to realize that if my neighbors were not voting on a bill, I had access to a number of votes over and above just mine. Our area on the House floor became known as "Sleepy Hollow," and I became a voting power with whom the more senior legislators had to deal.

Life in the House was not without its lighter moments. A member who sat next to me, Dr. Walter Sackett (D., Miami), was a veteran legislator in his 70's. He had written one of the first

"Death with Dignity" bills in the country. Dr. Sackett was prone to a brief siesta now and then, particularly during lengthy floor debates. During one of these interminable sessions, the Speaker, who was known for his great sense of humor and quick wit, looked over at Dr. Sackett, who was napping next to me, and slammed his gavel, announcing, "For what reason does the gentleman from the 110th, Dr. Sackett, *AWAKE*?" The Chamber and the gallery broke up and the debate tension dissipated.

As we continued into the session, I fell more out of favor with the Speaker, although I was able to hold on to my subcommittee chairmanship. Meanwhile, I had a crisis developing in my district. Sunrise Community, a not-for-profit based in the Redlands of South Dade County, was near financial bankruptcy. In addition, torrential spring storms had caused the roof of their main residence for developmentally disabled children to collapse. After meeting with them, and not having additional responsibilities during the session, I decided to devote much of my time and energies during session to save Sunrise. I worked closely with the governor's office, his staff, and parents of the children and the community, to develop a strategy to get the school back on its feet. With a lot of hard work by hundreds of individuals and some luck, we were successful. At the end of the session, the community and Sunrise were kind to recognize publicly my efforts. Years later, the president and chief executive officer of Sunrise, and my good friend, Les Leech, convinced its Board of Directors to name their new administration building "The Robert W. McKnight Administration Building." As noted later in this book, I accepted a request by Sunrise to represent them as a lobbyist in the late 1990s. In that regard, Republican Jeb Bush provided substantially more funds for the care of persons with disabilities than did his predecessor. Putting my ego aside, that was what it was all about—helping people who otherwise could not help themselves. That was a powerful motive for seeking public service.

As my first legislative session was coming to an end, my colleagues and I were subject to the seemingly never-ending race for Speaker of the House of Representatives. That year, the incumbent, Speaker Tucker, had decided to seek reelection, which had never happened before. His opponent was a respected legislator from Plant City, Representative Jim Redman. With over 50 freshmen in the House in 1975, it was difficult to predict the votes, but generally there was a question as to why the Speakership could not continue to be rotated. The campaign for Speaker intensified over the summer and I had decided to remain uncommitted until the outcome became clearer. The campaign became so intense that the unheard of happened—the lobbyists got involved, with most of them supporting Speaker Tucker. The speaker surrounded himself with some of the finest political operatives in Tallahassee, including Phil Blank, Gerry Sternstein, and Bob Hugli, among others. More on the Speaker's race later.

Lobbyists are often painted in a negative light, and that is really unfortunate, in my opinion. Admittedly, there have been, probably at all levels of government, abuses committed by lobbyists, especially as regarding campaign contributions. Yet, the good lobbyists provide a critical source of information regarding proposed legislation. Contrary to most conventional wisdom, most lobbyists are non-partisan. *The lesson here is that lobbyists are the fourth branch of government. Treat them with respect and never lie to them. Your word is your bond...keep it. I always made it a point not to spring a surprise on a lobbyist, but rather tell them in advance my plans on a particular piece of legislation. With some few exceptions, most of them did the same for me.*

As the committees began their meetings in advance of the 1976 session of the legislature, the Speaker's race was in the highest gear possible, so Speaker Tucker thought it best to call for the election. Although the election was to be by secret ballot, it was widely believed that the Speaker's supporters were able to identify those members voting for him, and they made no secret of the supporters' identities. The result was a one-sided victory for the Speaker, and rumors of retaliation for Representative Redman's supporters circulated widely. As Majority Leader Clark said to Representative Kutun, one of Redman's supporters, "If you are going after the king, Barry, you'd better kill him...whatever you do, don't wound him or you will be forever sorry." This historic warning proved true in 1976.

Election years almost always result in political surprises, although few had surfaced at the start of the session in April 1976. I retained my subcommittee chairmanship and joined my colleague Representative Bob Hector on a tour of all the prisons in the state. Bob chaired the House Governmental Operations Committee, so we both had a hand in dealing with the growing controversy over a federal lawsuit, *Costello v. Wainwright*, in which an inmate named Michael V. Costello was suing the state and Corrections Secretary Louie Wainwright over the poor quality of health care in the prisons. The tour was eye opening— running the gamut from seeing death row to meeting with Theodore Bundy; from touring Lowell, the women's prison, to filing amicus curiae briefs on behalf of the legislature in court.

Another issue that came before our Corrections Subcommittee was the sentencing of offenders. In general, there appeared to be public disdain for the wide variation of sentences rendered in Florida courts. My committee staff researched the issue as well as alternatives, which included more determinate sentencing authorization for the courts. I wrote an article on the subject for the *Florida Bar Journal* and to my surprise, I got a telephone call from Larry King inviting me to discuss the issue with him on his radio show. This was the same Larry King of CNN fame, but it was while he was on WIOD radio in Miami. He was a tactful and informed interviewer and as a result of my guest appearance he invited me to be on his show a number of additional times in later years. I also appeared on the popular *Allen and Bernice Courtney* radio show on WQAM in Miami, along with my good friend and former colleague Senator George Firestone (D., Miami), to discuss the same subject. Lastly, one of my favorite radio talk show hosts was the conservative, Steve Daily, of WVCG in Coral Gables—his interviews always helped keep me grounded in good values.

As a part of my Corrections Subcommittee activities, as chairman, I called for several public hearings around the state on the determinate sentencing model. One was in Tampa, and while there, I ran into my good friend Yvonne Burkholtz, of the United Teachers of Dade County. She invited me to dinner at a renowned Cuban restaurant owned by one of her members. The owner joined us for dinner that night and I was impressed with his personality and panache. He turned out to be none other than future Tampa mayor, Federal drug czar, and Republican governor, Bob Martinez. He won his election as governor by defeating the Democratic nominee, former representative Steve Pajcic (D., Jacksonville). Pajcic's statewide campaign co-chair was none other than one Senator Bob McKnight, confirming the adage that "politics makes strange bedfellows".

During the session, the Speaker reminded all of us that only one bill had to pass—the appropriations bill. No matter how important our personal bills were to each of us, the state could get by, thank you very much, without passing them. Another adage I remember about bills came from my mentor, Senator Thomas. He told me once, "Bob, a bill should not be easy to pass, but rather it should be extremely difficult. Yes, we are a nation of laws, but we should pass no more laws than are absolutely necessary for the peace, welfare, and advancement of our citizens." That was pretty powerful stuff.

Since the appropriations bill was so critical, I spent a lot of time working on amendments that I felt were important to issues in my district. One such area was the needed funding for neonatal care facilities in Florida. This was critical funding for newborn babies who might die or suffer lifelong diseases if not treated at birth. The Speaker's administration did not see this as a priority, in spite of my requests. Representatives Sheldon, Bell, Gordon, and I decided to take on the leadership by offering a series of amendments on the floor to fund the program. But the Speaker used the power of his office to oppose us by directing the rules chairman to declare that no amendment would be considered for new funding without identifying an existing source of revenue. In other words, we had to take another member's appropriation to fund ours. As you might imagine, that was a no-no, especially for a freshman. Nevertheless, we rebels laid out a game plan and took off the gloves. Even though we meant no ill will, we decided to get the necessary monies by canceling a large fleet of new highway patrol cars for the Department of Highway Safety and Motor Vehicles (a pet project of our friend, Representative Herb Morgan (D., Tallahassee). The debate on the amendment was spirited, with Representative George Sheldon on our side telling the members, "What we are talking about is the financial equivalent of one mile of asphalt on a state road." We continued to debate furiously and relentlessly, and when the vote went up on the board, we won—albeit by a narrow margin. The Speaker and his lieutenants were incensed with us, and used every parliamentary procedure possible to reverse the vote. We were bloodied, but kept swinging. One former member, who served with us at that time, predicted that this confrontation and the success for us would be the beginning of the end of the Speaker's regime. His prediction was correct. Needless to say, the four of us shared food tasters for a while, but just like with the Sunrise success, this was what it was all about.

During my first term in the House, I was fortunate to have the leading political columnist in the state, John McDermott of the *Miami Herald*, do a profile of me for a Sunday edition. It was an attempt to shadow a day in the life of a freshman legislator. John's column was so widely read that a number of lobbyists that I did not know started calling me by my first name. At the end of my first term, *Florida Trend* magazine conducted a poll among all 160 members of the House and Senate, and I was honored to be identified by my colleagues as a member *"Admired for Dedication, Honesty, Integrity and Regard for the Public Welfare."* In my estimation, I figured that future elections, if there were any, would be much easier to raise funds for by virtue of my growing public profile.

As with most organizations, the members had a tradition of presenting awards at the end of a term. The Speaker and his team predetermined, through arm-twisting, most of the awards. Even so, since there were so many freshmen from 1974 to 1976, there was some uncertainty as to who would receive the two First

Term Member Awards. The Speaker made it clear that he had a slate indicating his choices for them, and I later found out that I was not on it. Candidly, I am not sure I should have been, except for the fact that I was one of only two freshmen to chair subcommittees in the House. This vote was also to be in secret, but again everyone assumed the Speaker and his folks had the awards wired. When the *Florida Times Union*-sponsored Allen Morris Awards for *Outstanding First Term Member of the House*, were announced, I was selected as the runner-up, or second place award winner. Most Tallahassee observers wondered how that could happen with such tight oversight by the controlling officer, and frankly, I wonder about it myself.

As my first term ended, I wasn't sure what the future held for me, but I knew if I ran for reelection in 1976, that it couldn't get much better than my first term. There had been setbacks of course, but overall, I was gratified by the results of the first term. As a freshman, I had had success, from chairing a major subcommittee, to saving Sunrise School in my district; from successfully passing the back pumping amendment, to securing critical funding for newborns in the Neonatal Intensive Care Program; and to being selected by my peers as the Runner-Up for the *Outstanding First Term Member of the House of Representatives*. Susan, Michelle and I thanked God for the blessing of my being able to serve.

(Left to right) Swearing-in of State Representatives Bill Flynn, Charlie Papy, Billy Freeman, Bob McKnight and Dick Clark by Chief Justice B.K. Roberts, 1974.

Bob, Michelle, and Susan McKnight in House Chamber, 1976 (AP).

Michelle McKnight in House Chamber, 1976 (AP).

(Left to right) State Representatives Jim Eckhart, Dick Clark, and Bob McKnight, 1976.

State Representatives Bob McKnight and Dick Clark on House Floor, 1977.

Left to right: Governor Reubin Askew, Matthew Blumberg (page), and Representative and Mrs. Robert W. McKnight, 1976.

(Left to right) State Representative Bob McKnight, Governor Reubin Askew, and Elizabeth and Herb Williams (Susan's parents) in the governor's office, 1976.

Miami Herald *article by John McDemott, 1975.*

Now's the Term to Learn For Freshman Legislator

By JOHN McDERMOTT
Herald Political Writer

TALLAHASSEE — A day in the life of a freshman legislator can be exciting and suspenseful, or humbling and frustrating.

There is no set pattern for the high-pressure, often tense crises which seem to arise almost daily.

But it represents a challenge to first-term members like state Rep. Bob McKnight, one of nine first-term members of the Florida House from Dade county.

And while almost to a man or woman — there are three women among the newcomers to the Dade contingent — they are finding themselves working harder than ever before. Just the thrill of holding public office keeps them charged up.

McKNIGHT, 31, a partner in an investment company, says he has learned two hard lessons during the early days of the current 1975 session.

"Don't make the mistake of committing yourself on a bill until you are fully informed about what it does," he said.

"And once you have given your word, keep it."

McKnight sees the 22-member Dade delegation as having "a new place" in the House this year because of the changeovers which resulted from retirements and the 1974 elections.

"We lost such superstars as Murray Dubbin, Marshall Harris and Dick Pettigrew," he said. "But I think we gained in achieving a more cohesive delegation — one which seems able to work together as a unit."

The typical day of a first-term legislator goes something like this:

McKnight gets up about 6:30 a.m., has breakfast with his wife and baby daughter.

HE IS IN his office at the capitol shortly after 7:30 a.m. making local phone calls, studying the calendar for the day's action ahead in the House and checking on legislation of particular interest to himself.

Between 9 a.m. and noon, he attends committee or subcommittee meetings before returning to his office for a sandwich and answering phone calls which have piled up during the morning.

Most of the afternoon is spent in the House chamber — and this can be exhausting as floor debates erupt, points of order made and the freshman legislator forced to pay constant attention to keep up with the complex flow of activity, most of which is brand new to him.

In between, he studies the rules, so that when his time eventually comes to handle a bill, he will know the angles and the pitfalls and not get "snookered" by opponents who use the rules to their advantage.

THERE IS A fair amount of social life at night while the legislature is in session, but for McKnight he usually is too tired to participate.

One of the surprises he has found about being a legislator is how quickly impressions are formed and

'Don't make the mistake of committing yourself on a bill until you are fully informed about what it does. And once you have given your word, keep it.
—Rep. Bob McKnight

labels given to a lawmaker after he has made only two or three votes.

He doesn't see himself as fitting into any particular pattern yet. But some of his colleagues and the sideline observers seem ready to tag him.

However, there is little uniformity thus far to his designation as a conservative, liberal or middle-of-the-roader.

McKnight believes that a freshman lawmaker must keep his campaign promises — and be seen, not heard.

Thus, he voted for the Equal Rights Amendment "because I promised I would when I was campaigning although my district (Coral Gables-South Miami) is conservative."

ON THE FLOOR, he listens but stays out of debates.

During the environmental reorganization debate, McKnight was on the Natural Resources Committee taking up the bill. Although the measure was being pushed by the leadership of both House and Senate, he, along with Rep. Elaine Bloom, another Miami freshman, felt it needed some amendments.

They lost on eight but succeeded on one point. Knight admitted it caused him to perspire. "After all, (Rep.) Dick Clark (D, Miami) who is the majority leader, was looking right at us and he was pushing the bill."

Others in the Dade delegation who are serving their first time include Reps. Gwen Margolis, John A. Hill, Joe Gersten, Barry Richard, Nancy Harrington, James Eckhart and Bill Flynn.

The Golden Years ... 61 *Robert McKnight*

Speaker Don Tucker and President Dempsey Barron, Florida Trend *magazine, 1976.*

The Golden Years ... 62 Robert McKnight

CHAPTER 6

The "Plan"

Upon returning to my district, I immediately filed the paperwork to run for reelection to House District 116. After each session, the statewide newspapers typically published a "report card" on the legislators. No punches were pulled on who was effective and who was not. Since the report card could affect whether or not I drew opposition in my reelection bid, I was encouraged when the assessment of my first session was positive and quickly arranged a fundraiser to be held at the Miami Marriott Hotel. My good friend (and Susan's fellow Alabamian) Comptroller Gerald Lewis was invited as a special guest of honor for the event. It was well attended, and perhaps more importantly, received good press coverage. Although it was audacious of me, I was beginning to hope that I might get reelected without opposition. On the last day of qualifying, I got a call from friends in Tallahassee saying that I had just been reelected to District 116 in the Florida House of Representatives, without an opponent.

Although most of my professional time was spent on legislative work, I continued my real estate business. David Blumberg, a prominent Miami developer who had been a strong supporter since my election, had asked me to join his real estate company. I still had my securities license, and he was interested in possibly using me to structure private syndications of investors for his real estate developments. David and his wife, Lee, were recognized as among the finest community leaders in all of South Florida, and I was honored to join their organization. I worked very closely over the years with David's executive vice president Larry Kahn, who, like David, had an MBA from Harvard. I selected a new aide after my election, Sherry Halstead, who served ably in that capacity through the end of my legislative career.

As stated earlier, Speaker of the House Tucker was reelected to a second term and was organizing his new administration just as the next campaign for Speaker was starting. The candidates were John Forbes (D., Jacksonville), Hyatt Brown (D., Daytona Beach), and Ed Fortune (D., Pace). At the outset, the race was probably even, but Representative Fortune had the advantage of having the support of Speaker Tucker. I remained uncommitted for the time being. *The lesson here is a repeat of my remarks to John McDermott in his* Miami Herald *article about me: do not commit your vote until you are certain about it and its probable results. If you are confident about that, commit and never break your word. If something happens to change your mind, obtain a release of responsibility from the person to whom you pledged your vote. This lesson was sacrosanct during my service in the legislature, but I am told, adherence to it is quite rare today.*

Susan, who was expecting our second child, tragically miscarried around this time. There were some serious complications for her as a result, and I had to spend time away from Tallahassee to be with her. My colleagues and their spouses were sensitive to us, especially Senator Bob Graham's wife, Adele, who later gave Susan a lovely shirt for our son, Bobby.

As the first session of my second term approached, the Speaker appointed me chairman of the important Subcommittee on Health and Mental Health. I was hoping for a seat on the all-important Appropriations Committee, but as in almost all politics, to the victors (Speaker Tucker and his lieutenants) go the spoils. John Phelps became my subcommittee staff director, and David Coburn (future staff director of the Appropriations Committee) and Mike Cusick (future lead fundraiser for the Pajcic Campaign for Governor in 1986) became the remaining staff members. We worked on a major piece of legislation creating a bill of rights for the mentally retarded and helped Senator Bob Graham, chairman of the Senate Health and Rehabilitative Services Committee, create the Community Care for the Elderly Act. We also were involved in a national controversy dealing with the possible legalization of laetrile as a cure for cancer. I was included in pieces on the subject by the *60 Minutes* TV magazine and *Time* magazine. The legislation did not pass.

In my capacity as chairman of the House Health and Mental Health Subcommittee, I also faced a very difficult moral issue at that time. The court had issued conflicting decisions on the definition of brain death. It pleaded with the Florida legislature to provide some clarifying guidance. This was approximately 30 years before the Terri Schiavo case surfaced. As a non-attorney, I felt it incumbent upon me to seek as much scholarly advice as possible while our committee wrestled with the issue. It is one that I prayed over often and fervently. We finally passed a bill that was described by some observers as a landmark bill, and which stands today. I have included in the Appendix a letter related to this subject that I received from counselor and good friend Tom Horkan of the Florida Catholic Conference. As Senator Jack Gordon (D., Miami Beach) said, "Senator, this is not work for the faint of heart." He was right.

One humorous debate occurred on the floor of the House, shortly after the start of the 1977 session. Representative Gus Craig, the colorful rules chairman from St. Augustine, was sponsoring a bill drafted by the pari-mutuel gaming industry that would allow minors into racetracks. Craig was a staunch conservative, and claimed to be a bible-toting Baptist, which made it strange that he would introduce such legislation. The racetrack industry was renown for generous campaign contributions and that, plus perhaps the fact that the powerful rules chairman could dispense of the legislation quickly, suggested that the legislation was probably "wired" for passage. To his surprise, Representative Craig encountered stiff resistance from many of his conservative colleagues who realized what he was doing. Craig looked up at the Speaker and motioned that he was going to attempt to move the bill on for final consideration. The Speaker recognized Representative Craig to close on the bill, and Craig proceeded to proclaim into his microphone, "Mr. Speaker, *I believe a family that gambles together, STAYS TOGETHER* ... move the bill, Mr. Speaker." The bill did not pass, and the House laughed for almost fifteen minutes.

As in the earlier Speaker's race, the longer the campaigns went on, the more disruptive they were for the proceedings of the House. This Speaker's race became even more disruptive for me and even personal. While I was back in my district in Miami, one of the candidates, Hyatt Brown, called to say he was in town and asked if we could meet. Of course I said yes, and invited him to our house for dinner. Hyatt proceeded to tell me about his campaign, and then shocked me by asking me to join him as his running mate, a candidate for Speaker Pro-Tempore of the Florida House of Representatives. I was more than honored since I was only starting my second term in the House, but was uncertain if I wanted to risk everything if I ran with Hyatt and we lost. Also, at that time, Susan and I were discussing a "plan." We felt that we were comfortable with public service, including campaigning, although it was difficult at times. The office I aspired to was that of governor of the state, and since more governors were elected directly from a seat in the legislature rather than from the statewide-elected Cabinet, the only real question was whether to run from the House or the Senate. Since the Senate was smaller, with a higher profile, we felt that the Senate should be our goal. I told Hyatt the plan that night in Miami. Hyatt was a successful insurance executive, and was not accustomed to being turned down. We discussed it late into the night, but ended our talk with the understanding that I planned to run for the Senate in the future, and therefore would not accept his kind invitation to be his running mate.

Hyatt moved forward with his campaign, and selected a good friend and fine legislator, Dr. Dick Hodes (D., Tampa), as his running mate. I publicly announced my support for their ticket shortly after their announcement. The race was narrowing down to one between Brown and Fortune—sort of a young versus old and moderate versus conservative.

Hyatt honed his strategy to win the Speakership and he concluded that the best way to win was to initiate a clandestine roll call for the necessary 61 pledges. For a number of weekends straight, he secretly invited about a half a dozen members (I was the only one from Miami) to his apartment to plan a sneak poll to get the votes. One member of our team that I worked closely with on social service legislation and with whom I went to Florida Southern was Representative George Sheldon. He chose the night that members of the House were invited to a popular social function called The Redneck Party. The plan was carefully scripted and required precise timing, including how long Representative Sheldon and I were required to debate each other on the floor, while other members were picking up pledges. The solicitation went on through the night—I remember Representative Alan Becker and I had to get the pledges of Gwen Cherry and Bill Sadowski, both of whom were at their respective homes in bed. When the sun rose, the Fortune Campaign had no idea what had happened—during the night, we had secured the required 61 signed pledges for election of the Honorable Hyatt Brown as the next Speaker of the Florida House of Representatives. The press dubbed the sneak attack as the "Attack on Entebbe" after the famous Israeli attacks on Uganda. The next morning the *St. Petersburg Times* had a picture of me with a quote, "It was crazy, there we were running around in the middle of the night in dungarees and sneakers, picking up pledges." (Today's young people probably don't even know what dungarees and sneakers are.) Hyatt requested and received a Democratic Caucus that day, and was elected by a unanimous vote. *Many students of Florida politics described this as the defining moment signifying the end of the Pork Choppers' reign.* The methodology was somewhat unceremonious, but it was lasting and historic.

As an aside, the next campaign for Speaker was in the whisper stage, and although I had nothing to do with it, my name was being circulated as a possible candidate. Obviously, no one except Susan knew that our "plan," did not contemplate that.

The 1978 election would include electing a new governor. There were many candidates, including the favorite, Attorney General Bob Shevin, as well as banker Raleigh Greene, Secretary of State Bruce Smathers, Lieutenant Governor Jim Williams and state senator Bob Graham. The probable Republican candidate would again be drugstore magnate, Jack Eckerd. I had come to know all the candidates quite well, but some more than others. According to press accounts, Lieutenant Governor Williams had me included on a short list to be his running mate. He ultimately selected one of my best friends, Senator Betty Castor (D., Tampa). The race began in earnest, but as so many do, became acrimonious toward the end, especially between the two finalists, Shevin and Graham.

The surprise of the 1977 session was the rumor that Speaker Tucker might resign to take a post in the Carter Administration in Washington. Tucker was an early supporter of the president, and although a lawyer, did not have an active practice. President Carter was a former governor of Georgia and was close to Atlanta-based executives of the Coca-Cola Corporation. During the sessions, the Speaker brought up an obscure bill that, according to the press, could be interpreted as favoring Coca-Cola's interests in Florida. Tucker's critics quickly spread word that he was trying to do a favor for Carter supporters in Georgia to win support for his rumored appointment. In the meantime, the Speaker Pro-Tempore was low key John Ryals (D., Brandon), who was making plans to take over the House, if necessary. He asked to meet with me and a number of other members to solidify his ascension, if it occurred. I was assured of moving up from chairmanship of a subcommittee to chairmanship of a full committee, if he became Speaker. Rumors about the Speaker and his relationship with the president persisted, and he finally advised the White House that he was withdrawing his interest in an appointment.

Even though it was just 1977, the 1980 Speaker's race was starting and the front-runner was a good friend and Brown lieutenant, Ralph Haben (D., Palmetto). Although I had told all who cared to know that my plans were to run for the Senate, Representative Haben did ask me to consider being his running mate, as Speaker Pro-Tempore, but I declined. I always felt that Ralph was smart and capable, but he did not seem to have the seriousness about his legislative work to reach his full potential. I was wrong—in my opinion, he turned out to be one of the best Speakers ever, because, among other reasons, he was not afraid to surround himself with people whose opinions differed from his.

During this time, I made it a point to spend time with the Clerk of the House of Representatives Emeritus, Dr. Allen Morris. The venerable clerk had a wealth of knowledge on the House and its history. His *Florida Handbook* was the bible for students of Florida politics, and he always made himself available for curious House members like myself. He once told me that he felt our class of 1974 had more potential future state political leaders than any he could recall, and that I was among the best of the class. I was extremely pleased. Dr. Morris passed on a number of years ago, but he will always remain one of the greatest Floridians I have ever known.

With the end of the 1977 session, I got a call from veteran senator Ralph Poston (D., Miami) who advised me that he was not planning to run for reelection in 1978. Since we both represented South Dade County, I tried to work closely with him and considered him a friend. I told him of my "plan" and said if he felt comfortable that he was not going to run, I would announce for his anticipated open Senate seat. He said he did not object, and I then sought the approval of my employer, David Blumberg. David had always been so supportive of me and was happy to hear of this opportunity. David and I always agreed that I should be careful never to put myself into a potential conflict of interest while employed as senior vice president for sales and marketing at Planned Development Corporation ("PDC"). After informing Susan of my conversation with Senator Poston, we began quietly making the initial plans to announce for the Senate. Susan and I selected George DePontis and Stu Rose as our professional consultants, and they worked tirelessly on our behalf for the entire campaign. Two superb political communicators, my fellow Tallahasseean Ron Sachs and my close friend Seth Gordon ably assisted George and Stu.

As the 1978 session of the legislature convened, I taped the letters *NM* on my desk on the floor of the House of Representatives. It stood for *No Mistakes*. I knew that my race for the Senate would be the biggest and most difficult undertaking of my life. I had observed elected officials accidentally make comments or remarks that they later came to regret. *It is important to remember that anything said on the floor of the House or Senate Chamber is recorded and therefore public record forever. Many a candidate or elected official has wished that they could take back something said in jest and/or intended to be off the record. Say nothing unless you have to.*

I announced my campaign for Senate District 38, saying that it was my understanding that Senator Poston would not be a candidate for reelection. I added that if I was wrong and he was going to be a candidate or if he changed his mind, and decided to run, I would not reverse myself. This was awkward to say at the time, but it was based on my understanding from the earlier phone call I had gotten from the senator. In a matter of weeks, a shocker crossed the news wires—a citizen from Orlando accused Senator Ralph Poston of Miami of violating Senate rules of ethics. It so happened that the senator's crane erection business in Miami had encountered financial problems, and as an alternative line of employment, he had sought out an ambulance license in Orlando. The issuance of the licenses was political and the senator allegedly used his office to influence the license issuance process. One of his competitors apparently documented the senator's actions and advised the Senate president, Lew Brantley. The Senate alleged that Senator Poston had violated its rules, and perhaps state financial disclosure laws, and asked the attorney general to conduct an investigation. There I was running for Senator Poston's seat, and this potential scandal broke into the news. In the back of my mind I thought that this charge might prompt him to change his mind and run for reelection to clear his name. That was exactly what happened.

Needless to say, that revelation became the major state news for months. The attorney general, Bob Shevin, had served in the Senate with Poston, and both were from Miami, so that dynamic added to the public's interest in the matter. Ultimately the decision was referred to a select committee chaired by Senator Mattox Hair (D., Jacksonville). Many expected an impeachment vote from the committee, but instead they voted for a reprimand. The full Senate followed the committee's recommendation. One of the committee members, and one of the most respected lawyers in the Senate, Harry Johnston (D., West Palm Beach), told me once that it was really the only decision they could render, given the evidence presented by Assistant Attorney General Jim Whisenant.

President Brantley did not want the first official business in the new Senate office building to be the trial of one of its members, so after the vote he ruled that all future actions of the Senate would occur in the new offices. The House did the same, for the same reason. Both chambers placed a permanent plaque on the entrance to their respective new chambers, identifying the first members to serve there. Accordingly, I am shown as one of the first members of the Florida House of Representatives to serve in the new House Chamber in 1978.

As I anticipated, Senator Poston was angry about the public reprimand by his Senate colleagues, and reversed himself saying he would run for reelection to clear his name. Shortly thereafter, a former state senator, Don Gruber (R., Coconut Grove), announced that he would also run for District 38. Boy, now I had really done it. I went from a very safe seat in the House of Representatives, potentially the Speaker Pro Tempore of the Florida House of Representatives, to a hotly contested race for the Florida Senate. Added to that, I had elected a situation where I had to run against not one but two senators: the first, a 14-year veteran of the legislature and the second, one of the first Republican senators from Miami. What a summer I had in store for me in 1978.

Before we moved on to the 1978 campaign, Susan and I celebrated the birth of our son, Robert Joel, at South Miami Hospital. Regardless of any political outcomes, I considered myself the luckiest guy on earth to have such a wonderful and healthy family.

Bob and Susan McKnight at Longboat Key, 1987.

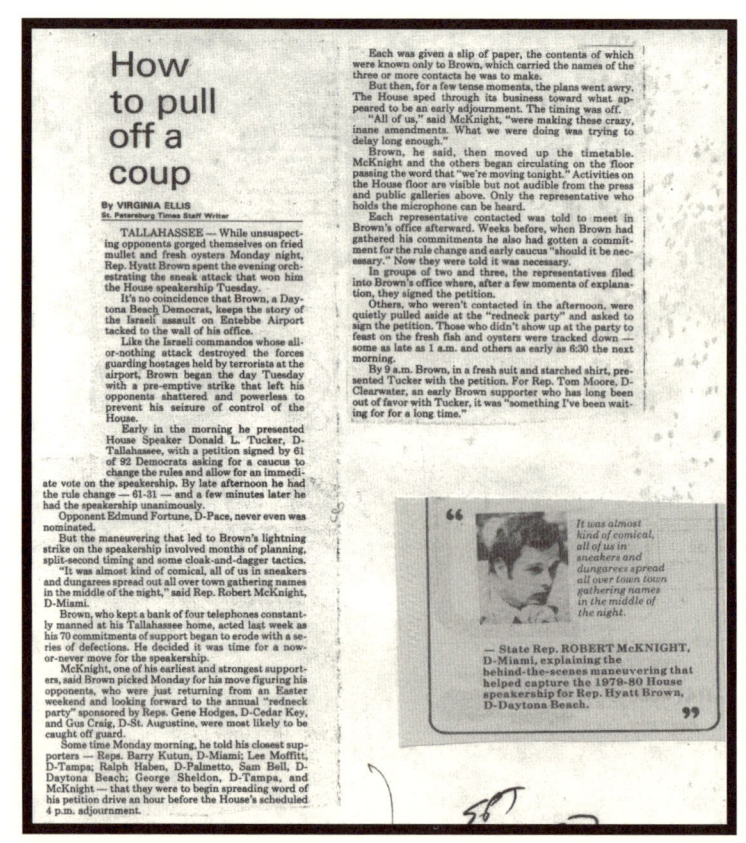

How to pull off a coup

By VIRGINIA ELLIS
St. Petersburg Times Staff Writer

TALLAHASSEE — While unsuspecting opponents gorged themselves on fried mullet and fresh oysters Monday night, Rep. Hyatt Brown spent the evening orchestrating the sneak attack that won him the House speakership Tuesday.

It's no coincidence that Brown, a Daytona Beach Democrat, keeps the story of the Israeli assault on Entebbe Airport tacked to the wall of his office.

Like the Israeli commandos whose all-or-nothing attack destroyed the forces guarding hostages held by terrorists at the airport, Brown began the day Tuesday with a pre-emptive strike that left his opponents shattered and powerless to prevent his seizure of control of the House.

Early in the morning he presented House Speaker Donald L. Tucker, D-Tallahassee, with a petition signed by 61 of 92 Democrats asking for a caucus to change the rules and allow for an immediate vote on the speakership. By late afternoon he had the rule change — 61-31 — and a few minutes later he had the speakership unanimously.

Opponent Edmund Fortune, D-Pace, never even was nominated.

But the maneuvering that led to Brown's lightning strike on the speakership involved months of planning, split-second timing and some cloak-and-dagger tactics.

"It was almost kind of comical, all of us in sneakers and dungarees spread out all over town gathering names in the middle of the night," said Rep. Robert McKnight, D-Miami.

Brown, who kept a bank of four telephones constantly manned at his Tallahassee home, acted last week as his 70 commitments of support began to erode with a series of defections. He decided it was time for a now-or-never move for the speakership.

McKnight, one of his earliest and strongest supporters, said Brown picked Monday for his move figuring his opponents, who were just returning from an Easter weekend and looking forward to the annual "redneck party" sponsored by Reps. Gene Hodges, D-Cedar Key, and Gus Craig, D-St. Augustine, were most likely to be caught off guard.

Some time Monday morning, he told his closest supporters — Reps. Barry Kutun, D-Miami; Lee Moffitt, D-Tampa; Ralph Haben, D-Palmetto, Sam Bell, D-Daytona Beach; George Sheldon, D-Tampa, and McKnight — that they were to begin spreading word of his petition drive an hour before the House's scheduled 4 p.m. adjournment.

Each was given a slip of paper, the contents of which were known only to Brown, which carried the names of the three or more contacts he was to make.

But then, for a few tense moments, the plans went awry. The House sped through its business toward what appeared to be an early adjournment. The timing was off.

"All of us," said McKnight, "were making these crazy, inane amendments. What we were doing was trying to delay long enough."

Brown, he said, then moved up the timetable. McKnight and the others began circulating on the floor passing the word that "we're moving tonight." Activities on the House floor are visible but not audible from the press and public galleries above. Only the representative who holds the microphone can be heard.

Each representative contacted was told to meet in Brown's office afterward. Weeks before, when Brown had gathered his commitments he also had gotten a commitment for the rule change and early caucus "should it be necessary." Now they were told it was necessary.

In groups of two and three, the representatives filed into Brown's office where, after a few moments of explanation, they signed the petition.

Others, who weren't contacted in the afternoon, were quietly pulled aside at the "redneck party" and asked to sign the petition. Those who didn't show up at the party to feast on the fresh fish and oysters were tracked down — some as late as 1 a.m. and others as early as 6:30 the next morning.

By 9 a.m. Brown, in a fresh suit and starched shirt, presented Tucker with the petition. For Rep. Tom Moore, D-Clearwater, an early Brown supporter who has long been out of favor with Tucker, it was "something I've been waiting for a long time."

> " *It was almost kind of comical, all of us in sneakers and dungarees spread all over town town gathering names in the middle of the night.*
>
> — State Rep. ROBERT McKNIGHT, D-Miami, explaining the behind-the-scenes maneuvering that helped capture the 1979-80 House speakership for Rep. Hyatt Brown, D-Daytona Beach. "

St. Petersburg Times article on "Attack on Entebbe," 1977.

The Golden Years ...   72   Robert McKnight

FLORIDA HOUSE OF REPRESENTATIVES
DONALD L. TUCKER, Speaker/JOHN L. RYALS, Speaker Pro Tempore
COMMITTEE ON HEALTH & REHABILITATIVE SERVICES

Elaine Gordon
Chairperson
David J. Lehman, M.D.
Vice Chairman

M E M O R A N D U M

TO: Representative Bob McKnight

FROM: John Phelps, Assistant Staff Director

SUBJECT: Opening Remarks at January 12, 1977 Meeting of the Subcommittee on Health and Mental Health

DATE: January 28, 1977

Attached to this memorandum is a copy of your introductory remarks before the Subcommittee on Health and Mental Health on January 12, 1977. Because these remarks represent an excellent introduction to the proper role of a House Subcommittee, we would appreciate your permission to use them in the future when the need arises for subcommittees to be created.

Marjorie R. Turnbull, Staff Director
Room 426, House Office Building, Tallahassee, Florida 32304 (904) 488-8315

Opening remarks by Chairman Robert W. McKnight to Florida House of Representatives Subcommittee on Health and Mental Health, 1977.

Health and Mental Health Subcommittee
Meeting of January 12, 1977
Opening Remarks by Rep. McKnight, Chairman

As you will note, those of you who are in the audience and also the Subcommittee members and the staff, we do have a brief agenda that we want to take up. I think, consistent with the Chairperson's format at our full Committee meeting this morning, it might be appropriate for just a couple of minutes, since two of our distinguished members are new, to touch on what the Chairman would envision as the role of this Subcommittee, some of my own personal preferences, and then open up the meeting for any comments or questions. I think that to do so is often helpful just in terms of setting a format for the Subcommittee.

I might first of all reintroduce the members. I think we did this earlier, but again we are very pleased to have Rep. Walter Young with us. Rep. Young is in his third term, and we're especially pleased to have that experience. Dr. Lehman, the Vice Chairman of the Subcommittee, is also a member; he's in his second term. Rep. Burnsed we're pleased to have with us from Lakeland and also Rep. Evans from the Melbourne area. We look forward to working with you.

Let me reintroduce also the staff, if I may, because I would like to reiterate Rep. Gordon's/sentiment (Chairperson of the full HRS Committee) regarding the professionalism of this staff and also reiterate the point that this staff does not work exclusively and solely for any of the full Committee or Subcommittee chairmen, for any of the individual members or even solely for the Committee, but rather for all members of the Legislature. If we can for coordination and for ease of operation, let's funnel all requests for staff assistance through Marjorie Turnbull, the staff director, so we can insure that we don't have a duplication. To my right, the assistant staff director, John Phelps. I have had the pleasure of working with John for one year, as Chairman of this Subcommittee, and I just really, if he doesn't mind, want to boast on his professionalism and his openness, so I'm glad to have John working with us again. Working very closely in the mental health area, Mike Cusick. Again, Mike has been with us since last year and has developed a

The Golden Years ... 74 *Robert McKnight*

real expertise in that area, and we look forward to working with Mike again. Fred Signs, who is a former employee of the Department of Health and Rehabilitative Services--and totally unbiased, he's told me--is in graduate school at Florida State. He will be joining us as a social work intern focusing in the area of health. And finally, our new secretary, welcome on board, Samm Seidel. We look forward to working with Samm.

Now, let me hit on a couple of areas; then we can go ahead and take up the two bills before us.

For the sake of the Subcommittee and also those people present, I consider this Subcommittee to be extremely important. Those of you who are familiar with the legislative process, and in particular with the history of this full Committee and this Subcommittee, recognize the significance of this Subcommittee's jurisdiction, both as it affects the largest state agency we have and as it affects so many different disciplines. As it affects total volume of legislation, I think the work load before this Subcommittee is as extensive, if not more extensive, than any other in the House. I have had the pleasure, as I indicated earlier, of chairing this Subcommittee for one year, and I know that the members enjoy serving on it because of the very diverse areas to which it addresses itself.

Now, picking up on what Speaker of the House Tucker has reiterated time and time again, an effective organization in the House of Representatives is one which has a strong subcommittee system. I think Representative Gordon in full Committee touched on this today. It will be the intention of this Subcommittee to hear any and every person that would like to discuss or comment on a bill. And I mean _all_ people. As a matter of fact, as the Chairperson pointed out, this may be, might be, the only opportunity that citizens have to comment to the extent they want and in any fashion they want regarding legislation which will come through the HRS Committee. So I want to reiterate, that it is the chair's intention for the meetings of this Subcommittee to be informal but to be totally exhaustive. It is my hope that not a single person will be able to say, "I didn't have a chance to comment" or "I didn't have a chance to express my feelings." I know

3

the staff is aware that I have made a special effort to do that on previous pieces of legislation, especially the controversial ones. So I want to make clear that it is my intention to take public testimony from any person who wants to speak. All we would ask is that they do fill out, pursuant to House Rules, the Committee appearance record.

Since the full Committee will be so reliant upon this Subcommittee, its members and the staff, I ask you to thoroughly screen, to digest, to amend, to change and, yes, in some cases, to kill legislation. We've all got a responsibility to be as thorough as we can. I need to emphasize this because I recognized, during my brief two years up here, that this isn't always done and, without trying to make a judgment on which way is better, I would prefer that we take our time. Our agendas will be full, but if we don't get to all of the bills, then that is fine. Those we get to we will thoroughly go through.

Additionally, this Subcommittee will have what I consider to be a serious responsibility. And that is not only to screen and review thoroughly and totally every bill filed which is referred to this Subcommittee, but, as well, if it is the will of this Subcommittee, to initiate legislation as Committee drafts and Committee bills. Pursuant to that responsibility, I am going to ask John Phelps to put out a communication to all members of the Subcommittee requesting and soliciting any broad areas of concern that the individual members have. They can be areas of concern to us individually or they may affect our own constituency more than they might others. So I would ask that the staff person for this Subcommittee request and solicit from each member of the Subcommittee your areas of concern. If you can be specific as to changes in the statutes that you would like drafted as a Committee bill or Subcommittee bill, I'd like you to communicate that to John and let us then have some time to begin working on Committee drafts.

For our two new members, one might wonder why would we want to put in a Committee draft when I can put in a bill myself. Having authored some of the worst legislation ever considered by this Legislature, I can tell you my preference is that the staff do alot of research rather than the individual members. Additionally, there are political considerations such that, if a bill does find its way to the floor, it probably has a better ability to be received if it is a Committee draft. It simply reflects more than one person's thought has gone in it. So unless you have a strong feeling that you prefer to be the sole initiator of the legislation, I think you will find the staff analysis to be objective, to be independent, and I think frankly it will probably be a little more comprehensive than your own research might be. So, repeating, it is my request of all members, identify the areas as they relate to health and mental health that you are concerned about, and we'll certainly ask staff to provide the resources necessary to screen those subject matters and solicit information from the various departments and other interested persons about their feelings on the legislation.

I might add a point that I think the Chairman of the House Appropriations Committee would feel is appropriate. Many of us run for public office because we sincerely feel we want to make the system better. It doesn't take long to realize that to change it significantly probably affects dollars, especially as you look at the jurisdiction of this Subcommittee, again having the broad area of responsibility of the largest department in state government. With that being the case, I would ask that each Subcommittee member in his or her own legislation, as well as as a member of this Subcommittee, be sensitive to the very difficult area of social service and human need in juxtaposition to the cost of those social services and social needs. Specifically, what I'm saying is you are entitled to vote the way you feel on every single bill, but if there is a significant fiscal impact, it may be just cruel to both the sponsor of the bill and potential recipients of those services to lead them to believe that that bill is going to become law. The likelihood of that bill passing is minimal and, make no mistake, every bill that has a fiscal impact either will be referred to the Appropriations Committee or can be re-referred at a later point. What I am simply saying is each member should evaluate the cost impact in a very serious and sobering way because we are going to be held accountable for that, and I don't think it's fair to our colleagues in the Appropriations Committee to pass legislation, albeit good, worthwhile legislation, that has additional dollars impact, knowing full well that they are going to have to kill it in that Committee. I think we ought to be bigger than that in the sense of recognizing what the bill can do and what it costs to do it.

Let me add one final point, and then I'll hit a couple of administrative matters. I touched on it earlier. Speaker Tucker has said it rather clearly, that it is his feeling that once we make it into this very august body, we ought to be big enough to recognize that some of our thoughts may be appropriate but maybe the timing is wrong. It just would not be right to just pass a bill out for "good ole Charlie" just because he or she is a good ole guy or a good ole gal. Therefore, I will reiterate the Speaker's suggestion that if there is a negative aspect to a bill, we ought to be big enough to come forward, certainly having the mutual respect of our colleagues, and flat out kill the bill or, if you want, to have a little more mercy and temporarily pass it. All I am saying is this Subcommittee and, as I understand Speaker Tucker's directions, all Subcommittees of the House should have the responsibility and the authority to kill legislation. It just is not right to waste the time of the full Committees and other subsequent Committees on legislation for "good ole Charlie" when the bill should have been killed and each of the members knows it. So I would suggest we have the courage and the kind of will that is necessary, and I think that all of us, after we have had our first half a dozen bills killed, will recognize it is more common than we might think.

Okay, with that as some brief introductory remarks and recognizing the presence now of our distinguished Vice Chairman, Dr. Lehman, let me hit on a couple of administrative matters, see if any Subcommittee members have any comments--staff as well can comment if they wish--then we'll go ahead and take up our two pieces of legislation.

A couple of my personal preferences, if you will. Number one is as this Subcommittee takes up legislation, I prefer that the sponsor of the legislation be here to move it. I recognize that we all have difficult time constraints and we all have heavy schedules. I will commit to the members of the Subcommittee that I will adjust the schedule any way I can for the convenience of the members, but I think if a member has a strong enough conviction to file a piece of legislation, even if it's by request, I'd like the benefit of his thoughts personally, or her thoughts, so it will be my will, as we did last year, to not take up any bills--we'll certainly be glad to temporarily pass them--unless the sponsors of the bills are here personally to move the bills.

Secondly, I think, as a courtesy to each of the members, we should make every effort to start the meetings on time and end them on time. I happened to have had the honor of serving in the military, and I regret to say I'm just conditioned that way. If we have a quorum (whatever point after the starting time we have a quorum), it's my intention to start the meeting. Again, Dr. Lehman and I have served together, and he knows that's sort of the way I work. I recognize that politically maybe you lose a couple of votes, but I just don't think it is courteous to others, and I think if we all make an effort, I think we can meet that time schedule or else notify the staff or the chairman. All questioning and dialogue will go through the Chair. I'm not doing this to try and control the meetings, and only time will prove whether I'm sincere when I say that, I'm doing it because after taking up bills such as Death with Dignity and others, it is the only efficient way to run a meeting. I will not make it so formal and stiff that we can't have good communication. But I am going to insist on it, and I will rule out of order any dialogue with people in the audience as well as among Subcommittee members unless it goes through the Chair. I'll be reasonable, but I am asking for at least your courtesy in that regard.

I repeat, anybody who wants to speak on a bill will be heard before this Subcommittee, any amendment at any time that any member wants to move will be heard. I'll commit that to these members and I'll reiterate it again. And I'll finally reiterate the point of the request for areas of concern as far as the members

7

are concerned. Now, Dr. Lehman, do you have any comments, before we get to your bill.

DR. LEHMAN: Oh, I'm sorry I was late. I was with Mr. Page. I had a meeting and I just couldn't . . .

MCKNIGHT: Fumble the ball one more time and you're out of the game.

LEHMAN: And I'm out, that's all. Okay. And I can tell you that we have a very fine Subcommittee Chairman, excellent.

MCKNIGHT: You were supposed to add another paragraph on that, you're supposed to go into my background, remember. Alright, Rep. Burnsed, do you have anything you want to go to the Subcommittee or otherwise comment?

BURNSED: Not at this point.

MCKNIGHT: Rep. Evans? Okay, any staff members, who I might add-- there is a temptation occasionally to refer to the staff members and ask them questions, "What do you think of this bill?" I'll repeat what all of us who have been in for a short time know, they don't have any opinions; at five o'clock they do, unless we're still meeting. So staff is independent and I'll repeat again, I think they're the finest group around. Further comments or questions? Alright, anybody now, before we take up these two bills, who wants to testify on HM 5 by Dr. Lehman or HB 35 by Rish, we need you to sign an attendance card. Okay, further discussion? Okay, take up HB 5 by Dr. Lehman. Dr. Lehman is recognized on the bill.

State Representative Bob McKnight debating back-pumping amendment on House Floor, 1976.

Reverend Joseph Coates from Perrine and Representative McKnight in new House Chamber, 1978.

Final photo of the Florida House of Representatives in the Old Capitol, 1977.

CHAPTER 7

The Campaign Against Two Senators

The day after qualifying ended, I received an invitation from Hal Bergida, executive director of the Tiger Bay Political Club in downtown Miami's Dupont Plaza Hotel, to debate Senator Ralph Poston for District 38. The invitation said that the media would be invited, and I was told that the debate was going to be televised live, which was unheard of then. As has always been my practice, I had done extensive research on Poston's voting record and public positions. One vote that stood out above all the rest was that on the Equal Rights Amendment ("ERA") to the U.S. Constitution.

The Congress had authorized states to adopt the amendment, and a number of them had done so at the time of the debate. Legislation to adopt the amendment had been introduced in Florida, but it had not yet been adopted. During the 1978 session of the legislature, the ERA was taken up and defeated, *by one vote*. Poston, who was one of the co-sponsors, had decided, apparently without a clear explanation, to withdraw his sponsorship of the amendment, and he became a decisive no vote. Women all over the state and even the country were outraged. I had previously expressed support for the amendment and declared that I would continue to support it.

So two high profile issues had surfaced in the District 38 campaign, even before the race started—the reprimand of Senator Poston by his colleagues and his vote against the ERA amendment, which was subsequently defeated, ironically, by one vote. We were to find out that there was an even more volatile issue to be introduced at the Tiger Bay Debate.

In driving to the debate, I mentioned to Susan that I thought Poston might bring up my missed votes when I was with her after the loss of our baby, described earlier. Sure enough, as I sat down at the podium, I noticed a Poston campaign brochure highlighting my absent votes. But he went further and said that, although I was considered to be a nice person, I was absent from important votes and added something to the effect that I was not committed enough to my responsibilities to stay in Tallahassee and vote for my constituents. He amplified on this theme in his introductory debate remarks, and needless to say, I was steaming. You should know that the room was packed to overflowing. All the South Florida news outlets including TV, radio, print news and even some national news (because of the ERA angle) were present. The anti-ERA crowd was dressed in red and the pro-ERA crowd was dressed in green. There appeared to be about equal numbers of both. When I was asked to respond to Poston's opening remarks, I paused to get my breath and then pointed toward Poston and said, "Senator, during the time you cited that I was absent from the House of Representatives, I was with Susan after we lost our baby, and you knew it—Senator, if it were ever to happen again, I would be with her again!" The crowd noise was beyond description, and interestingly, the crowd in red probably yelled approval the loudest, because of their proud support of families. I overheard one political pundit say, "The District 38 race is over!" The senator was visibly shaken and compounded his problem by saying something to the effect that he did not mean to suggest I should not support my wife. The campaign contributions flowed to us from people I did not know. Because of the ERA, I received campaign contributions from actor Alan Alda, actress Valerie Harper (Rhoda Morgenstern of the *Mary Tyler Moore* TV series), philanthropist Stuart Mott (of the Mott beverage family), and feminist Gloria Steinem. It took me a while to come down from the emotions of the debate, but we finally hunkered down for a long summer campaign.

In previous campaigns, we were not able to afford television advertising, but it appeared this campaign would be different. Two veteran producers of political commercials, Mike Vasalinda and former Leon County commissioner Gary Yordon, both from Tallahassee, shot a number of commercials featuring our family. That "family" theme was a perfect follow-up to the

Poston debate gaffe. To my surprise, ours was the fifth highest fundraiser among all the state legislative races in 1978.

During the campaign, Poston's reprimand seldom surfaced, except when it was brought up by newspaper editorial boards. One exception was in Islamorada, a part of the central Keys, which was a part of the senatorial district. During a town hall meeting, one of the people in the audience asked Senator Poston why the people in that area should vote for him in light of the reprimand, and he responded poorly, looking harshly at me as if I planted the question, which was certainly not true.

In planning the Senate campaign, we wanted to come up with a lasting media brand. We settled on a very straightforward message, *Bob McKnight...Senate...Integrity*. It was intended to convey a positive message about me, but it could also have been interpreted to convey a negative message about Poston. We used the University of Miami colors, orange lettering against a dark green background, over a picture of me at a press conference at the Tiger Bay Club. The photograph of me at the press conference was real, and reflected the logos of the media covering the event. When our billboards went up, I got a call from an executive with ABC affiliate WPLG asking me to remove their logo. I told them I would if I had put it there, but that it was the work of their reporter. The picture was not altered. Once again, the endorsements were a key element of our campaign.

A third person, Ellen Allen, whom I did not know, entered the primary at the last minute, and managed to garner a surprising number of votes because of her name—the same as Representative Joe Allen (D., Key West), one of my strongest supporters. However, when the votes were counted, Senator Poston was defeated and I was now the Democratic nominee for the District 38 Senate seat. Although there was great celebration on victory night, Susan kept me grounded by interrupting an interview with a reporter from the Associated Press, saying, "Bob, how about being a good new senator-designate and taking the garbage out." I smiled and thought to myself, it is only for the rest of my natural life. If I have not stated it, I love my wife.

During the general election, my opponent was former senator, Don Gruber. Don had won an upset election over former senator, Eddie Gong (D., Miami), hammering away on Senator Gong's absenteeism from the Senate, while lecturing at his alma mater, Harvard University, in Boston. Most political observers felt we would win, because it did not appear that Gruber had any smoking gun issues on me. Still, since our campaign had raised so much financial support, he decided to run ads alleging that I was a tool of the special interests. In reality, that couldn't have been farther from the truth, and the editorials refuted that assertion for me. Even the Republican Senate leader, Ken Plante (R., Oviedo), told me that he had rejected Gruber's request for financial campaign support from their party. We won the election big, totaling almost 100,000 votes. As Robert Redford asked his wife in the 1972 movie, *The Candidate*, and I repeated to Susan on election night, "Well, now what do we do?" The answer was to make plans to accept the people's mandate, and be the best junior senator from the 38th possible.

Campaign bumper sticker (above) and brochure
for Senate campaign (below), 1978.

Campaign brochure for Senator Ralph Poston District 38, 1978.

Campaign advertisement for Senate District 38, Bob McKnight, 1978.

The Golden Years ...　　　　88　　　　Robert McKnight

CHAPTER 8

The Junior Senator from the 38th

The day after the election, I got a call from Senator Sherman Winn inviting me to a meeting of the eight Dade County senators with the leading candidate for Senate president in 1980, Dan Scarborough (D., Jacksonville). One of the supporters of Senator Scarborough was prominent Southeast Bank lobbyist, John Roberts. Also present at the meeting was newly elected Broward County senator, Ken Jenne (D., Hollywood). I later found out that Jenne and I had attended Lake Worth High School at the same time, although I was two years ahead of him. We shared the fact that we had both beaten incumbent senators (he beating Bill Zinkell) to win our seats. At that time, our wives had become good friends as well. As of this writing, sadly, I have learned that Ken's promising political career has come to an end as he has resigned from office as Sheriff of Broward County and pleaded guilty to a number of serious finance-related charges. One of the Dade Delegation's most senior and respected senators, the late Ken Myers (D., Miami), attended the meeting, and expressed surprise at its intended purpose. It turned out that he also had thoughts of running for president in 1980 and argued against committing to Scarborough at that meeting. The meeting turned out to be a non-event, and the race for Senate president continued.

That evening, I was invited to another get-acquainted meeting, this one with the new Senate president, Phil Lewis (D., West Palm Beach), and the new governor, Bob Graham. The meeting was held at the Miami Airport Sheraton Hotel and was attended by all of the Dade senators. I knew President Lewis well and had worked with him on the back pumping legislation described earlier. He was one of the only senators who could bridge the gap between the older, more conservative senators led by the Dean, Dempsey Barron (D., Panama City), and the more moderate new senators led by Buddy MacKay (D., Ocala) and Harry Johnston (D., West Palm Beach). When the governor-elect arrived, he knelt before Lewis and bowed, suggesting that he understood the equal separation of powers between the executive and legislative branches. In actuality, Graham and Lewis were best of friends.

I mentioned earlier the touching moment when I stood on the floor of the Senate to be sworn into office by the Chief Justice of the Supreme Court, alongside my wife, Susan, and my longtime mentor, Senator Jerry Thomas. Years before, he had switched to the Republican Party because of his frustration with the liberal trend of the Democrats. (It was ironic that I as a Democrat, was being mentored by Senator Thomas, then the leading Republican in the state.) Jerry and I talked about the numerous conversations we had had about my interest in following his path, and the fact that by the grace of God, I had been successful. Unfortunately, that demon cancer took the senator's life shortly afterward. I, of course, missed my mom and dad's presence at the swearing in, but was comforted by the presence of the senator and Susan's family; her parents, Herb and Elizabeth Williams; her sister and her husband, Dianne and Billy Adkins; and Susan's grandfather, "Big Daddy," Willy Williams. It was a day I will never forget.

After being sworn into office in Tallahassee, I was surprised to find that the president had appointed me vice-chairman of both the Committee on Natural Resources and the Committee on Health and Rehabilitative Services. This was quite unusual for a freshman, even one with experience in the House. My other committee assignment was Community Affairs. I was invited to join a group of new senators who seemed to have mutual interests: George Stuart (D., Orlando), Pat Frank (D., Tampa), Paul Steinberg (D., Miami Beach), Gwen Margolis (D., Miami Beach), Ken Jenne (D., Hollywood), Pat Neal (D., Bradenton), and the late Pete Skinner (D., Lake City). A member of the House who followed us into the Senate who became a special friend was Senator Tom Brown (D., Daytona Beach). Tom's wife, Jo, is one of Susan's closest friends today. Also, a special senator who provided me sage counsel over the years was none other than the distinguished (and only) former Senate president and Speaker of the House, Mallory Horne (D., Tallahassee). They just didn't get any better than President Horne. The veteran senators began paying attention to the Class of 1978 because of our numbers as well as our talent.

As indicated earlier, Senator Dempsey Barron was the Dean of the Senate, with over 30 years of legislative service. He was a very interesting person—bright, engaging, unpredictable, tough, and, most importantly, the most knowledgeable on the rules. When he was first elected he was an outsider, never joining the infamous "Pork Choppers" from North Florida. The Pork Choppers strongly opposed increased urban representation as provided by the Court's directive of "one man, one vote." The choppers formed a tight bond and generally voted as a conservative bloc of votes from North Florida. But as Barron continued to get reelected, he expressed concern about the potential power imbalance of the urban, South Florida senators. I believe he was always suspicious of manipulation of the voter rolls under the Court's decree of "one man, one vote." In any event, Senator Barron had taken a personal interest in the election of the president of the Senate for the last decade. His actions were so recognized, that they became the stuff of legends and rumors. It was said that one could not be elected president of the Senate without his blessing. You will recall I mentioned the 1974 election when Dick Pettigrew upset George Hollahan, and it was most significant because Hollahan was the first Senate President-Designate from Miami. With Hollahan's loss, Dempsey Barron became the Senate president in 1974, declaring on the floor of the Senate that Governor Askew should, "Stay the hell out of my Senate." Askew, who was not present at the time, quickly called a press conference and declared sternly, "Senator, I wish to inform you that the Senate does not belong to you, but rather to the people of the great state of Florida." Score one for the governor, but make no mistake, Barron had clout and he knew how to use it. He had a plaque on his desk reading, "Assume Nothing," and he always practiced it. Repeatedly, in campaigns for Senate president, senators had assumed their election, only to have Barron replace them with senators of his own choosing: Bob Saunders was replaced by Lew

Brantley in 1976, the late Jack Gordon was replaced by Phil Lewis in 1978; Dan Scarborough was replaced by W.D. Childers in 1980; Mattox Hair was replaced by Curtis Peterson in 1982; and Ken Jenne was replaced by John Vogt in 1986.

The results of Barron's influence were catastrophic when the leaders were toppled—careers were literally created or destroyed. Barron always had excellent peripheral vision. I remember once sitting with him in the waiting room of the governor's office for a meeting with the governor, when two individuals walked out in front of us. Senator Barron leaned over to me and said, "Senator, I think we did not get invited to the more important meeting before the meeting." He was completely correct.

I neither voted with Senator Barron, nor was I considered a supporter of his. But I did respect him and, yes, I will admit now that I had a little bit of fear when I found he was opposing me. He was a skilled lawyer and a ferocious debater. My criticism was not of Dempsey, but of the weak lemming-like senators who blindly followed him. When Barron was described as a fighter, it was meant to be literal. In 1982, he parted ways with his longtime friend W.D. Childers and later they ended up in a fistfight on the floor of the Senate. He passed away a few years ago, but those who were fortunate to serve with him will always remember the landmark impact of the "Red Barron" on the Florida Senate. I should also point out how supportive his wife, Terri Jo, was of the senator, both in and out of office. Terri Jo was an excellent attorney with a sharp political mind, which was of great benefit to Dempsey. I had the pleasure of visiting with both of them at their ranch in Bonifay a few years ago, and found them following with great interest the activities of the legislature.

The legislature was still under the multi-member apportionment formula, and my two colleagues representing the same constituents were Dick Anderson (D., Miami) and Vernon Holloway (D., Miami). Dick was elected in 1978 in his first campaign, and he was obviously helped by being an All-Pro Safety with the Miami Dolphins. Although Dick and I did not vote alike very often, Susan and I developed a very close relationship with

Dick and his terrific wife, Joy. That was not the case with Holloway, who lost his reelection in 1980. You may recall that when Holloway vacated his House seat in 1976 to run for the Senate, I ran for his old House seat and was successful. At the start of the 1979 session, the president asked the three of us who should sit on a new select committee, Areas of Critical State Concern ("ACSC"). All three of us represented Monroe County and the Florida Keys, and that area was directly affected by ACSC. Holloway did not want to serve on the ACSC because he felt he might have to vote against his constituents and he was up for reelection in two years; and Anderson was swamped with critical issues affecting the Commerce Committee, which he would later chair. I accepted the appointment, and it was indeed controversial. We dealt with a fundamental issue covered by the state and national constitutions, which was private property rights. The argument essentially was that if the government declares the use of private land at less than its highest and best use, then the constitution defines that as a taking, and the government should compensate the owner for it. This was an issue of foremost importance to Governor Graham. I was aided in my work on the ACSC by one of my best friends in legislative service, and one of the most courageous public officials I have ever met, Representative Joe Allen (D., Key West). As they say in Key West, Joe was always my bubba.

As always, my family came to Tallahassee with me each legislative session. Michelle was then six years old, so we had to make arrangements for her in public schools. Over the years, she met many outstanding individuals, and I was always so impressed how at ease she was in meeting new people. Susan became close friends with many of the spouses of the legislators and Cabinet members. She even hosted a tea for her good friend, the First Lady, Adele Graham. Although just a baby at the time, Bobby still talks today about joining the governor for a swim in his outdoor Jacuzzi. I mentioned earlier Michelle's connection to press conferences. One that comes to mind occurred in my district at a ribbon cutting for an expansion of Coral Reef Hospital in Kendall.

Since I was chairman of the Senate Committee on Health and Rehabilitative Services, with jurisdiction over hospitals, I was invited to cut the ribbon and make remarks at their press conference in front of the local electronic and print media. It took place on a Saturday, and I invited Michelle to join me. She was playing with her marbles at home and asked if she could bring them to the press conference. I said sure. While I was speaking, I heard Michelle in the background exclaim, "Uh, oh, Dad, there go my marbles." The floors were newly polished and the marbles went everywhere. All of us were crawling on our hands and knees to find them, because, after all, this was a hospital where injuries were not supposed to happen, but be treated. That day, Michelle could have easily beaten her dad in an election at Coral Reef Hospital.

Although I was not on the ballot in 1980, there were a number of very important races underway around the state. One in my district became a poster civics lesson for the voting public. In Monroe County, encompassing Key West and the Florida Keys, a political dichotomy existed between the pro and anti-development factions. That year pitted a well-entrenched county commission incumbent favoring more development in that district, against a newcomer who supported conservation named Curt Blair. I tried not to get directly involved in that race because I had friends and supporters on both sides of the campaign. Still, I could not help but be impressed with how Blair shaped the race into a David and Goliath fight, with himself in the role of David. You will recall my first recommendation back in Chapter One—be careful of the public sentiment for the underdog. Sure enough, against all odds and a massive financial war chest, Curt Blair squeaked out a victory in that highly watched county commission race. You ask how close was the election? Can you recall all of the times you have heard people say, "Make sure and vote! You never know—the outcome could be decided by one vote!" Folks, the Honorable Curt Blair was sworn in as the new Monroe County commissioner with the cushion of one vote!!! That may bring back recollections for you political junkies of the "landslide Lyndon" race in which U.S. Senator Lyndon Johnson won a close and questionable election and went on to become president of the United States. Some have said that President Kennedy's father was the financial support of his son's whisker-close race in West Virginia, which resulted in Kennedy's election as president. So, the razor-thin election of Monroe County commissioner Curt Blair that year is again empirical evidence that every vote counts.

With experience, I found myself getting more and more comfortable debating my colleagues on the floor of the Senate. Yet, one day I met my match and then some. A very smart attorney, Dick Langley (R., Clermont), was debating me on legislation affecting water management districts in the state. I was becoming frustrated because I could not overcome some of his objections to my position. He then startled me by asking, "Senator, where does the water come from in these districts?" I stumbled and stammered thinking, what would it be, the ground, or God or what? Since I could not answer him, he was gentle with me and said, "I am sure you were about to say the rain." Man, did I feel like a jerk, and deservedly so. I looked up in the gallery and saw Susan laughing. I knew I was going to get razzed when I got home.

Another favorite Republican of mine was Warren Henderson (R., Sarasota). Warren was a longtime veteran of the Senate who had a passion about protecting the environment. A bill came up on the floor that opened up a small area of his district for commercial fishing. He told me he could not vote that way because it would harm his conservationist voting record back home. Several senators debated on behalf of the commercial fishermen, and when they did, he began debating the other side, especially when the TV cameras were running. The legislation passed, which I believe Warren might have actually favored, and yet he was able to show his folks back home that his conservation record was intact. I am not sure if that is what you call a win-win, but now you know why it is said that making laws often reminds one of making sausage.

I mentioned Senate president W.D. Childers (D., Pensacola) earlier—he served in that capacity from 1980-82. W.D.

was an impetuous, spunky legislator whose nickname, "Banty Rooster," was given to him by his mentor, Dempsey Barron. Senator Childers was never long on details and facts. Allegedly, he once called a press conference in his district to announce that he had secured initial funding for the construction of a football stadium for his hometown college, the University of West Florida. At the press conference one of the reporters present asked, "Senator, although your efforts are appreciated, are you aware that the University of West Florida does not have a football team?" I was told that those funds were quickly transferred to a critical need in the senator's district, without further discussion.

Childers was involved in another historic skirmish, that being between him and first term state representative Roberta Fox (D., Coral Gables). At that time, President Nixon had initiated diplomatic discussions with Red China by encouraging ping-pong matches between players from the two countries. It became known as ping-pong diplomacy, which Childers, a strident conservative, violently opposed. Meanwhile, Representative Fox represented the Hialeah Race Track, and their racing dates had to be approved every year by the legislature. Innocently, Roberta had voted in favor of a rather harmless resolution supporting ping-pong diplomacy with Red China. Childers heard about Fox's vote, found her bill authorizing the racing dates of Hialeah, and pulled it from consideration by the Senate. Roberta was shocked, and stood on the floor after asking to be recognized on a point of personal privilege. She could not believe that in the 1970's she was being asked by one of her colleagues to trade a vote dealing with Red China (against the ping pong resolution) for a vote dealing with Hialeah (in which case Childers would release her bill on the voting dates). Little did the fine people of Hialeah know that they were so important that they were traded that day for Red China!!!

One initiative that I introduced while I was in the legislature, and for which I was extremely proud, was the Florida Management Fellows career development program. I first got the idea from my IBM work experience. The company had a highly regarded Fellows Program for the best of the best of the company.

IBMers were exposed, early in their careers, to some of this country's greatest challenges—famine, civil rights, blighted communities, economic development, the arts, and politics. Although I would have given anything to be considered for the program, I never had the opportunity. Since I was involved in social service public policy in the legislature, I noticed very few "up and comers" who wanted to make that area a career. Former Florida Health and Rehabilitative Services secretary David Pingree and South Florida HRS District director David Dunbar helped me draft the legislation. Because I had such strong influence over the HRS department, I started with the program in that agency. After Governor Graham signed the legislation, you would have thought that the bureaucrats who had to implement it were going to go nuts—who ever heard of a state employee placed on a fast track with multiple assignments and tasks? The first graduate of the program, Joe Pankowski, was a model for those who followed. He and his wife, Dr. Mary, became good friends of Susan's and mine, and to my knowledge, the program continues to flourish. Andy McMullen, my friend and wonderful sentry for state employees, still thinks I lost my head when I introduced the idea in the early '80s.

Another program I introduced that did not fare as well as Management Fellows was the Artificial Reef program. Since I represented Miami and the Keys in the Senate, I was very familiar with the strong sport and commercial fishing interest as it pertained to the creation of artificial reefs. I usually got deathly sick to my stomach during trips on small boats into the Atlantic to sink abandoned navy and coast guard vessels. However, there was no statutory authority to sink the reefs, so I introduced a bill and a modest amount of funding for local governments to match, to help get the program started. I mention later Senator Barron's coalition of Democrats and Republicans created to unseat President Childers's leadership team in the Senate. One of Barron's most vocal allies was Senator Curtis Peterson (D., Eaton Park). Although his son and I were fraternity brothers at Florida Southern College in the '60s, Curtis and I never saw eye to eye. After my retirement from the Senate in 1982, Peterson led an assault on the Artificial Reef program, taking all of its funding and transferring it to sponsor a beauty pageant in his district. I still occasionally get calls from sports enthusiasts asking what happened to the program. As I said in the Speaker Tucker stories, this is another example of the old adage, "to the victor go the spoils."

As you have noted from the title of this book, political observers have often referred to the '70s and '80s in the legislature as the "Golden Years." Veteran Capitol reporter and author Martin Dyckman of the *St. Petersburg Times*, once described the time as the "Golden Age" in a 2002 column. A fair question is why? I think as best it can be determined, the time was largely the result of court-mandated reapportionment to reflect one man, one vote. I made reference to this in the portion of the book featuring Senator Barron. Prior to that ruling in the '60s, Florida was considered to be the most mal-apportioned legislature in the country, largely attributed to the political clout of the Pork Choppers. The nefarious manipulation of the legislative process in the '50s was legendary. *But, Florida's legislative apportionment framers in the '60s came up with the unusual formula of multi-member district governance in the urban areas.* The argument for single-member districts was increasing minority participation and accountability. Conversely, multi-member districts appeared to the framers to have the potential of electing representatives with broader thinking, and less self-interest. Add to that the altruism of the John Kennedy era among emerging baby boomers in the late '60s, and early '70s, and many felt the result would be that the very best Floridians would make themselves available for public service. This was expected to be particularly true in the urban areas of Miami, Tampa, and Jacksonville, with so many residents with professional experience and advanced education. The radical change was adopted and the urban delegations, in my opinion, may have included the best legislators ever elected in the state. Fortunately, it generally seemed, the electorate selected the most able representatives around the state after reapportionment. This was reflective of the era referred to as the Golden Years as well as being central to the message of this book.

One of the most important pieces of legislation to pass during my service was the so-called Sunset Act. It was so popular that it was essentially replicated in the federal government as well as in most states. The authors were two outstanding legislators, Senator Ken Myers (D., Miami) and Representative Pat Neal (D., Bradenton). The idea was to dissolve all of state government and require the legislature to reauthorize its existence agency by agency. It was argued that this would force us to look carefully at all of the agencies, reauthorizing only those essential to the state. After the novelty wore off, it became unbelievably time-consuming and almost drudgery. I recall one hot afternoon in the Senate, taking up some very unexciting agencies—the watch repair folks, the foresters, the clinical psychologists, and massage parlors. I think I remember standing in a corner with senators Barron, MacKay, Carlucci, and Kirkpatrick discussing what these professionals did in their jobs. None of us knew much about any of the agencies and I seem to recall one of us saying something to the effect that we might as well draw straws on whom to reauthorize. I am not sure what happened from there, I just know that the next day the headline in the state press said that the Senate had decided to deregulate clinical psychologists. Watch repairers, foresters, and massage parlors were reauthorized. Again, as stated in an earlier chapter, sometimes law-making is described as making sausage.

I received a wonderful award at the end of my 1980 session from the Florida Jaycees. With the support of a former Florida Jaycee president and fellow legislator, Randy Avon, I was selected as one of the *Five Outstanding Young Men In Florida*. This is an extraordinary award, especially in light of the august previous winners including the Selmon Brothers of the Tampa Bay Buccaneers and a former colleague and now the senior United States senator from Florida, Bill Nelson. My membership in the Coral Gables Jaycees was a memorable experience, one I will be grateful for always. Also, in 1980, I was elected chairman of the 30-member Dade County Legislative Delegation. On paper, this made me one of the most powerful politicians in the state, but as most political observers know, it is one thing to chair the largest delegation in the state, and quite another to get them to vote together. As Senator Harry Johnston (D., West Palm Beach) once quipped to me, "Bob, you can't even get your Dade Delegation to vote together for a resolution honoring Mother's Day." Unfortunately, he was right, but I tried an experiment to leverage the voting clout of the urban south Florida members. I formed a caucus made up of Palm Beach, Broward, and Dade County legislators to vote as a bloc. I specifically had members from one county sponsor legislation benefiting another county to emphasize to the legislators that the problems of the state do not recognize county boundaries. I was commended for an unusual strategy, but it found only limited success.

Another honor afforded me in 1980 was receiving an invitation from President Carter to attend a briefing at the White House on his Strategic Arms Limitation Agreement ("SALT II"). The president was having difficulty getting bipartisan support on the initiative in the Congress, and decided to solicit grass-roots support among legislators from the 50 states. Speaker Brown and I were the two legislators invited from Florida. I had an opportunity to spend some time with my old friend and former legislator Dick Pettigrew, who was then on the president's senior staff in Washington. Later in the year, I also had a chance to meet and spend time with the late president Ronald Reagan, future president George Bush (the 41st), Vice President Walter Mondale, U.S. Senate Armed Services Committee Chairman Sam Nunn (D., Georgia), and the senior U.S. senator from Massachusetts, Ted Kennedy. The meeting with Kennedy was somewhat tense because he was asking me to support his candidacy against another Democrat, the incumbent president Jimmy Carter. I have never figured where the bad blood came from between those two, but it sure ran deep.

As an aside, I have often been asked, of the national figures I have met or followed closely, which ones do I think would have made the best presidents? As you can guess, my two favorites are the governors with whom I served in legislature, Reubin Askew and Bob Graham. Putting those two aside, five great Americans who would have made outstanding presidents in my opinion are: former senator Sam Nunn (mentioned above), former congressman Lee Hamilton (D., Indiana and of recent fame as the co-chairman of the Baker-Hamilton Commission on U.S. National Security), the late senator Henry "Scoop" Jackson (D., Washington), Senator Richard Lugar (R., Indiana), and the late senator Mike Mansfield (D., Montana). All of these gentlemen seemed to have the common traits of intellect, integrity, balance of thought, measured response and, of critical importance, a sense of humor. Mansfield's response to reporters' questions stands out in my mind: he reportedly answered most questions, even the complex ones, with a simple and direct, "yes, no, or maybe." When is the last time you heard that response from a politician? Clearly, our selection process for presidents in America is far from perfect, but it is the best we know.

As happened after my first two years in the House of Representatives, the Senate conducted its survey of members for the *Florida Times-Union*-sponsored awards. The presiding officer, as before, spread the word among his lieutenants regarding who should win the awards. I had heard that the president's favorite was my good friend and an outstanding first-term member of the Senate, Clark Maxwell (R., Merritt Island). Clark and I were first elected to the House in 1974, and he was, by most accounts, a late political bloomer. We found that we were fraternity brothers at Florida Southern, but at different times. I certainly felt that Clark was deserving of the award. But again, to my surprise, I was selected as the runner-up for the Allen Morris Award, *Most Outstanding First-Term Member of the Senate*. I was flattered because as I previously pointed out, we had an outstanding group of first-term members of the Senate in 1978. Later in my term, I received recognition from the *St. Petersburg Times*, which was based upon the voting by its Capitol bureau reporters, without influence from elected legislators. They correctly, in my opinion, selected Harry Johnston as the *Most Valuable Member of the Senate*, but senators

Barron, Jack Gordon and I were also nominated for the award. This was again surprising since I was still a freshman in the Senate.

One individual whom I truly enjoyed serving with was my former colleague in the Dade Delegation, former governor and senior U.S. senator, Bob Graham. As previously indicated, Bob and Adele were special friends to Susan and me during our service together. Those who know Bob well know of his brilliance and kindness, but you may not know that he has a terrific sense of humor. I can recall joining House Appropriations Subcommittee chairman and future speaker Jon Mills (D., Gainesville) on a trip to Washington with the governor. Jon and I had decided to hold up the governor's funding request for his pet project Community Care for the Elderly as a way to get his attention. While on the plane to Washington, the governor was not upset with us nor did he even raise his voice toward us. He simply began describing how he and Adele were recently talking about all the senior citizens who would be impacted by this draconian measure of the legislature. The governor asked if we knew who was behind this atrocity and Jon and I burst out laughing. The funds were restored by a telephone call from Mills and me to our staff, when our plane landed at Reagan International. Bob also had some sage advice for me just after my election to the House. He said that I should focus on one or two issues, and become an expert in those areas. I took his advice and selected as my priorities the areas of social services and natural resources.

As a sidebar on Graham, he was known to keep careful notes on small note pads in his pocket. Many of us who worked closely with him knew this and we once schemed to lift one from him to put some bogus notes in it. When we got our hands on one of the pads, we did not realize that he had them color-coded for certain days and events. He caught us and quickly discovered who the guilty parties were. A new school in my district mysteriously disappeared from the Department of Education construction list, but, thank goodness, later reappeared.

Like Speaker Tucker, Governor Graham had a good relationship with President Carter. Governor Graham was given the prestigious invitation to deliver the keynote address at the Democratic Convention in 1980. At that time, rumors circulated that the president might appoint the governor to his Cabinet. Immediately that triggered rumors that Lieutenant Governor Wayne Mixson would become governor and have the opportunity to appoint a new lieutenant governor. I got a call from a senior staffer to Governor Mixson, Ron Villella. He said Mixson wanted to make a trip into my district in the Keys and asked if I would like to join him. I said I would be honored, as it would be an opportunity for us to get to know each other better. We had served together in the House, and Susan and I had had a very fine relationship with him and Margie. We had a pleasant trip into Monroe County, and as I somewhat expected, nothing came up about any possible future roles for me in the current administration. Wayne went on to serve out the remainder of Bob Graham's term as governor and I always felt that he combined those rare attributes of a good personality with no-nonsense decision-making capability. He made a wonderful speech on the floor of the House in 1977 praising the military service of a great African American from Pensacola, Florida, Air Force General Chappy James.

An event at that time that made national and even international news was the release of thousands of prisoners from Cuba by their president, Fidel Castro. I can recall getting an urgent call from the governor's office asking me to meet with him and Representative Joe Allen (D., Key West). It was a Saturday morning, and senators Holloway and Anderson had left to return to their district for business. Susan was with me as we were going to have lunch across from the Capitol at Andrew's. When we got to the governor's office, he was on a speakerphone with the chairman of the U.S. House Foreign Relations Committee and our South Dade congressman Dante Fascell. There was live television coverage of the flotilla from Cuba to Florida, which became known as the Mariel Boatlift. We later found out that the prisoners who were released were those who had committed the worst kind of crimes and many, allegedly, had communicable diseases. My district office had already called to say that some of my constituents from the Keys had started across the Gulf Stream in small boats en route to Cuba to pick up some of the prisoners and return them to Florida for a healthy bounty. Unlike the original 1960 Cuban Air Lift initiated by President John Kennedy, this one had no order and chaos quickly set in. There was a backlash against the boatlift from Miami's Cuban community—they felt they had assimilated successfully among Floridians, and they were resentful that the prisoners selected by Castro were given their freedom, rather than their law-abiding relatives. President Carter was blamed for the fiasco, because he was not prepared for it. As you know, he was blamed for the hostage crisis in Iran at the end of his term. An interesting sidebar to this situation was that then-Arkansas governor Bill Clinton offered to incarcerate a large number of the released Cuban prisoners, over the strenuous objection of many of his constituents. When they were finally released, they committed some serious and alarming crimes in Arkansas, and it has been said that that is the reason Governor Clinton was not reelected to office. The impact of that crisis carried over for many years in South Florida.

During the Childers administration, a rift developed between the Democrats from urban areas and conservative Republicans. Senator Barron had fashioned the dissenters into a coalition of Republicans and conservative Democrats, and they actually totaled a majority of the 40 senators. I was in the Childers' camp and because of Barron's in-depth knowledge of the rules we had to be careful about ceding control of the Senate to his team. Childers decided to change the committee chairmen to strengthen his hold on power. I was already the chairman of the powerful Appropriations Subcommittee funding all of social services and the legal/prison system. Childers appointed me to also chair the Senate Committee on Health and Rehabilitative Services at the same time. I found out that this was history in the making. Only one senator had ever chaired both this committee of jurisdiction and its funding committee at the same time and that was my former and late colleague, Senator Ken Myers (D., Miami). I was told that as it related to social services and crime, I had more political power than the governor. Nonetheless, Susan continued to remind me to take out the garbage.

My role in the appropriations process became important for the state due to the large appropriation required for social services and the criminal justice system in the '80s. I was fortunate to have the support and recommendations of our subcommittee staff director, Patsy Eccles. As a result of the feuding described earlier, most appropriations issues were worked out directly between me and the House of Representative conferees on the Appropriations Conference Committee. I did observe one very effective technique for reminding members of the importance of frugality in the appropriations process. At that time, it was commonplace for the presiding officer of each chamber to receive a "trophy" appropriation for their district—a new school, new road, or new program of some kind. The closer a legislator was to the presiding officer, the more probable that a member would also get a trophy, just with a smaller price tag. In Congress today, these are referred to as earmarks (for example, U.S. Appropriations Chair and Senator Ted Steven's new road to nowhere in his home state of Alaska). Senate president Phil Lewis introduced the self-correcting technique. He had the appropriations chairman, and his best friend, Harry Johnston, put in the draft-spending bill a huge appropriation for a new school named after Lewis. He then came down to the committee meeting and asked that the appropriation for the school to bear his name be withdrawn from further consideration because he said the state could not afford it. All of a sudden, all of the other members of the committee looked embarrassed, and quietly asked that their "trophies" also be removed from the bill. That was one of the best cases of legislating by example, not by what was said.

From those appropriations subcommittee days, I recall the seemingly endless requests for social service needs. Florida was about to become the fourth-largest state, and its social needs then were substantial. As a result, I was subject to some of the most effective lobbyists in Tallahassee—representing the wealthy doctors, the politically powerful hospitals, and the thousands of recipients of the billion-dollar Medicaid program. But far and away, the lobbyist who hit me the hardest was none other than the polite and gracious former first lady, Donna Lou Askew. Facing a directive from my Senate appropriations chairman, Jack Gordon, to hold the line on spending, I froze appropriations increases for existing programs. One of those was of great and personal interest to Mrs. Askew (and as I came to find out, her husband, one former governor Askew), dealing with the cherished Children's Home Society. I can still recall my assistant saying, "Mr. Chairman, there is a Mrs. Askew on the phone—she says you and Susan know her." I picked up the phone and greeted her. She responded by saying, "Bob, what has happened to you? Rube and I were just talking the other night and we remember when...." I cringed and thought to myself, "I am not sure which is worse, getting lobbied by a wonderful lady like Donna Lou Askew or getting a root canal." I thought about it, and felt that I would opt for the root canal. The Children's Home Society got their full appropriations request. *Donna Lou Askew was the toughest lobbyist I ever faced.*

Probably the second toughest lobbyist for me was again, not a professional lobbyist, but in this case my colleague and good friend, Senator Harry Johnston (D., West Palm Beach). Harry was a very respected member of the Florida Bar, and, not surprisingly, had a sincere interest in adequate funding for the judiciary. Since I was the appropriations subcommittee chairman for judicial funding, Harry asked for a meeting to discuss it. He introduced me to Florida Appellate Judge Gavin Letts of Palm Beach County and later, Chief Justice Alan Sundberg of the Florida Supreme Court. Both gentlemen enjoyed great reputations and I listen intently to their plea for increased funding for the judiciary. I pointed out to them the freeze under which I was working, based upon Senator Gordon's directive described earlier, but said I would do what I could. Johnston appeared to feel uncomfortable pushing me further on the issue, so I moved forward with the appropriations process. When it became time to handle that appropriation on the floor, I noticed an amendment filed by Senator Hair (D., Jacksonville) proposing increased funding for the judges. It sounded exactly like what Johnston was seeking, but Harry was nowhere to be seen and he had said nothing to me about it. I looked at the back of the Senate Chamber where the pages and messengers sat, and saw a person sitting there covered by a rattling (because the individual was laughing) newspaper. Johnston had quietly put our friend Senator Hair up to the assignment of filing the pay raise amendment to throw me off. Harry was a one-of-a-kind lobbyist—always accomplished his objective, but with subtlety and finesse. He and his wife, Mary, were good friends and neighbors of Susan's and mine in Tallahassee.

As the end of the 1982 session approached, Susan and I talked of our plans. In principle, I believed in Florida's citizen legislature, where there would be a periodic turnover, and hopefully the introduction of fresh ideas. I did not oppose career politicians in Washington, but felt the states should be more open to change. Also, the legislature had become exceedingly acrimonious, and I felt I could make contributions to the state in other capacities. Lastly, as previously indicated, running for governor was in the back of my mind. The next election was in four years, and if I did not run for reelection in 1982, I could spend the time getting prepared for a statewide race, if it happened. Susan was disappointed, but supported my decision as I had always tried to support her decisions. At my old stomping ground, the Tiger Bay Club, I announced that I was retiring from the legislature at the age of thirty-eight. Because I served in the state's largest media market, South Florida, I was fortunate in my relatively short political career to be able to participate in all of the major television public affairs programs. These included WTVJ/CBS, WPLG/ABC, and WSVN/NBC, in addition to the radio programs previously mentioned. I also had an opportunity to meet and discuss important political issues on the record with Steve Croft, then with WTVJ, now *60 Minutes*; Richard Schlesinger, then WTVJ, now *48 Hours*; Michael Putney of WTVJ; the late Ralph Renick of WTVJ, and the late Ann Bishop of WPLG.

In wrapping up this part of my legislative journey, I have had a chance to reflect on many of the great people I observed in the legislative process who did not find their way into this book for one reason or another. I wish I could include all of the 640 members with whom I served, but I obviously cannot. However, since this will probably be the only such book I will write, I want to be sure to recognize a few members of the House and Senate who, along with those identified in the book, served Florida well by their stewardship, while I was in office with them: Senators Ed Dunn, Pat Thomas, John Vogt, John Ware, Mary Grizzle, David McClain, Gwen Margolis, Bob Crawford, Carrie Meek, Van Poole, Ron Silver, Bud Gardner, Dennis Jones, Toni Jennings, Curt Kiser, Jon Thomas, Jim Scott; and Representatives Jane Robinson, Jere Tolton, Hamilton Upchurch, Betty Easley, James Harold Thompson, Ron Richmond, Barry Richard, Bill Andrews, Bill James, John Culbreath, Dick Batchelor, Fred Jones, Billy Joe Rish, Tom Gustafson, Linda Cox, John Mica, Jim Brodie, Joe Lang Kershaw, Pete Dunbar, Dale Patchett, T.K. Wetherell, and Dan Webster. Their mark on lawmaking in Florida will long be remembered. It has been somewhat forgotten over the years, but in the early '70s, the respected Council of State Legislatures identified Florida as having the most independent and effective legislative body among the fifty United States. Perhaps that is one reason the era was known as the golden years.

Five individuals with whom I did not serve in the legislature, but to whom I must make reference are the former executive director of the Florida Senate, Howard Walton, former insurance commissioner and state representative, Phil Ashler, Sarasota County Tax Collector, Barbara Ford-Coates, former attorney general Bob Butterworth, and former commerce secretary and banker, Bill Sutton.

To the general public, Walton was unknown—he wasn't even listed in the official Clerk's Manual. But make no mistake, Howard Walton was a political power in the Golden Years of the Florida Legislature. He was a fanatic for detail and probably the person who was the closest parallel to him that I can think of would be J. Edgar Hoover. The Senate staff was large in numbers and impressive in academic credentials (I think I had three lawyers and two PhDs as staff on one committee I chaired), but Howard was on top of their every move. It was rumored that he was quite a liberal in his early years, but it was not evident when I was in the Senate. I believe all senators recognized that the heralded power of Dempsey Barron was to a significant extent possible because of his close relationship with Howard. Like Barron, I always respected Howard and made it a point to watch his every move when he began circulating around on the Senate floor.

Phil Ashler did serve in the legislature before me, and with great distinction I understand. Phil, from Pensacola, was a retired Admiral with his master's degree from Harvard. His close friend Governor Askew appointed him to serve as insurance commissioner on an interim basis. Phil was one of the most respected public servants on both sides of the aisle, and I consider it an honor to have worked with him, while he was both in and out of office, over the years.

Barbara Ford-Coates is really cut from the same cloth as Phil—a good solid Floridian who is as bright as they come. Governor Graham appointed her tax collector after she served so ably in the Sarasota League of Woman Voters. She was appointed by Governor Bush to the prestigious Florida Constitutional Revision Commission, and continues to get elected handily as a Democrat in a Republican county.

General Butterworth has had a long and distinguished career in public service at every level of government. He has served as a judge, agency head twice, sheriff, and of course, was elected and reelected as attorney general of Florida. Bob, a Democrat, left a position as the dean of a law school in South Florida to take a somewhat thankless job as Secretary of Children and Families under the administration of Republican governor Charlie Crist. Upon accepting the job, Bob said it best, admonishing all of us, "If not us, then who?" He and his wife, Marta Prado, are outstanding examples of Floridians who are making a difference.

Bill Sutton has been actively involved in civic and political affairs in South and Central Florida as well as in Tallahassee. He served as secretary of commerce under Governor Martinez and in my opinion would have been a terrific addition to our Florida Congressional Delegation. Bill comes from a pioneer South Florida family and I have found him to be an outstanding businessman who has made so many significant contributions to our state.

I have not included in this writing all of the legislation I sponsored over the years, but have included selections in the index for your review. Also provided is a summary of my major legislative achievements from 1974-1982. For history buffs, I have also listed in the index the names of the members of the Senate and House with whom I served.

Finally, one piece of legislation that I would like to bring to your attention due to its historic significance is the law directing that apportionment of legislative districts be drawn based upon single-member districts. Earlier in this chapter, I discussed the contrast between multi- and single-member districts and their intended purposes. During my last year in elected office, 1982, Florida was faced with a reapportionment challenge—should we redraw the map again based upon multi-member districts in urban areas or should we base all districts on single-member apportionment? My good friend and colleague, the late senator Jack Gordon (D., Miami Beach), often made brilliant speeches on the floor detailing how shifting back from multi-member to single-member districts would create narrow and self-serving thinking among elected legislators. Others even argued that apportionment change would result in a far different makeup of the legislature, certainly nothing resembling what we had been privileged to enjoy during the era known as the Golden Years. For African Americans, voting for single-member districts was a litmus test for earning their support, but without exception, no one ever questioned Jack Gordon's commitment to civil rights. I struggled with that vote, and today wonder sometimes if I did the right thing. I voted for single-member districts, which did help African Americans and Hispanics win seats, and I think that reflects pure representation. As long as the people are free to vote, I cannot fault their choices. Further, I felt the problems of narrow thinking and self-interests would abate over time. I really think that depends on the individual, and I can think of examples of both good and bad results.

It has been widely argued over the years that the legislative process today does not really resemble the earlier era known as the Golden Years. If you accept that, then you would probably ask why? Many tell me that the answer is the negative consequence of the introduction of a combination of single-member districts and term limits in the 1980s. As I previously said, the single-member district issue was debated on the floors of the Florida House and Senate extensively in 1982. In fact, it passed as a part of a political trade between the House, which favored single-member districts, and the Senate, which favored a reapportionment plan that did not require all senate members to run for reelection in 1982. Both got what they wanted—that is how politics works in real life. Limiting legislative terms to eight years passed as a constitutional amendment shortly after that, perhaps because many wanted to express their frustration with their elected officials. Critics say term limits not only impair the quality of the legislative process, but also give inordinate power to the lobbyists and staff, at the expense of elected legislators.

On reflection, maybe Senator Gordon's assertions went further that we thought…perhaps legislators lose some of that visionary and broad perspective if the governance model is based on single-member apportionment and it is further compounded with term limits. Looking back, it is around the time of the shift from multi-member districts to single-member districts and the introduction of term limits, that many feel the type of representatives elected began to change. *Could it be that single-member districts and term limits caused, at least partially, the dearth of legislators such as the ones who served during the era of the golden years in Florida's legislature?* I must admit the question is personal to me—I was there during the Golden Years, or at least a portion of them, and I voted for single-member districts in earnest. I stepped down from my legislative career after eight years by choice. I don't have all the answers, I only know that what we observed during the years after the 1982 reapportionment appeared to be based on a cause and effect of some kind, be it single-member districts, term limits, a combination of the two, or something else. To definitively answer the question, I believe that you will have to look at each legislative seat in question over a period of time. In some cases, single-member districts and term limits negatively impacted the legislative process, and in other cases, they may very well have improved it. Perhaps this apportionment experience is further evidence that democracy and our form of government is awful…but it is simply the best known to us. I believe we need to keep working to make it better.

As of this writing, this whole issue of narrow versus broad governance is spreading across the country—California and other states are considering splitting up their Electoral College votes along congressional districts lines to further restrict their legislative governance.

I would like to state clearly that in my opinion, the years of my service, 1974-1982, are not the only ones comprising that period of the legislature referred to as the Golden Years. I recall some outstanding legislators elected in the 1966 class and beyond, and many fine members were elected throughout the '80s. Further, we do have fine legislators who have served since 1982 to the present. However, I still cannot help but join many in suggesting that the legislature today is just not the same, in a positive sense, as it was then … and it may never be again.

In any event, it means a great deal to me that many Floridians seem to recall the legislative era of the '70s and '80s and describe it as being part of what has been known as the Golden Years of the Florida Legislature. That description of that era encapsulates the diligence and devotion to public service of the outstanding individuals with whom I had the honor of serving.

Standing left to right: Willy and Elizabeth Williams, and Susan McKnight. Below: Herbert Williams, Senator Bob McKnight holding son Bobby, and Michelle McKnight, at Swearing-in ceremony in Senate Chamber, 1978.

Senator McKnight and U.S. Senator Bob Graham, 1994.

The Golden Years ...   *Robert McKnight*

Bill-signing ceremony in Governor's office, (left to right) David Gluckman, Wayne Maleny, Representative George Sheldon, Governor Graham, Representative Frank Mann, Senator Bob McKnight and Susan McKnight, 1981.

Vice President Walter Mondale meeting with Senator McKnight, 1980.

The Golden Years ... 114 Robert McKnight

> **JANET RENO**
> 1351 N.W. 12TH STREET
> MIAMI, FLORIDA 33125
>
> February 15, 1984
>
> Dear Bob and Susan,
>
> Thank you so much for your contribution and for your encouragement and support. Bob, you are one of the best public officials I have ever worked with and I am very proud to have your support.
>
> I will do my best to deserve your confidence.
>
> Sincerely,
> Janet

Letter from former U.S. Attorney General Janet Reno to Bob and Susan McKnight, 1984.

Former president George H.W. Bush meeting Senator McKnight, 1980.

U.S. Senator Ted Kennedy with Senator McKnight, 1980.

Sen. W. D. Childers, D-Pensacola, and Sen. Dempsey Barron, D-Panama City, fake a puppet routine during the 1982 press skits. Months before, the two were engaged in a bitter battle for control of the Senate. The two later made up.

Senate President W.D. Childers and Senator Dempsey Barron at Annual Press Skits, 1980 (photo by Donn Dughi).

Senator McKnight at press conference at Coral Reef Hospital, 1980.

The Golden Years ...   117   Robert McKnight

SEN. ROBERT McKNIGHT

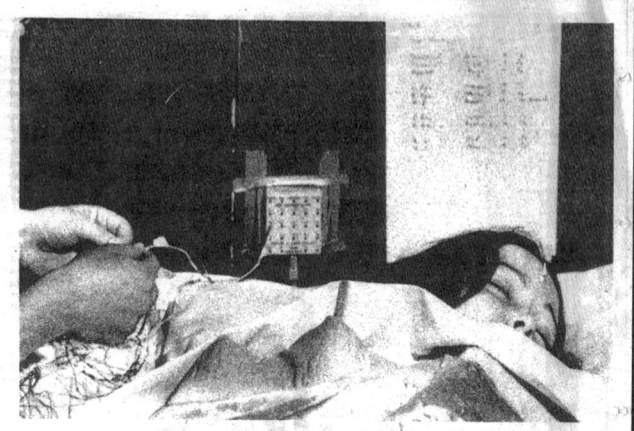

The bill would set a standard for declaring a patient dead if his brain shows no function, in accordance with nationally recognized standards approved by the American Medical Association and the American Bar Association.

Pulling the plug: Will the Legislature confront death?

By Ardith Hilliard

TALLAHASSEE — While police waited to charge his mother with murder, a 3-year-old child lay in a Miami hospital and his body kept functioning only with the help of machines.

Those marvelous machines, created to sustain life, in this case were to become a shield for a murder suspect.

Although by most medical standards the child was dead, the mother fought in court to keep him on a respirator, staving off the murder charge.

MEANWHILE, the tiny body deteriorated, slowly obscuring the medical evidence that would be necessary to prove what had happened to him.

The grim drama went on through three court hearings. Finally, the child stopped breathing because of pneumonia.

By that time, his brain had deteriorated to the consistency of toothpaste, said the medical examiner, making it useless in determining a cause of death.

That Miami case is just one of many that must be grappled with each year by doctors hospitals and medical examiners because Florida does not have a legal description of death among its laws.

IN A DARK TWIST of fate, the technology that has been developed to save lives has given rise to a whole set of mind-rending dilemmas.

State Sen. Robert McKnight, D-Miami, and representatives of the Dade County government will try to solve one of these questions during this legislative session. They are sponsoring a bill that would establish the death of the brain as conclusive in deciding whether a person is dead.

The bill has already passed the Senate Committee on Health and Rehabilitative Services.

The legislation would not apply to comatose patients where some brain activity survives.

And it would not involve terminal patients who try to assert their right to die by being disconnected from life-support machinery — those people still have full control of their mental faculties.

The committee approved a change in the bill stating that the definition would neither preclude nor specifically allow pulling the plug on life-sustaining equipment in cases of a conscious or comatose patient.

BUT THE BILL would set a standard for declaring a patient dead if his brain shows no function, in accordance with nationally recognized standards approved by the American Medical Association and the American Bar Association.

Besides sometimes interfering with the prosecution of suspects in crimes such as child abuse, the current silence of the law on what constitutes death causes other problems.

Doctors and hospitals are understandably reluctant many times to take on the responsibility of pulling the plug on a brain-dead patient. The result is prolonged suffering for the family and monumental hospital bills, say the bill's supporters.

"It's just awful what these people go through — weeks and months of suffering for no reason," said Dade Assistant County Attorney Elly Middlebrooks, one of the bill's authors.

FINALLY, the delay in disconnecting those patients from machines often robs doctors of the chance to use organs for transplants.

Kidneys and other organs deteriorate to the point where they become useless while a brain-dead patient is being kept artificially alive, said Dr. John Shinner, Pinellas County's medical examiner.

"There are problems sometime when people don't want to give up — often (that person is) the doctor caring for the patient," said one Pinellas County doctor involved in location of organs for transplant. "Yet the longer the damaged by infection, making it useless," he said.

One medical examiner, Ron Wright of Miami, has achieved nationwide fame for taking an active role in determining when a patient should be disconnected from machines.

WRIGHT, WHO also has a law degree from the University of Miami, said he has "all the hospitals locally beaten down," so that most of them do not hesitate to disconnect a patient whose brain is dead.

Wright said he will often intervene in some of the estimated 300 cases of brain death in Dade County each year, helping the family, the doctor and the hospital accept the inevitable.

But he and others agree that a statutory definition of brain death would make the process easier.

So far, the proposed legislation has little opposition. But the Florida Catholic Conference, the lobbying arm of the church, already has sent Sen. McKnight a letter of protest, warning that "the worst thing that can happen to the problems of the dying patient and of the medical profession would be legislative intervention. Whatever problems might be solved by this bill, additional problems would undoubtedly arise."

Catholic Conference spokesman Thomas Orkin said the state should not interfere in life-and-death matters.

McKNIGHT BELIEVES, however, that the bill could be written in such a way as to avoid any possibility of prematurely ending a person's life.

Twenty-five states have faced the same problems and have decided to establish the death of the brain as the legal definition, said Ms. Middlebrooks.

Most have done so very cautiously, with wording that leaves room for advancement in technology. Several different tests should be applied to determine brain death, she said, before a doctor is allowed to cut the patient off from the machinery.

Among the most widely accepted criteria are:
✓ Total unresponsiveness;
✓ No movement or independent breathing for at least one hour;
✓ No reflexes of the eyes and pupils fixed and dilated;
✓ A "flat" electroencephalogram (EEG), indicating no electrical brain activity. ■

FOR A BETTER FLORIDA

ST. PETERSBURG TIMES ■ SUNDAY, APRIL 6, 1980

St. Petersburg Times *article on McKnight's landmark Brain Death Definition legislation, 1980.*

FLORIDA CATHOLIC CONFERENCE
314 BARNETT BANK BUILDING
POST OFFICE BOX 1571
TALLAHASSEE, FLORIDA 32302

PHONE (904) 222-3803

THOMAS A. HORKAN, JR.
EXECUTIVE DIRECTOR

September 17, 1982

Senator Robert W. McKnight
1440 Brickell Avenue
Miami, Florida   33131

Dear Bob:

Re: Brain Death Statute

It is now two years since you very skillfully guided to adoption CS/SB 293, which provided the procedures to be followed before doctors could determine brain death. That bill is now Section 382.085, Florida Statutes, entitled "Recognition of brain death under certain circumstances."

As you are well aware, the Florida Catholic Conference has taken many strong stands on medical ethics, especially as they relate to the very questions of life and death. We have vehemently opposed the so-called "death with dignity" proposals throughout the years and continue to maintain that opposition. When brain death proposals were first introduced in the Florida Legislature, we expressed extreme concern, and opposed several of the early versions, fearing that they could lead toward euthanasia. Brain death is greatly different from death with dignity. It deals with a person who is actually dead, but has not been diagnosed as dead; whereas death with dignity deals with a living patient whose life is yet to be terminated. However, because of the technicalities of legislative draftsmanship and various conflicting interests, we were concerned that the two would be confused.

Throughout your handling of this legislation, you were most open to all of our concerns, and took a strong moral view toward the entire subject, and especially insisted that the question of death with dignity and euthanasia be eliminated completely from your bill. For this we are very appreciative.

I would also point out that in the development of the bill, the Medical Association, the trial lawyers and many others had strong concerns, and you were able to satisfy not only them, but us. You will recall that our original position of non-opposition was changed to one of support for your bill, and this was done by a specific action of the Catholic Bishops of Florida.

Since the adoption of the legislation, I have heard from several hospital administrators concerning their experiences with the law. They felt that it had greatly reduced any support for death with dignity amongst their medical staffs or their fellow administrators, and that it had been applied exactly as the law was written. I think this should be considered to be a compliment to you, since you were the primary developer of the legislation.

With best wishes on your leaving of the Florida Senate, I am

Yours very truly,

THOMAS A. HORKAN, JR.

TAH/sp

Letter from Counselor Tom Horkan of Florida Catholic Conference to Senator McKnight regarding his authorship of Brain Death Statute, 1982.

THE WHITE HOUSE
PRESIDENT GEORGE W. BUSH

Jimmy Carter

Jimmy Carter aspired to make Government "competent and compassionate," responsive to the American people and their expectations. His achievements were notable, but in an era of rising energy costs, mounting inflation, and continuing tensions, it was impossible for his administration to meet these high expectations.

Carter, who has rarely used his full name--James Earl Carter, Jr.--was born October 1, 1924, in Plains, Georgia. Peanut farming, talk of politics, and devotion to the Baptist faith were mainstays of his upbringing. Upon graduation in 1946 from the Naval Academy in Annapolis, Maryland, Carter married Rosalynn Smith. The Carters have three sons, John William (Jack), James Earl III (Chip), Donnel Jeffrey (Jeff), and a daughter, Amy Lynn.

After seven years' service as a naval officer, Carter returned to Plains. In 1962 he entered state politics, and eight years later he was elected Governor of Georgia. Among the new young southern governors, he attracted attention by emphasizing ecology, efficiency in government, and the removal of racial barriers.

Carter announced his candidacy for President in December 1974 and began a two-year campaign that gradually gained momentum. At the Democratic Convention, he was nominated on the first ballot. He chose Senator Walter F. Mondale of Minnesota as his running mate. Carter campaigned hard against President Gerald R. Ford, debating with him three times. Carter won by 297 electoral votes to 241 for Ford.

Carter worked hard to combat the continuing economic woes of inflation and unemployment. By the end of his administration, he could claim an increase of nearly eight million jobs and a decrease in the budget deficit, measured in percentage of the gross national product. Unfortunately, inflation and interest rates were at near record highs, and efforts to reduce them caused a short recession.

Carter could point to a number of achievements in domestic affairs. He dealt with the energy shortage by establishing a national energy policy and by decontrolling domestic petroleum prices to stimulate production. He prompted Government efficiency through civil service reform and proceeded with deregulation of the trucking and airline industries. He sought to improve the environment. His expansion of the national park system included protection of 103 million acres of Alaskan lands. To increase human and social services, he created the Department of Education, bolstered the Social Security system, and appointed record numbers of women, blacks, and Hispanics to Government jobs.

In foreign affairs, Carter set his own style. His championing of human rights was coldly received by the Soviet Union and some other nations. In the Middle East, through the Camp David agreement of 1978, he helped bring amity between Egypt and Israel. He succeeded in obtaining ratification of the Panama Canal treaties. Building upon the work of predecessors, he established full diplomatic relations with the People's Republic of China and completed negotiation of the SALT II nuclear limitation treaty with the Soviet Union.

There were serious setbacks, however. The Soviet invasion of Afghanistan caused the suspension of plans for ratification of the SALT II pact. The seizure as hostages of the U. S. embassy staff in Iran dominated the news during the last 14 months of the administration. The consequences of Iran's holding Americans captive, together with continuing inflation at home, contributed to Carter's defeat in 1980. Even then, he continued the difficult negotiations over the hostages. Iran finally released the 52 Americans the same day Carter left office.

President Jimmy Carter, 1976-1980.

```
DEPT 9002212962
P.O. BOX 185
MCLEAN VA 22101                    western union Mailgram


1-094081U221011 08/09/79 ICS WA16614      MIAA
 00304 MLTN VA 08/09/79



THE HON ROBERT W MCKNIGHT
1440 BRICKELL AVE
MIAMI FL 33131




ON BEHALF OF THE PRESIDENT, I AM PLEASED TO INVITE YOU TO A
BRIEFING REGARDING THE STRATEGIC ARMS LIMITATION AGREEMENT
(SALT II). THE BRIEFING WILL BE HELD ON WEDNESDAY, AUGUST 15,
1979, IN THE EAST ROOM OF THE WHITE HOUSE.

THE BRIEFING WILL BEGIN PROMPTLY AT 2:00 P.M. A RECEPTION WILL
FOLLOW IN THE STATE DINING ROOM OF THE WHITE HOUSE.

THE BRIEFING WILL BE CONDUCTED BY THE PRESIDENT AND DR. ZBIGNIEW
BRZEZINSKI, ASSISTANT TO THE PRESIDENT FOR NATIONAL SECURITY
AFFAIRS.

PLEASE RESPOND TO THE WHITE HOUSE SOCIAL SECRETARY, AT (202) 456-
7787 REPEAT (202) 456-7787. IF YOU WILL BE ATTENDING, THE SOCIAL
SECRETARY WILL NEED YOUR SOCIAL SECURITY NUMBER AND DATE OF BIRTH.

YOU WILL ENTER THE WHITE HOUSE VIA THE SOUTHWEST GATE. I LOOK
FORWARD TO SEEING YOU ON AUGUST 15.

ANNE WEXLER, ASSISTANT TO THE PRESIDENT

9002
16:49 EST

MGMCOMP MGM
```

Original available

Invitation from the White House to Senator McKnight to attend SALT II briefing by President Carter, 1979.

Keys News
Thursday, July 9, 1981   The Miami Herald   Section C

McKnight to retire in 1982

Bob McKnight: 1982 will be his last.

Miami Herald *article on McKnight's retirement announcement, 1981.*

Miami Herald *article on Senator Robert W. McKnight, 1981.*

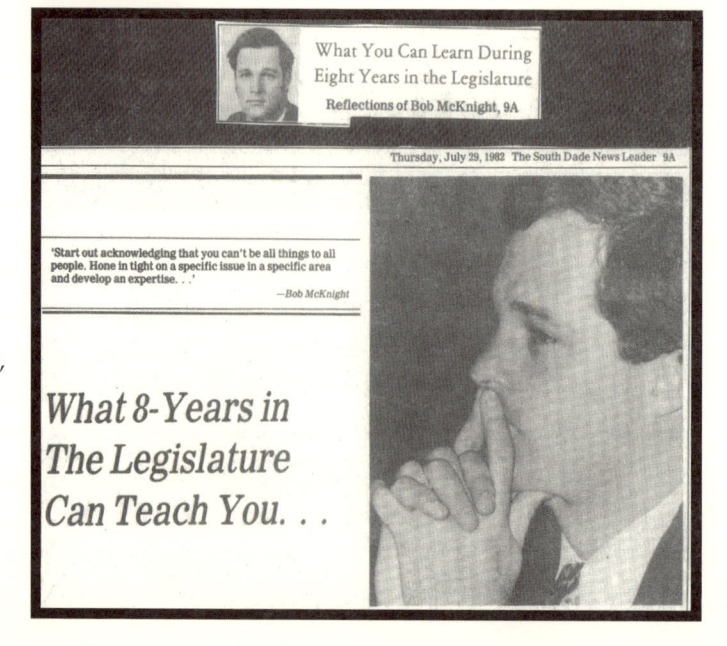

What You Can Learn During Eight Years in the Legislature
Reflections of Bob McKnight, 9A

Thursday, July 29, 1982   The South Dade News Leader   9A

'Start out acknowledging that you can't be all things to all people. Hone in tight on a specific issue in a specific area and develop an expertise...'
—Bob McKnight

What 8-Years in The Legislature Can Teach You...

The Golden Years ... 122 Robert McKnight

McKnight starts early to build unity among Dade legislators

GLENDA WRIGHT-McQUEEN
Miami News Reporter

In January, when the Dade County delegation returns to the Legislature, the organization will be a more effective lawmaking group — or so its newly-elected chairman hopes.

But before that time the delegation will have to make some major changes, says Democratic Sen. Bob McKnight.

"The session will begin in five months," McKnight said yesterday in a meeting with The Miami News' editorial board. "We have to get it together internally here before we get up there in Tallahassee."

McKnight acknowledged that he "will need every tool and technique I have to keep this delegation together," and conceded "We have not done a good job in the past." But, he added, "I think we can become more effective as time passes."

McKnight said he will focus on unifying the delegation and polishing up some of its members' oratorical and decision-making skills.

The group will take part in a decision-making and problem-solving seminar at Florida International University sometime before the session begins, he said. The delegation will also hold social and recreational activities to promote closer ties between the members.

The main objective will be to "put some unity back into the delegation," he said.

Task force groups to work on the seminar and other activities will also work on organizing the delegation's key issues.

Democratic Rep. Bill Sadowski of the delegation believes the focus on unity is a move in the right direction.

Bob McKnight

The session will begin in five months. We have to get it together internally here before we get up there in Tallahassee

McKnight is "on a solid course that will increase the effectiveness of the delegation over a period of time," Sadowski said in a telephone interview. "It can't hurt; it can only help."

Last year, the delegation's effectiveness was stifled by intense in-house fighting between members on and off the Legislature's floor.

"This is a big county and we had a lot of egos to deal with," explained McKnight. "There has been some friction in the past but we are working to get to know each other better."

This year the organization will have to pull itself together quickly to prepare for a battle with conservative North Florida legislators on the heated issue of reapportionment — the redrawing of Senate and House boundaries to reflect population changes documented in the 1980 U.S. Census.

The delegation also plans to try to improve funding of education, transportation, criminal justice and social services — program which have not been the favorites of North Florida legislators in the past.

But the population growth in urban South Florida during the past decade — if reapportionment reflects that properly — virtually guarantees that the Senate in particular will be more sensitive and responsive to urban needs, said McKnight.

As part of the effort to reform the Legislature's traditional power structure, he said, he hopes to align Dade with Monroe, Broward and Palm Beach counties to form a strong South Florida coalition.

Dade and other highly urban counties are facing problems of rising crime rates and escalating costs related to refugees, McKnight noted. Because of the Reagan Administration's cutbacks on refugee aid, McKnight said, these counties will probably look to the state for financial help.

McKnight said the Dade delegation plans to hold hearings to make the public more aware of the lawmakers' role, as well as a seminar teaching citizens lobbying skills.

The delegation will take on a "broader scope than ever before, he said.

Miami News *article on McKnight's chairmanship of Dade Delegation, 1981.*

The Golden Years ...   *Robert McKnight*

MIAMI MAGAZINE/JUNE 1979

Some of
The Best and the Brightest

It's time you met some local people who have made a mark in the fields of Art, Music, Government-Politics and Business

Sen. Bob McKnight
...calm problem solving

When Bob McKnight decided to end a four-year career in the Florida House of Representatives last fall by challenging incumbent State Sen. Ralph Poston, his campaign radio jingle (sung to the tune of *Baby Face)* included a line for Dist. 38 voters to *"pull that lucky lever, McKnight will serve us better."* Enough voters sang that tune at the polls, dumping Poston's past to embrace McKnight's future.

"I'm not a grandstander," explains McKnight. "I try to be as candid as possible, whether it's in the campaign, talking to voters, or in the legislature, talking to other legislators."

At 35, he's a successful businessman (Masters in Business from Florida State University) who is marketing vice president for Planned Development Corp. In addition, he is an officer of a real estate leasing and management firm. But, McKnight concedes, it is in government that he has found the greatest challenges. He has been active in strong advocacy for legislation dealing with water—quantity and quality—and has sponsored bills for restoration programs in north Biscayne Bay and greater public access to the amenities of south Biscayne Bay.

In addition, McKnight has pushed for residential treatment facilities for emotionally disturbed children as an alternative to institutionalization.

Perhaps the highest accolade accorded McKnight came from legislative colleagues who critiqued each other in a 1976 *Florida Trend* magazine poll. McKnight, it was said, is "admired for dedication, honesty, integrity and regard for the public welfare."

Miami Magazine *article about Senator McKnight, 1979.*

Lieutenant Governor Wayne Mixson and Senator McKnight campaigning in the Florida Keys, 1980.

Senator McKnight with Dr. Allen Morris, Clerk Emeritus of the Florida House of Representatives, 1980.

Florida Times-Union's *Allen Morris Award, Runner-up, Most Effective First Term Senator, 1980.*

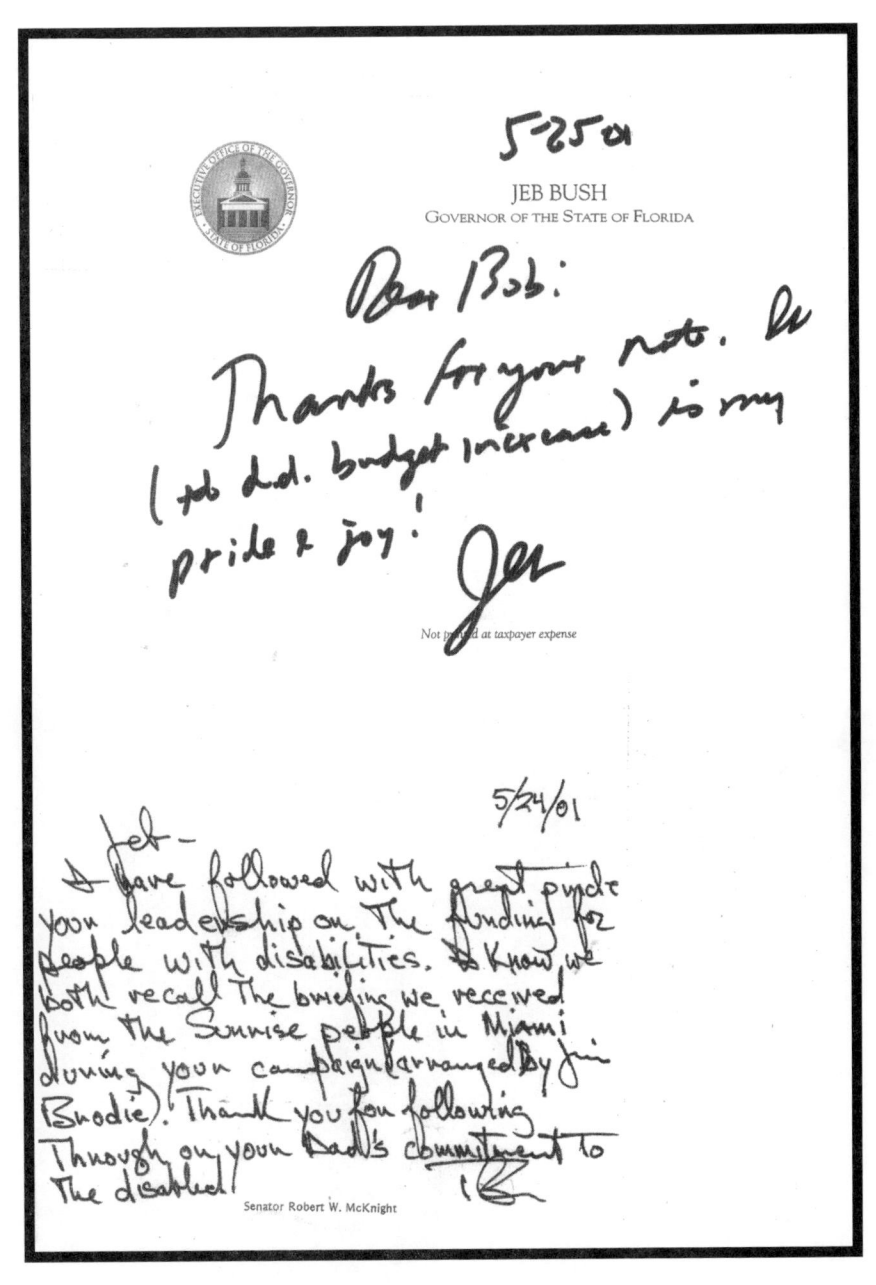

> 5-25-01
>
> **JEB BUSH**
> GOVERNOR OF THE STATE OF FLORIDA
>
> Dear Bob:
>
> Thanks for your note. It (Job ded. budget increase) is my pride & joy!
>
> Jeb
>
> *Not printed at taxpayer expense*

> 5/24/01
>
> Jeb —
>
> I have followed with great pride your leadership on the funding for people with disabilities. I know we both recall the briefing we received from the Sunrise people in Miami during your campaign (arranged by Jim Brodie). Thank you for following through on your Dad's commitment to the disabled!
>
> Senator Robert W. McKnight

Correspondence between Governor Jeb Bush and Senator McKnight regarding funding for Sunrise Community, 2001.

(Left to right) Senator McKnight, Dr. George Spelios, Michelle, Bobby, and Susan McKnight at Robert W. McKnight building dedication at Sunrise Community, 1982.

South Dade News Leader *article on Senator McKnight's retirement, 1982.*

The Golden Years ... 128 Robert McKnight

LECTURES BY SENATOR ROBERT MCKNIGHT

THE ROLE OF GOVERNMENT IN MEDICINE AND HEALTH CARE

Florida Senator Robert McKnight is a veteran legislator who first served in the House and was elected to the Senate in 1978. He has been an outspoken proponent of hospital care cost containment and is chairman of the Senate's Health and Rehabilitative Services Committee. He also brings concern to that legislative body for Florida's environmental, natural and water resources. McKnight is considered an expert in the area of natural resources management and is past vice-chairman of the Senate's Natural Resources Committee. His other legislative service includes:
— Chairman, Senate Appropriations Subcommittee C
— Member Senate Appropriations Committee
— Member Senate Subcommittee on Employees Group Health Insurance Program
— Chairman of the Dade County Legislative Delegation

McKnight is a member of the Florida Health Coordinating Council and once served on the State Emergency Medical Services Committee. He is a recipient of the Florida Council for Community Mental Health Legislative Award and the Dade County Mental Health Association's Distinguished Service Award.

9:00 a.m.
South Campus,
11011 S.W. 104th Street
Room 2105
and
12:00 Noon
Medical Center Campus,
950 N.W. 20th Street
Room 1175

M-DCC DISTRICT BOARD OF TRUSTEES
Garth C. Reeves, Sr., Chairman
Daniel K. Gill, Vice-Chairman
Jack Kassewitz, Maria C. Hernandez, Talbot D'Alemberte
College President: Robert H. McCabe
Miami-Dade is an equal access/equal opportunity community college and does not discriminate on the basis of handicap in compliance with the Rehabilitation Act, Section 504. The collegewide coordinator for compliance is the Director of Minority Affairs and Equity Programs. 8/82

Lecture by Senator McKnight at Miami Date Community College, 1983.

'Citizen legislator' may leave power-broker politics behind

Associated Press

TALLAHASSEE -- Sen. Robert W. McKnight, D-Miami, seems like a clean-cut, upwardly mobile, nose-to-the-grindstone politician with a promising legislative future.

He paid his dues as a House member from 1974 to 1978 and as a senator since then, weaving the intricate web of friendships and alliances that are often so useful for achieving legislative goals.

He is chairman of the Senate Appropriations subcommittee for social services and was recently mentioned as a possible future choice to head the full Senate Appropriations Committee.

He belongs to the Democratic faction loyal to Senate President W.D. Childers, ostensibly the ruling party's choice to lead the Senate until November 1984.

But McKnight, a 36-year-old real-estate developer, seems likely to give it all up next year even though he is on the threshold of real influence and unabashedly admits he would like to be governor. For now, he says only that he is "thinking seriously" about stepping down, but in recent public meetings he has said unequivocally he won't run again.

Why would McKnight give up a seemingly bright future in the Legislature? The answer helps illuminate why some young legislators end their legislative careers early. For example, highly regarded Rep. William E. Sadowski, D-Miami -- who won widespread acclaim for his role in reforming Florida's workers compensation law in 1979 -- planned to retire last year after only two terms but ran again when Gov. Bob Graham appealed to him to stay on.

McKnight says he wants more time for a growing family, budding business and ambitious political preparations, and less hassle from a time-consuming job in a legislature that too often lets powerbrokers abuse the policy-making process.

"My thought when I came up here was to serve a reasonable period of time in the true sense of a citizen legislator," says McKnight. "I've seen so many people up here not necessarily abrogate their principles but lose their independence to perpetuate themselves."

He says the power struggle between Childers and conservative Senate Dean Dempsey J. Barron, who has been in the Senate saddle for a decade, did not trigger his decision, but it clearly has been an unpleasant experience that reinforced the idea of quitting McKnight doesn't want to talk about his decision to bolt the camp of long-time friend Sen. Harry A. Johnston, D-West Palm Beach, and support Childers to help unhorse Barron.

McKnight won his seat by ousting veteran Sen. Ralph Poston, D-Miami, in a nationally celebrated 1978 campaign tied to ratification of the Equal Rights Amendment When Poston double-crossed ERA supporters in 1977 by voting against the ERA after promising to support it they vowed to see that, in the words of one out-of-state booster, "Ralph Poston never gets elected to anything again, even church deacon."

The instrument of their revenge was McKnight, who favored the ERA and wanted a promotion.

Since then, McKnight has been rising in the Senate constellation. He was supposed to have been elevated to Senate Natural Resources chairman this year, but Childers backed out on that understanding. Instead, he got an important slot on the budget-writing committee.

An ardent reformer and serious-minded if ambitious lawmaker since his days as a House member McKnight says he is disturbed by the abuses of power in the Legislature, the bills held hostage by rival factions, the complex end-of-session deals involving as many as a half-dozen unrelated bills, the frenzied manhandling of delicate legislation with not enough attention to the merits.

"As long as I've been here -- from 1974 until now -- it seems so much more commonplace now than it did in the beginning," says McKnight. "I'll be talking to people and they'll tell me, 'I've got to get my bill out before the hostage-taking starts.'"

Diplomatically, he puts much of the blame on the Senate's dominance by Barron.

But McKnight has personal reasons, too.

He says he wants to stop uprooting his two school-age children for the two-month move to Tallahassee every spring and devote more time to his real-estate development business. He also wants to begin building a statewide constituency in case he runs for governor in 1986, although that path involves challenging the tradition of governors being selected from the ranks of incumbent office-holders, most often state senators.

"It's difficult to walk away from something when you could step up if you stayed around," says McKnight.

> I've seen so many people up here not necessarily abrogate their principles but lose their independence to perpetuate themselves.
>
> — Sen. Robert McKnight
>
> Sun Sentinel 5/10/81

Associated Press article about Senator McKnight's retirement, 1982.

The Golden Years ...   130   Robert McKnight

(Left to right) Michelle, Susan, Senator Robert and Bobby McKnight at Senate swearing-in ceremony, 1980.

1980-1982 Florida Senate on steps of new Capitol.

The Golden Years ... 131 Robert McKnight

CHAPTER 9

The McKnight Commission and the 1986 Gubernatorial Election

One of the bills that passed at the end of the 1982 session of the legislature dealt with affording and paying for health care for indigent Floridians. As mentioned earlier, the Mariel Boat Lift added thousands of new people requiring health care who were without employment or money to pay for it. The bill provided for the creation of an advisory group to make recommendations for funding indigent health care. The study group was unusual in that it was mandated as a two-year study rather than the typical one-year, and carried a substantial appropriation to fund the work thoroughly. The governor had passed along word to me from his respected chief of staff, Dr. Charlie Reed, that he wanted me to chair the group. I was told I would have complete access to the governor and his senior staff, and would have input in terms of the selection of the members. Since I was chairman of the Senate Health and Rehabilitative Services Committee that handled the legislation, I was aware of the heavy influence the medical industry lobbyists had on the bill. They were ably represented by Ralph Glatfelter and Dr. Steve Wilkerson of the for-profit hospitals, John French of the medical industry, Ronnie Book and Billy Rubin of various medical interests, and Scotty Frazier of the Florida Medical Association and former Speaker of the Florida House of Representatives, John Thrasher; and they were not pleased when they heard the governor planned to appoint me as chairman. *This lesson is a good one to remember. If you do not have the votes, yield to the person who does, and try to work within the system. In this case, the lobbyists knew that I was close to the governor and if I would accept the appointment, it would be mine. I elected to meet with them and told them I was going to accept the appointment, but wanted to work with them. Although they did not really have a choice, they did the wise thing and offered to work with me and our staff to create the best public policy on health care possible.*

The members of the study group were among the most knowledgeable about health care in the state. Also, because we had a substantial appropriation with which to work, we were able to hire some of the nation's best minds to assist us. I was pleased that the group became known as the McKnight Commission. Two task force individuals who stood out during both the deliberations and the creation of the final work product were staff member Ree Sailors and Lester Abberger, representing member Bill Gunter. I had worked with Ree when she was on the staff of the Senate Health and Rehabilitative Services Committee, and knew of her extraordinary energy and talent, especially in the areas of health policy. She was instrumental in the success of the group's effort. Lester was the cabinet aide to Insurance Commissioner Gunter, and provided excellent counsel on a bipartisan basis. Over the years, I have found Lester to be a great Floridian, making contributions in health policy, the environment, and the acclaimed Leadership Florida Program. His work on this study group was pivotal. Representing the governor's office were Graham's chief of staff, Dr. Charlie Reed, and senior executive assistant Patsy Palmer. Our success, to the degree we enjoyed it on the final work product, can to a significant extent be attributed to Charlie and Patsy.

We completed our study and recommendations for submission to the governor and the legislature in 1984. The governor enthusiastically embraced the report and even highlighted it in his annual State of the State Address to the legislature. My former colleagues and goods friends, senators Johnston and Jenne, and representatives Bell and Lippman provided the leadership to pass the recommendations into law that same year.

Being out of legislative office at that time, I was invited to join a number of important state and community organizations: the Florida Chamber of Commerce board of directors, Greater Miami Citizens Against Crime ("GMAC"), the Visiting Committee for the University of Miami School of Business, the United Way, and the Greater Miami Chamber of Commerce ("GMCC"). The crime problem was becoming an epidemic in Miami—the nation watched with horror on national TV while Liberty City burned during the Orange Bowl festivities. As a member of GMAC's board of directors, I developed a close working relationship with some of the most respected community leaders in South Florida including David Blumberg, my employer; Alvah Chapman of the *Miami Herald*; Chuck Cobb of Arvida; developer Armando Codina; Burger King founder Jim McLemore; former Miami commissioner Mamma Althea Range; lawyers Marty Fine, Bill Colson, and Bob Traurig; Tad Foote of the University of Miami; department store executives Bill Ruben and Stu Thomas; developer Lou Fisher; Walter Revell, former secretary of the Florida Department of Transportation; public relations executives Hank Meyer and Leslie Pantin; architect Willy Bermello; Tal Fair of the Miami Urban League; the late Ray Goode of the Babcock Companies and GMCC executive directors Lester Freeman and Bill Cullom, among others. Most of the community kindly embraced me and asked that I use my political experiences to assist in community causes. I was asked to represent organizations as a professional lobbyist, especially since I had a close relationship with the governor, cabinet, and the leadership of the legislature, but I felt that my strengths as a lobbyist should be directed pro bono toward community and state needs.

Occasionally I received invitations to public events by virtue of my previous service in public office. One I received while in office in 1982 was to deliver the commencement address to the graduates of the Florida Keys Community College in Key West. Their outstanding president, Dr. Bill Seeker, extended the invitation, and was kind enough to make a hotel room available to help me prepare for my address. Dr. Seeker failed to tell me that the hotel, the magnificent Pier House, was known then for its topless beach. I tried my best, but I am sure that my graduation ceremony remarks were disjointed and probably hard to understand given my surroundings during my stay there. For the record, I disclosed that situation to Susan.

In the early '90s, I received an invitation from my good friend Dr. Ed Massey, President of Indian River Community

College ("IRCC"), to deliver their commencement address. I was honored, and wrestled with a germane subject for my remarks. There seemed to be a growing drift toward isolationism internationally in the country, so without getting overly political, I tried to plant a seed for the new graduates to think about. I started my address by repeating the words of a popular Simon and Garfunkel song from the '60s—*I Am a Rock*, reflecting isolationism and despair.

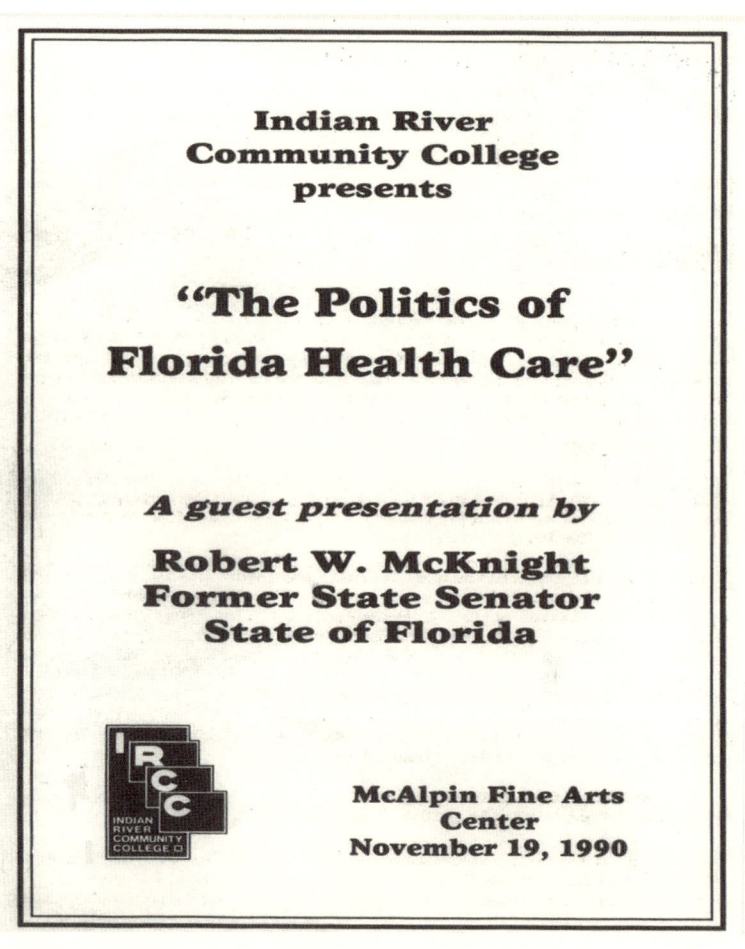

> **Indian River Community College presents**
>
> ## "The Politics of Florida Health Care"
>
> *A guest presentation by*
>
> **Robert W. McKnight
> Former State Senator
> State of Florida**
>
> **McAlpin Fine Arts Center
> November 19, 1990**

Commencement Address Program for Indian River Community College Graduation.

My message to the graduates was, of course, that America and its people could never exist without feelings and love for others. I urged them to take up causes, any causes, and dared them and the IRCC faculty to risk making mistakes pursuing those causes. I guess the theme of my message was not unusual for a graduation keynote, but I think linking that song up with the message got their attention.

I still had in the back of my mind running for governor in 1986. *The Miami Herald*, the *Miami News*, and the *Orlando Sentinel* had features identifying me as one of the possible candidates for governor. As a result, a number of people around the state contacted me to set up meetings that would develop better relationships among us. One matter I had somewhat decided upon was who would be my running mate. While in negotiations with the House on the Appropriations Conference Report, I often found myself across the table from Representative Bev Burnsed (D., Lakeland). Bev was smart, aggressive and a lot of fun to be around. Although I never discussed us running together for governor and lieutenant governor with her, I did mention it to her in later years. After Bev completed her distinguished legislative service, she served as vice president for External Affairs at our alma mater, Florida State University.

During the mid '80s, Florida's housing and commercial developments fell into a lull—with the usual culprits being the national economic downturn, oversupply of real estate, uncertainty internationally, and high interest rates. Susan and I had owned property in central Florida, in Vero Beach. Our company was considering branching into either central or southwest Florida in order to develop commercial and residential real estate. It was decided that I would move to Vero and open a central Florida office for the company. I did so, but retained many of my Miami responsibilities for a number of years, and commuted almost regularly between the two locations. Working with PDC executive vice president Larry Kahn, construction manager Rick Taylor, and our terrific counsel (and former legislative staffer) Bill Caldwell, PDC developed a number of award-winning projects out of the Vero office, including the acclaimed 60 Oaks zero-lot line single-family residential development.

We had a number of projects under development when I got a call in 1985 from my former colleague and good friend, Representative Steve Pajcic (D., Jacksonville). Steve said he was coming to Miami and asked if we could meet. Steve and I were elected together in 1974 and worked together on *Save Our Rivers* legislation. Steve was one of the brightest and most pleasant legislators I ever met—he had attended Princeton on a basketball scholarship, and was a Harvard law school graduate. I gave Steve his handle, "Magic Pajcic." Steve's only negative, at least in some people's mind, was that he was an unashamed liberal, in the George McGovern mold. I knew his late brother Gary, as he was the star quarterback at FSU during my years there and threw the touchdown pass (that was never counted) to Lane Fenner to beat Florida and Heisman Trophy winner Steve Spurrier in 1966. I saw the play in Doak Campbell stadium.

I knew Steve wanted to meet to discuss the 1986 Democratic nomination for governor. As I have stated earlier in the book, that is the only position that really appealed to me, and I still harbored the thought of running. However, I found that time has a way of sometimes diminishing the sharpness of appeal of things, and that certainly was the case regarding the governor's race and me. Also, I was gaining much professional satisfaction from my PDC development activities in Miami and Vero Beach. Lastly, and probably most important, Michelle and Bobby were both entering the challenging years of child development. Essentially, I felt it came down to whether I felt the majority of my energies should be spent on my political ambitions or helping Susan steer the children through the tricky formative years. I did notice that the quality of the legislators seemed to have lessened after my leaving office, with a number of members being tainted with improper use of campaign contributions. All in all, after conferring with Susan and praying about it, I decided that I would not be a candidate for governor in 1986. I did not make a public statement, and felt that I could still serve in some worthwhile public capacity. Little did I know that I would become the statewide co-chairman of the Democratic nominee for governor campaign.

In any event, I met with Steve and he told me he was thinking about running for governor, but did not think it would be wise for both of us to run. I told him that I was getting completely immersed in my development activities and my family, and therefore would probably not run. He seemed relieved, and surprised me by asking if I would co-chair his campaign, along with former speaker Fred Shultz (D., Jacksonville). I was quite honored by Steve's offer, especially since Shultz had just completed his service to President Carter as a governor on the Federal Reserve Board.

For the next two years, I spent almost all of my non-family and development time working on Steve's campaign. His opponents were formidable: former insurance commissioner Bill Gunter; former attorney general Jim Smith; and former senate president Harry Johnston. With incredibly hard work, good professional advice, and a surprising financial war chest, compliments of the trial bar, Steve won the Democratic nomination to face future governor Bob Martinez. The final election was difficult for Steve because one of his primary opponents, Jim Smith, not only did not endorse Steve, but also crossed over party lines to support Martinez. Steve's running mate, by the way, was another good friend, Senator Frank Mann (D., Fort Myers). Frank won my district 38 seat upon my retirement in 1982. The Pajcic-Mann ticket had two primary professional advisers—

one who impressed me, the other one, not so much. I had worked with Sergio Bendixen previously in campaigns and found him in this race to be just short of a genius. I remember then-U.S. Senator Bob Graham describing the campaign as "textbook." I knew of Pat Caddell prior to the campaign, but had not worked with him before this race. Admittedly, he was instrumental in helping to orchestrate Jimmy Carter's upset win of the presidency in 1976, but I never felt he really "clicked" with the Pajcic-Mann campaign staff. Martinez went on to win the general election with a comfortable margin.

For the remainder of my career I had a limited involvement with politics and campaigns. I worked briefly for Governor Lawton Chiles and Lieutenant Governor Buddy MacKay, after their election in 1990. They asked me to assist them in their transition from the campaign to setting up their administration. One assignment I particularly enjoyed was creating a marketing program for the state's recoverable waste. It occurred to me that the state might make available recyclable waste materials for the private sector to remove, along with the concurrent opportunity to sell products back to the state that included the waste materials. Examples of materials, which could be included in the program, were plastic garbage cans, paper products, and engine oil. I saw the program as an economic development initiative because I envisioned creating what I called Recycling Business Ventures. Although the plan was featured in the *Wall Street Journal*, *BusinessWeek*, and the national recycling trade press, it enjoyed only limited success because of the disinclination of the government agencies to implement the plan. Governors Chiles and MacKay, and their general counsel Dexter Douglass were among the finest public servants I have met and had the honor with which to work.

In 1992 I accepted an invitation from my longtime friend Frank Ryll to join the senior staff of the Florida Chamber of Commerce, the leading business advocate in Tallahassee. While at the Chamber, I worked closely with their fine general counsel, Roy

Young, to expand their lobbying presence as well as improve their financial condition. I also broke my previous prohibition of lobbying professionally for clients, when I agreed to represent the good people at Sunrise Community in front of the executive and legislative branches. Their dynamic leader Les Leech and their chairman Dr. George Spelios grew that not-for-profit provider of services for developmentally disabled citizens to one of the largest and most successful organizations in the country. For the last eight years, I have been working with my dear friend Mike Sheridan in a senior position at Fringe Benefits Management Company ("FBMC"), the premier benefits company in the United States. As I recounted earlier, Mike made the first contribution to my campaign and I often kid him saying, "Mike, your check didn't even bounce." Mike and his daughter (and FBMC president and chief executive officer) Lorraine Strickland had discussed with me an association for a number of years. Several years ago they acquired certain assets of my company, McKnight Financial Corporation, and I have been honored to be associated with them since then. A political connection for me within the company has been its twenty-five-year board member and rising star in the Democratic Party, Tallahassee mayor John Marks.

Susan has continued her lifelong passion of teaching children—first our two children, and now our five grandchildren. Since our return to Tallahassee in 1991, Susan has renewed her love of early childhood classroom education at Epiphany Lutheran School and Timberlane Church of Christ. I am so proud of her as a true professional educator—I have often said if the schools didn't pay Susan to teach her classes, she would probably offer to pay them. She has been the best partner, political and otherwise, that I could ever have hoped for.

As my old friend and respected lobbyist Jim Krog said in retiring as chief of staff to Governor Chiles in the '90s, "It has been quite a ride." We were fortunate to have along with us, as listed in the index to follow, a number of people on our exciting ride. To be clear, there have been ups and downs. *All in all, the traditional naval blessing, "May you have fair winds and a following sea," certainly has applied to the McKnight family's political journey.*

I'd like to close with the sage advice of the late president Theodore Roosevelt:

> *"It is not the critic who counts, nor the man who points out how the strong man stumbled or where the doer of deeds could have done better. The credit belongs to the man who is actually in the arena; whose face is marred by dust and sweat and blood; who strives valiantly; who errs and comes up short again and again; who knows the great enthusiasms, the great devotions and spends himself in a worthy cause; who at the best knows in the end the triumphs of high achievement; and who at the worst, if he fails, at least fails while daring greatly; so that his place shall never be with those cold and timid souls who know neither victory nor defeat."*

Governor Lawton Chiles and Senator McKnight, 1992.

FSU end Lane Fenner catching touchdown pass from quarterback Gary Pajcic to beat UF 26-22, 1966 (photo by Julian Clarkson).

The Golden Years ...   *Robert McKnight*

(Left to right) Ray Goode, McKnight, Democratic gubernatorial nominee Steve Pajcic, Former U.S. Federal Reserve Governor Fred Schultz, Dr. Eduardo Padron, and Chesterfield Smith, Pajcic for governor campaign, 1986.

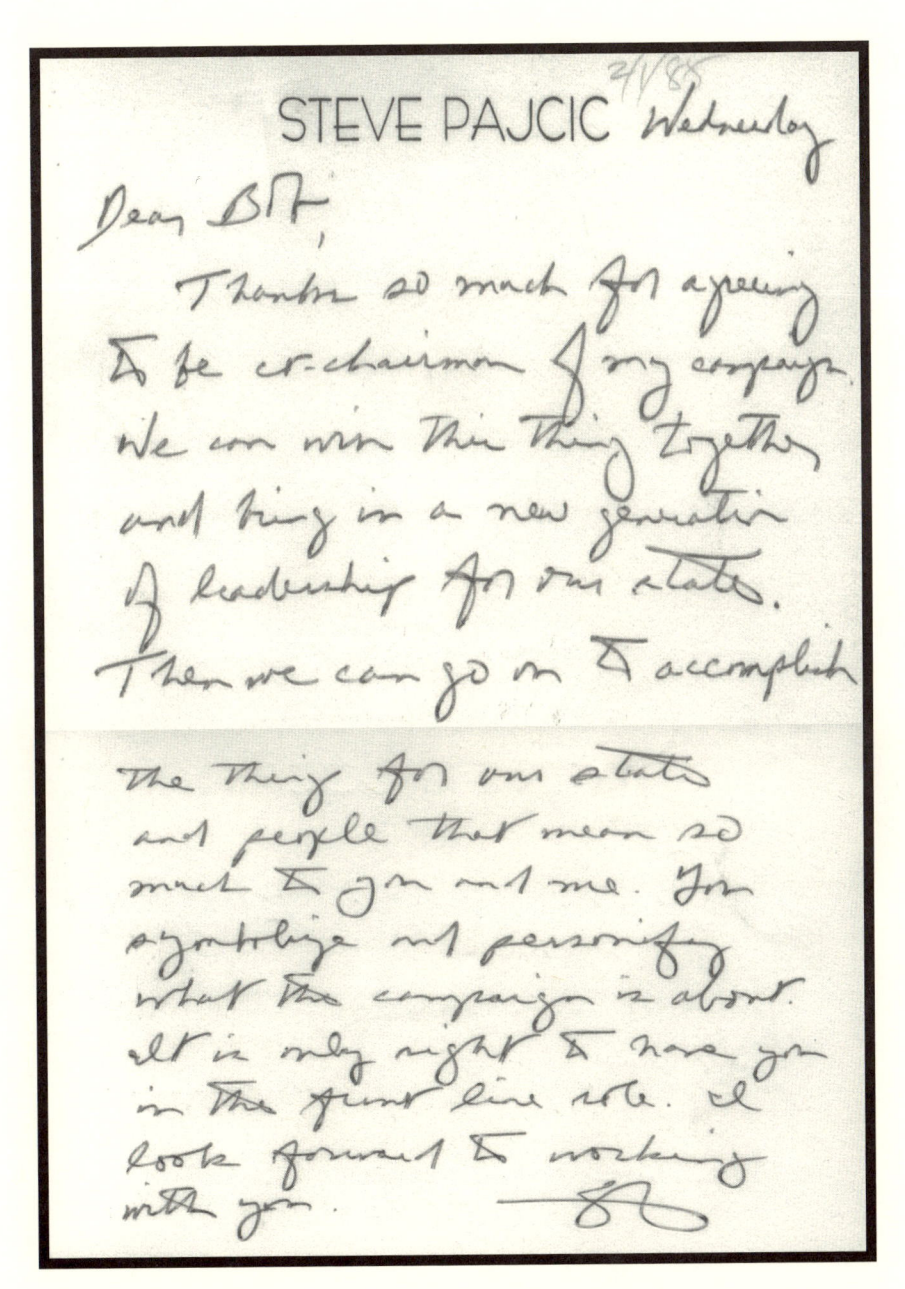

> **STEVE PAJCIC** Wednesday 2/1/85
>
> Dear Bob,
>
> Thanks so much for agreeing to be co-chairman of my campaign. We can win this thing together and bring in a new generation of leadership for our state. Then we can go on to accomplish the things for our state and people that mean so much to you and me. You symbolize and personify what the campaign is about. It is only right to have you in the front line role. I look forward to working with you.
>
> — S.P.

Note from Democratic nominee for governor in 1986 to Senator McKnight.

Final report of McKnight Commission on Health Care, 1984.

FLORIDA HEALTH ISSUES

"AN OPPORTUNITY FOR LEADERSHIP"

Report and Recommendations
of the Florida Task Force on Competition
and Consumer Choices in Health Care

March 1984

FLORIDA TASK FORCE ON COMPETITION AND CONSUMER CHOICES IN HEALTH CARE

MEMBERS

Chairman
Robert W. McKnight
Senior Vice President
Planned Development Corporation
Miami, Florida

Samuel P. Bell, III
Representative, District 28
Ormond Beach, Florida

Douglas W. Coffey
Senior Vice President
Burdines of Florida
Miami, Florida

Marie E. Cowart, R.N., Dr. P.H.
Associate Professor
Community Health Nursing
Florida State University
Tallahassee, Florida

Fred J. Cowell
President and Chief Executive Officer
Public Health Trust
Jackson Memorial Medical Center
Miami, Florida

Ronald Dunbar
Senior Vice President
Ryder Systems, Inc.
Miami, Florida

William E. Flaherty
President
Blue Cross/Blue Shield of Florida
Jacksonville, Florida

Alvin Goldberg, FACHA
Executive Vice President
Mount Sinai Medical Center
Miami Beach, Florida

Jack D. Gordon
Senator, District 35
Miami Beach, Florida

James T. Howell, M.D., M.P.H.
Deputy Secretary
Department of Health and
  Rehabilitative Services
Tallahassee, Florida

Margaret H. Jacks
State Long-Term Care
Ombudsman Committee
Tallahassee, Florida

Toni Jennings
Senator, District 15
Orlando, Florida

Fred Lippman
Representative, District 97
Hollywood, Florida

Joseph L. Marcille, CLU
President
Gulf Life Group Insurance
Jacksonville, Florida

Roland H. Rolle
Director of Collective Bargaining
United Teachers of Dade
Miami, Florida

Dirk W. R. Suringa, M.D., M.S.
Private Physician
Tampa, Florida

Maria Elena Torano
President
META, Inc.
Miami, Florida

Dick VanEldik, M.D., P.A.
Private Physician
Lake Worth, Florida

Robert A. Vraciu, Ph.D.
Vice President
Hospital Corporation of America
Nashville, Tennessee

EX OFFICIO MEMBER

Bill Gunter
State Treasurer and Insurance Commissioner
Tallahassee, Florida

STAFF

Del Lawrence
Executive Director

Ree Sailors
Health Policy Analyst

Cynthia Valencic
Executive Secretary

STATE OF FLORIDA

Office of the Governor
THE CAPITOL
TALLAHASSEE 32301

BOB GRAHAM
GOVERNOR

FOR IMMEDIATE RELEASE   CONTACT: Del Lawrence
March 15, 1984   Ree Sailors
                                        487-3336

MCKNIGHT RELEASES HEALTH COST FINAL REPORT

TALLAHASSEE--Former State Senator Robert W. McKnight, chairman of the Florida Task Force on Competition and Consumer Choices in Health Care, today released the final report and recommendations of the group's 16-month study.

The report entitled <u>Florida Health Issues: "An Opportunity For Leadership"</u>, lays out 42 wide-ranging recommendations designed to increase competitive activity among health care providers and purchasers, increase incentives for efficiency, and heighten consumer knowledge and awareness.

Governor Bob Graham received the report enthusiastically.

"This report will make a difference in the debate on how to control the cost of good health in Florida," Graham said. "I am grateful to Senator McKnight and the entire Florida Task Force for their months of hard work and their attention to detail.

"Their work product will help find the balance point between regulation of the health care industry by government and free market competition. I salute the men and women of

(MORE)
An Affirmative Action/Equal Opportunity Employer

ADD ONE

the Task Force for their efforts to help keep health care within the financial reach of all Floridians."

In the case of hospital revenues, which have risen 118.7 percent between 1979 and 1983, the Task Force recommended the establishment of an annual maximum allowable rate of increase for hospital revenues which if exceeded would trigger increased scrutiny and control by the Hospital Cost Containment Board. The recommendations also include a six-part plan to address the ever-growing problem of medical care for the indigent. The plan outlines a financing mechanism which calls for funding from the State, counties, the Federal government and hospitals.

Spurred by rapid and dramatic increases in health care costs, the Task Force, composed of consumer, provider, and business and labor representatives, was appointed by Governor Bob Graham in September 1982 and directed to examine Florida's health care system, federal and private health care policy, and to layout actions necessary for Florida to develop and maintain a cost-efficient, quality health care system.

Legislative mandate also included direction that specific attention be given to stimulating market price and service competition as a means of disciplining the costs of health care.

(MORE)

ADD TWO

McKnight said, "After 16 months of study and discussion by the members among themselves and with experts in many fields from throughout Florida and the country, this report represents the forged wisdom of the Task Force and the collective wisdom of the diverse groups represented."

The Executive Summary lists all 42 recommendations of the Task Force. The first chapter discusses the establishment of the Task Force and the methodology it used to accomplish its work. Chapter 2 lays the foundation for the Task Force's recommendations by exploring the problem and discussing the underlying caluses of rising costs in the health care marketplace.

The final four chapters present a wide ranging discussion of the many topics explored by the Task Force over a series of 15 meetings; and, weaves in the 42 recommendations made by the group that would directly affect incentives, aimed at cost-effective behavior, and focus on improving government regulation.

Attachment: Florida health issues: "An Opportunity For Leadership"

- 30 -

McKnight might run for governor in '86 race

By ROBERT RIVAS
Herald Staff Writer

State Sen. Bob McKnight, chairman of the Monroe and Dade county delegations to the Legislature, said Saturday he might run for governor in 1986.

McKnight, the wealthy 37-year-old South Dade land developer, was elected chairman of the Dade delegation Tuesday. A day later, he announced to the Tiger Bay Political Club luncheon in Miami that he would not run for reelection when his current term ends in spring 1982.

In an interview Saturday, the Democrat said only the governor's office would interest him.

"Yes, I am considering it, but no, I really have no specific decision and I really won't make a decision, probably until a year or so after I retire in '82," said McKnight, a Florida Southern College and Florida State University alumnus.

"I really think that that's the only position I would really like to consider running for and serving in, but it is such a serious responsibility."

McKnight said he would not consider running against Gov. Bob Graham next year because he and Graham and their wives are close friends. "I believe in Bob Graham, what he stands for and what he's trying to do," McKnight said.

Like McKnight, Graham is a Miami developer who built his reputation on being a liberal in a Florida Senate dominated by North Florida conservatives.

The Associated Industries of Florida, a big-business lobby, said McKnight's votes deserved a 69 per cent approval rating from industry in the 1980 session. McKnight ranked 28th in Associated Industries approval out of 40 senators.

He won election to a House seat in 1974 and served two terms, becoming active in health and rehabilitation committees and winning several leadership awards. In 1978, McKnight won election to the District 38 Senate seat vacated by discredited Sen. Ralph Poston.

McKnight became one of the principals in an unprecedented political battle between Senate President W.D. Childers (D., Pensacola) and arch-conservative former President Dempsey Barron (D., Panama City), who unabashedly tried to take control of the Senate from Childers. McKnight was a key Childers supporter.

Although it is unclear who won the battle — and, indeed, it will continue in 1982 — McKnight is in line to retain his chairmanship of an Appropriations Committee subcommittee that controls spending on prisons, health and rehabilitative services and criminal justice.

He is also likely to be in a "leadership position" on the reapportionment committee, which next year will draw new district lines that could seriously affect many members' seats. He is likely to be chairman of the Natural Resources Committee in next year's session.

McKnight said he is retiring because he is sold on what he calls a "citizen legislature." He cites Barron, a 25-year veteran of the Legislature, as a classic example of the kind of "career politician" he wants to avoid becoming.

"We really ought to have a Legislature in which citizens come from communities all over the state, meet in Tallahassee, deliberate on one essential issue — and that's the budget — but beyond that formulate some policy, and then go on back to the communities and live there and become a part of the community, raise your family, conduct your businesses, so that you get a better, more direct understanding of what the effect is of that legislation," McKnight said. "The longer you stay up there, the more potential there is for contaminating that concept."

Miami Herald *article about Senator McKnight's possible race for governor, 1981.*

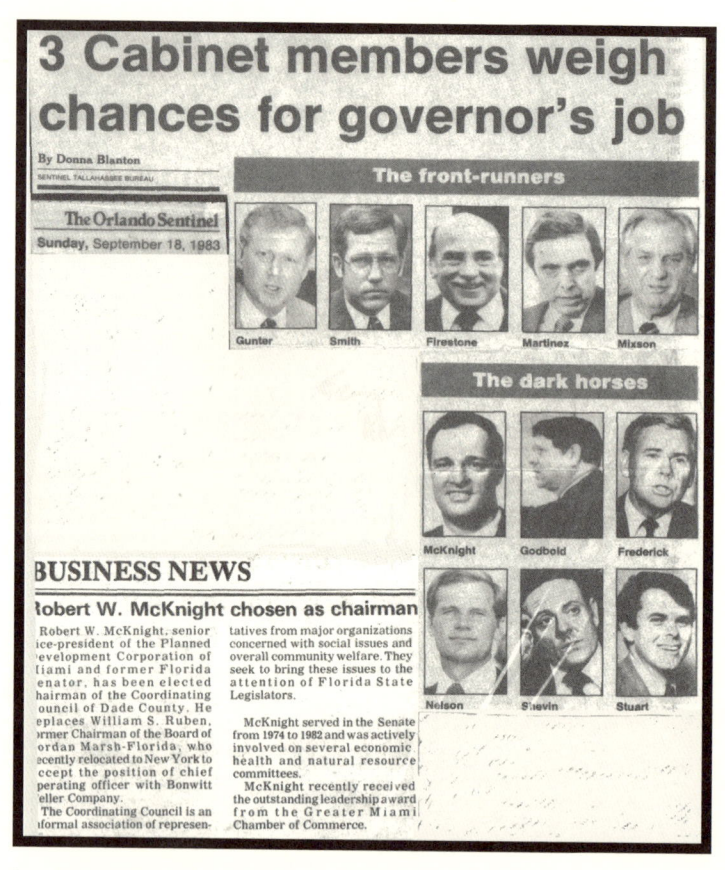

Orlando Sentinel *article about potential candidates for governor, 1986.*

St. Petersburg Times *article about potential candidates for governor, 1986.*

The Golden Years ...   152   *Robert McKnight*

The Miami Herald

Friday, April 10, 1987

Vero Beach project wins state marketing award

SIXTY OAKS SINGLE-FAMILY attached county homes are located on State Road 60 in Vero Beach. The developer of the community is Planned Corp.

Robert W. McKnight, senior vice president of Planned Development Company announced that his company's Sixty Oaks single-family residential development in Vero Beach received notification that its development received the Best Marketing Materials Award in the state wide Florida Achievement in Marketing Excellence ("FAME") program. The award is made annually by the largest home builder's association in the state, The Builder's Association of South Florida, and it was announced at the annual awards ceremony held on Key Biscayne at the Sonesta Beach Hotel on Saturday, March 28.

McKnight said the award was particularly appreciated by his colleagues and associates at Planned Development, as it was associated with the company's first venture in the Vero Beach and Treasure Coast area. McKnight attributed the success of the marketing program from graphics to market development to the advertising and marketing firm of Highsmith & Company in Miami.

Sixty Oaks, a planned residential community located immediately west of Kings Highway on State Road 60, is comprised of 60 single-family attached homes, featuring two- and three-bedroom homes with volume ceilings, skylights, ceramic tile foyers and breakfast nooks. Among the options available are a private enclosed garage, pool or spa and screened patio. The community, with a private security entrance, is clustered around the cul-de-sac, Sixty Oaks Lane, which is accented by mature oak trees, sabal palms and grapefruit trees.

The developer of Sixty Oaks has been a recognized builder in South Florida for over 40 years. The scope of the company's achievement is evident by the development of the 1,400 acre community of Cutler Ridge. This town was planned and developed by PDC and includes over 5,000 homes; parks; recreation facilities; churches and public schools; an office park incorporating professional buildings; hotels and financial institutions; a 1.5 million square foot regional mall; and a government center including library, fire, police, courthouse and administration buildings.

Award winning Sixty Oaks Residential Development by PDC in Vero Beach, Florida, 1987.

Former senator McKnight in PDC Vero development office, 1987 (photo by "The Best Gold Coast Fashion and Lifestyle").

CHAPTER 10

Reflections on Campaigns and Public Service

1. *The lesson here is not new, but still very important—assume nothing and recognize that the unrecognizable is what can hurt you. In other words, be careful of the underdog or "longshot."*

2. *Communicate often with your constituents whether it be in person or in writing. People appreciate being remembered. Perhaps more important than formal correspondence are handwritten personal notes or phone calls, which are often remembered for a lifetime. The best I ever saw at staying in touch with his constituents was Alabama-born and later U.S. Senator and member of the U.S. House of Representatives, Claude Pepper of Miami. The senator always remembered me and my wife, Susan, and something personal about us. I think he remembered us because he genuinely cared about us.*

3. *Serving in public office affords an opportunity to meet influential people you might otherwise not meet. However, it is important that one be very careful to avoid not only conflicts of interest but even the appearance of such. Do not cross the line of using your office to benefit financially in any way. Today, most governmental bodies allow elected officials to seek legal opinions, along with full disclosure, to avoid the potential conflicts.*

4. *It is important to seek the advice of people you respect, even if you disagree with their position. I adopted a policy in politics of always seeking contrarian views on controversial positions. If persuaded that a position other than the one you hold is correct, have the courage to admit it, and adapt to the correct position.*

5. *There is no such thing as too much research in pursuing a political issue. It is also important to thoroughly understand your opponent's position. Always understand the pros and cons*

of the issue and leave some room for your opponent to maneuver if you are winning the issue. Former attorney general Robert Kennedy wrote a great book about counseling President John F. Kennedy during negotiations with the Russians during the Cuban missile crisis in the early 60s. The attorney general emphasized the need to craft a face-saving position for one's opponent in negotiations. The basis for that design is research, research, and more research.

6. *Have a sense of humor in politics. As Senator Louis de la Parte (D., Tampa), once declared, while being slaughtered in debate by the Dean of the Senate, Dempsey Barron (D., Panama City), "Curse You, Red Barron." That quip resulted in the debate reverting to civil discourse and served both senators with honor. Perhaps the legislator with the best sense of humor during my legislative service was Senator Warren Henderson (R., Venice). Injecting humor into acrimonious debates can be difficult, but my experience is that it can pay big dividends in the long run.*

7. *Live every day as if it is your last, as it could be. I have had a successful political and business career and have had a blessed family life. I know my mom and dad would be proud.*

8. *Plan every detail of a campaign event, and include a contingency plan. In this case we not only should have confirmed the attendees, but provided rides for them to the event as well. Some candidates even use "Rent a Supporter," to give the event every appearance of success. Also, I recommend never scheduling a function in a location that looks empty—if necessary move the function to a smaller location so it has the appearance of SRO—Standing Room Only.*

9. *Get out your vote. Analyze where you got your votes in the primary and unleash all of your resources to get out that vote. Best of all, if you canvass those votes door-to-door or by phone, your opponent will never know. This is how many of the major*

upsets in political campaigns occur. It was a painful and expensive lesson for the McKnight campaign to learn in 1972.

10. The real heart of the legislative process occurs in the committees and subcommittees. That is where legislation is first heard and is subject to the apparent never-ending amendatory process. It is in committee that the staff influence is greatest on lawmaking and it is also the place where lobbyists have the best chance to influence legislation. The veteran legislators work the committees and leave the flowery speeches on the floor to the less effective lawmakers.

11. With few exceptions, the staff represents the members. In most cases they have more knowledge of and experience with the legislation being considered, so use them. They are supposed to be nonpartisan and they also have political ambitions. As stated in the golden rule, treat the staff with respect and they will respect you.

12. It is important to not only learn, but also memorize the rules of the chamber in which you are serving. This is the most important tactical advantage you can secure in the legislative arena.

13. Lobbyists are the fourth branch of government. Treat them with respect and never lie to them. Your word is your bond…keep it. I always made it a point to not spring a surprise on a lobbyist, but rather tell them in advance my plans on a particular piece of legislation. With some few exceptions, most of them did the same for me.

14. Do not commit your vote until you are certain about it and its probable results. If you are confident about that, commit and never break your word. If something happens to change your mind, obtain a release of responsibility from the person to whom you pledged your vote. This lesson was sacrosanct during my service in the legislature, but adherence to it is quite rare today, I am told.

15. *It is important to remember that anything said on the floor of the House or Senate Chamber is recorded and therefore public record forever. Many a candidate or elected official has wished that they could take back something said in jest and/or intended to be off the record. Say nothing unless you have to.*

16. *In my opinion, the certain three influences on political decisions are either, or all of: sex, religion and money. When evaluating a political situation, always consider those three influences during the decision-making process and attempt to make the most informed decision accordingly.*

17. *Success at politics is often as simple as keeping track of votes — yours and others. If you agree to support a position, especially if it is controversial, it is natural to feel that it should not be forgotten by the beneficiary. This is sometimes referred to as, "you scratch my back, I scratch yours." In legislative jargon, the votes are known as chits. Keep track of your chits and do not be afraid to use them. Few of your colleagues will forget your chits, especially on close votes.*

18. *Always respect the office. You can be upset with people and things people do. But know that you are a professional with an important craft. The individual with whom you are upset was elected, just like you. Treat the person with the respect of the office he or she holds. Always remember that democracy is a terrible form of government, but it is the best that we have.*

19. *Always seek bipartisan support. You are expected to enjoy the support of your like-thinking colleagues. Those who do not share your view will look to those who are supporting your position for comfort. The greater the breadth of support, the greater your chances are of success. Always remember the adage: politics makes strange bedfellows. My experience is that it is true.*

20. *"Do unto others as you would have them do unto you." This golden rule applies every day in life as well as in politics. Said another way, put yourself in the other person's shoes. Good negotiators often lead with a concession that satisfies the opponent's needs, before the opponent even fights for his position. In politics, be respectful of your friends and foes alike.*

APPENDICES

Appendix A: Biography

Robert W. McKnight
2546 Noble Drive
Tallahassee, FL 32308

Cell Telephone: 850-322-5566
Office Telephone: 850-425-6200 ext 2452
Office Fax: 850-425-6220
Email: bmcknight@FBMC-benefits.com

National Accounts Business Development and previously Senior Vice President for Sales and Marketing of Fringe Benefits Management Company, Third Party Administrator of public and private employer benefits. Also, President of McKnight Financial Corporation, a marketing, consulting, and outsourcing firm.

Previously, Executive Vice President of Florida Chamber of Commerce. Mr. McKnight served as a member of the Executive Staff of former Governor Lawton M. Chiles and former Lieutenant Governor Kenneth "Buddy" MacKay, upon their election in 1990; and was Senior Vice President of Planned Development Corporation, a real estate development, and management and investment firm for fifteen years. Prior to that, Mr. McKnight was Director of Marketing of three publicly-traded real estate partnership programs, raising over $21 million of equity capital and was associated with the IBM Corporation for five years. He has been a partner and developer in realty estate projects valued at over $50 million. He is a past member of the Board of Directors of Southeast National Bank of Tamiami; Miami National Bank; The National Association of Industrial and Office Parks, South Florida Chapter; and a member of the Visiting Committee, University of Miami School of Business.

Mr. McKnight is a former member of the Florida Senate (1978-82) and the Florida House of Representatives (1974-78). He was runner-up, *Florida Times Union*, Allen Morris award, "Most Effective First Term Member of the Florida House of Representative," in 1976. He served as chairman of the Subcommittee on Corrections and Offender Rehabilitation, and chairman of the Subcommittee on Health and Mental Health, House of Representatives. Mr. McKnight was runner-up for the *Florida Times Union*, Allen Morris Award, "Most Effective First Term Member of the Florida Senate," 1980. He was chairman of the Committee on Health and Rehabilitative Services and the Appropriations Subcommittee Funding Health Care and the Criminal Justice System in the Senate. He was nominated for the *St. Petersburg Times* award, "Most Valuable Member of the Florida Senate," in 1981. He served as chairman of the Dade-Monroe Legislative Delegation in 1982, and was listed in "*Who's Who in American Politics*" in 1982.

Mr. McKnight received his M.B.A. degree from Florida State University and B.S. degree from Florida Southern College. He was President of Omicron Delta Kappa, National Leadership Society; and a member of Beta Gamma Sigma, National Business Scholastic Honorary; and was elected president of his sophomore, junior and senior classes in undergraduate school. Mr. McKnight was a trustee of Florida Southern College and recipient of the college's Alumni Achievement Award in 1995.

Mr. McKnight is a former U.S. Army officer with service in Korea, a recipient of the U.S. Army Commendation Medal, and was a Distinguished Military Graduate, Reserve Officers' Training Corps, in 1966.

Former Governor Bob Graham appointed Mr. McKnight to serve as chairman of the Florida Task Force on Competition and Consumer Choices in Health Care, which proposed landmark legislation enacted in 1984. Previously, he served as chairman of the Florida Chamber of Commerce Foundation; Executive Committee and Board of Directors, Florida Chamber of Commerce; on the board of directors of WPBT Channel 2 Public Television in Miami; and on the Advisory Council of the School of Public Health, University of South Florida in Tampa.

Mr. McKnight received the Distinguished Florida Jaycees Award as one of the "Five Outstanding Young Men in Florida" in 1980.

Appendix B: Major Legislative Achievements by Senator McKnight, 1974-1982

THE FLORIDA SENATE

SENATOR ROBERT W. McKNIGHT
38th District

District Office Address:
1440 Brickell Avenue
Miami, Florida 33131
(305) 358-3764

COMMITTEES:
Health and Rehabilitative Services,
  Chairman
Appropriations, Sub. C,
  Chairman
Economic, Community & Consumer Affairs,
  Vice-Chairman
Natural Resources and Conservation,
  Vice-Chairman
Rules and Calendar

Major Achievements 1974 - 1982

House of Representatives

1974 - 1975 (1975 Session)
- Directly involved in the reorganization of the Florida Department of Health and Rehabilitative Services, to include serving on the Select Reorganization Oversight Committee.
- Directly involved in the reorganization of the Florida Department of Natural Resources and the Florida Department of Environmental Regulation.
- Sponsored the law which provided for parental involvement in offenses of juvenile crimes through counseling and restitution.
- Actively involved in the law providing for a Bill of Rights for retarded citizens (1975).
- Actively involved in and co-sponsor of the legislation establishing the Local Government Comprehensive Planning Act.

1975 - 1976 (1976 Session)
- Floor manager for the Urban Coalition in passage of the 1976 Water Management Act.
- Actively involved in the law reforming administration of nursing homes in the State of Florida.
- Sponsored a major determinate sentencing bill, as highlighted in the *Florida Bar Journal*.
- Responsible for the state aid which saved the Sunrise School for Retarded Children in South Dade.
- Supported the sunset legislation of all governmental agencies.

1976 - 1977 (1977 Session)
- Sponsored an appropriation for the establishment of a Drinking Water Quality Research Center at Florida International University.
- Sponsored the law amending the perinatal intensive care statute to provide for more urban participation in the program, and increased funding.
- Sponsored the law establishing the Management Fellows Program (a management development program) within the Department of Health and Rehabilitative Services.
- Sponsored the law providing for purchase of services and appropriations for treatment of emotionally disturbed children.

W. D. CHILDERS	CURTIS PETERSON	JOE BROWN	JOHN D. MELTON
President	President Pro Tempore	Secretary	Sergeant at Arms

1977 - 1978 (1978 Session) - Strongly supported the establishment of the community care for the elderly program.
- Sponsored the law establishing a screening program for infant diseases.
- Sponsored an appropriation for the restoration and enhancement of Biscayne Bay (1978-1982, approximately $2 Million).
- Sponsored an appropriation for establishing an impoundment program within the Kissimmee River Valley Tributaries.
- Supported state appropriations for the replacement of the Florida Keys' aqueduct pipeline and bridges.
- Sponsored an appropriation for development of Indian Key as a historic site in the Florida Keys.
- Urged support of the Water Management District for the establishment of linear parks along water management easements in urban areas.

Senate

1978 - 1979 (1979 Session) - Sponsored the law establishing a Recreational Trails Program within the Department of Natural Resources.
- Sponsored the law providing for a streamlined Industrial Siting and Permitting Act for the Florida Department of Commerce.
- Sponsored the law establishing Biscayne Bay as a lobster sanctuary.
- Supported establishment of a Cost Containment Board within the Florida Department of Insurance.
- Amended the Florida Conservation and Recreational Lands Act to provide that a priority be placed on urban purchases.

1979 - 1980 (1980 Session) - Sponsored the landmark law establishing a definition of brain death.
- Sponsored the law providing for local government planning for community based residential treatment facilities.
- Actively supported the establishment of tax exemptions for foreign bank transactions.
- Served on the Joint Select Committee for re-enactment of the Critical State Concern Program.
- Supported the establishment of Florida International University as a four year curriculum.
- Supported the temporary transfer of the Florida Keys Aqueduct Authority to the South Florida Water Management District.
- Actively supported the Medicaid Reform Act of 1980.
- Successfully lobbied the Cabinet on behalf of the acquisition of the ITT parcel in Coral Gables under the Conservation and Recreational Lands Act.
- Successfully lobbied the Cabinet on behalf of a special allocation of Florida Highway Patrol troopers for Miami's crime problem.
- Successfully lobbied the Cabinet on behalf of an accelerated appropriations distribution for the construction of the Downtown Miami Dade Community College Campus.

1980 - 1981 (1981 Session) - Sponsored the law establishing the first incentive plan for state employees to reduce health insurance costs.

- Joined in sponsorship and support of the Governor's Save Our Rivers Program
- Sponsored the law establishing an Artificial Reef Program within the Florida Department of Natural Resources
- Sponsored the law providing for tax increment financing for transportation needs in blighted areas.
- Provided an appropriation for an Education Joint Use Facility in Marathon.
- Provided for an appropriation for the expansion of the Bahia Honda State Park in the Florida Keys.
- Supported a Cabinet appropriation for the development of Jose Marti Park in Miami.

1981 - 1982 (1982 Session)
- Provided a first time statewide appropriation for the Guardian Ad Litem Program.
- Led the Dade Delegation's support for the one cent sales tax increase and proviso language for the fight against crime in Dade County.
- Supported the establishment of a study of a high speed rail program between Orlando and Miami.
- Sponsored the legislation providing for the re-enactment of the Cost Containment Board, re-enactment of the licensure and inspection of hospitals, and provided for local involvement in health planning (and the administration of certificates of need).
- Appropriated funds for continued development of Jose Marti Park.
- Increased the perinatal intensive care funding to $25 Million (funding in 1974, $1.5 Million).
- Sponsored legislation revising and reforming the Baker Act.
- Provided the first appropriation for implementation of the Gainesville Plan for nursing home medicaid reimbursement.
- Sponsored legislation providing for a child abuse prevention program.
- Provided the first appropriation for the state absorption of expert witness fees and court appointed counsel cost, under Article V of the State Constitution.
- Sponsored a $536,000 appropriation for the establishment of a wilderness youth camp prevention program for emotionally disturbed children in South Dade County.

Summary of Bills Enclosed:

1975-House Bill 736
1977-House Bill 739
 -House Bill 1270
1978-House Bill 562
 -Committee Substitute for House Bill 783
 -House Bill 784
1980-Committee Substitute for Senate Bill 293
 -Committee Substitute for Senate Bill 583
 -Committee Substitute for Senate Bill 584
1982-Senate Bill 425
 -Senate Bill 737
-Senate Bill 900

Appendix C: Selected Legislation sponsored by Senator McKnight, 1974-1982

HB 736
(Regular Session 1975)

By Representative McKnight and others

3 A bill to be entitled
4 An act relating to juveniles; adding a new sub-
5 section (6) to s. 39.02, Florida Statutes, and
6 adding a new subsection (8) to s. 39.11, Florida
7 Statutes; authorizing the circuit court, upon
8 recommendation by the Department of Health and
9 Rehabilitative Services, to order the natural
10 parents or legal guardians to participate in fam-
11 ily counseling and other activities necessary for
12 the correction of a child; providing an effective
13 date.
14
15 Be It Enacted by the Legislature of the State of Florida:
16
17 Section 1. Subsection (6) of section 39.02, Florida
18 Statutes, is renumbered as subsection (7) and a new subsection
19 (6) is added to said section to read:
20 39.02 Jurisdiction.--
21 (6) The court shall have jurisdiction over the parents
22 or custodians of a child subject to the provisions of this
23 chapter for the purpose of requiring the involvement of the
24 parents or custodians in activities deemed necessary for the
25 correction of the child.
26 Section 2. Subsection (8) of section 39.11, Florida
27 Statutes, is renumbered as subsection (9) and a new subsection
28 (8) is added to said section to read:
29 39.11 Powers with reference to a dependent or delinquent

1

CODING: Words in struck through type are deletions from existing law; words underlined are additions.

The Golden Years ...   *Robert McKnight*

173-129-12-4

1 child or child in need of supervision.--
2 (8) In carrying out the provisions of this chapter, the
3 court, upon the recommendation of an authorized agent of the
4 Department of Health and Rehabilitative Services, may order the
5 natural parents or legal guardian of a child subject to the
6 jurisdiction of this chapter to participate in family counseling
7 and other recognized activities deemed necessary for the cor-
8 rection of the child.
9 Section 3. This act shall take effect upon becoming a
10 law.

LEGISLATIVE SUMMARY

Provides that, for purposes of the judicial treatment of juveniles, the court having jurisdiction over the juvenile also has jurisdiction over the parents or custodian of the child for purposes of involving them in activities necessary for the correction of the child. Authorizes the court, upon recommendation of the Department of Health and Rehabilitative Services, to order the parents or guardian of a child to participate in family counseling or other activities necessary for the correction of the child.

Florida House of Representatives - 1977   HB 739

By Representative McKnight

1 A bill to be entitled
2 An act relating to state capital projects for
3 environmentally endangered lands and outdoor
4 recreation lands under the Land Conservation
5 Act of 1972; amending s. 380.05(1)(a), Florida
6 Statutes; providing that the state land
7 planning agency include, in its recommendations
8 to the Administration Commission for
9 designation of an area of critical state
10 concern, recommendations as to the purchase of
11 lands within such area as environmentally
12 endangered lands or outdoor recreation lands;
13 adding s. 259.04(3), Florida Statutes;
14 providing that the Department of Natural
15 Resources be required to make recommendations
16 to the head of the department as to purchase of
17 lands within an area of critical state concern
18 for such purposes; providing an effective date.
19
20 Be It Enacted by the Legislature of the State of Florida:
21
22   Section 1. Paragraph (a) of subsection (1) of section
23 380.05, Florida Statutes, is amended to read:
24   380.05 Areas of critical state concern.--
25   (1)(a) The state land planning agency may from time to
26 time recommend to the Administration Commission specific areas
27 of critical state concern. In its recommendation the agency
28 shall specify the boundaries of the proposed areas and state
29 the reasons why the particular area proposed is of critical
30 concern to the state or region, the dangers that would result
31 from uncontrolled or inadequate development of the area, and

CODING: Words in struck through type are deletions from existing law; words underlined are additions.

275-50-2-7

1 the advantages that would be achieved from the development of 1.23
2 the area in a coordinated manner and recommend specific 1.24
3 principles for guiding the development of the area. <u>The</u> 1.25
4 <u>recommendation of the state land planning agency shall also</u>
5 <u>include recommendations with respect to the purchase of lands</u> 1.26
6 <u>situated within the boundaries of the proposed area as</u> 1.27
7 <u>environmentally endangered lands and outdoor recreation lands</u> 1.28
8 <u>under the Land Conservation Act of 1972.</u> However, prior to 1.30
9 the designation of any area of critical state concern by the
10 Administration Commission, an inventory of lands owned by the 1.31
11 state shall be filed with the state land planning agency. The 1.32
12 state land planning agency shall request all political 1.33
13 subdivisions and other public agencies of the state and the 1.34
14 Federal Government to submit an inventory of lands owned
15 within the State of Florida. 1.35
16   Section 2. Subsection (3) is added to section 259.04, 1.35
17 Florida Statutes, to read:
18   259.04 Board; powers and duties.-- 1.37
19   <u>(3) Within 45 days of the designation by the</u> 1.38
20 <u>Administration Commission of an area of critical state concern</u>
21 <u>under s. 380.05, the Department of Natural Resources shall</u> 1.40
22 <u>make recommendations to the board with respect to the purchase</u> 1.41
23 <u>of the fee or any lesser interest in any lands situated in</u> 1.43
24 <u>such area of critical state concern as environmentally</u>
25 <u>endangered lands or outdoor recreation lands.</u> 1.44
26   Section 3. This act shall take effect October 1, 1977. 1.44/1

2

CODING: Words in struck through type are deletions from existing law; words <u>underlined</u> are additions.

275-50-2-7

***   1:sbs
SENATE SUMMARY   1:sbs

The state land planning agency is required to include, in its recommendations to the Administration Commission (Governor and Cabinet) for an area to be designated as an area of critical state concern, recommendations as to the purchase of lands within such area as environmentally endangered lands and outdoor recreation lands under the Land Conservation Act of 1972. Within 45 days of the designation by the commission of an area of critical state concern, the Department of Natural Resources is required to make recommendations to the head of the department (Governor and Cabinet) whether such lands should be purchased as state capital projects under that act.

1.47
1.50
1.52
1.53
1.54
1.55
1.56
1.57
1.58
1.60

CODING: Words in struck through type are deletions from existing law; words underlined are additions.

The Golden Years ...   171   *Robert McKnight*

Florida House of Representatives - 1977   HB 1270

By Representative McKnight

1 A bill to be entitled
2 An act relating to the Department of Health and
3 Rehabilitative Services; providing legislative
4 intent; adding subsection (24) to s. 20.19,
5 Florida Statutes, 1976 Supplement; authorizing
6 the establishment of a management fellows
7 program; providing that such program shall be
8 developed and implemented within existing
9 resources; providing an effective date.
10
11 WHEREAS, the reorganization of the Department of Health
12 and Rehabilitative Services in 1975 created a consolidated but
13 decentralized organizational structure for the provision of
14 integrated human services, and
15 WHEREAS, existing personnel development and training
16 programs in state government are generally limited to meeting
17 specific program or professional needs, and
18 WHEREAS, a demonstrable need exists to develop and
19 retain qualified candidates for key positions in the
20 department who have broad administrative capabilities, and
21 WHEREAS, a program which identifies high potential
22 individuals and provides them adequate training and experience
23 in various units of the department will greatly help to meet
24 this need, NOW, THEREFORE,
25
26 Be It Enacted by the Legislature of the State of Florida:
27
28 Section 1. It is the intent of the Legislature to
29 provide a program whereby the Department of Health and
30 Rehabilitative Services may identify, train, and promote
31 employees with high levels of administrative and management

CODING: Words in struck through type are deletions from existing law; words underlined are additions.

This public document was promulgated at a cost of $7.66 per page for 900 copies and $.83 per page for distribution for the information of members of the Legislature and the public.

The Golden Years ...   172   *Robert McKnight*

potential in order to meet the department's need for broad-based administrative skills in key positions within the department.

Section 2. Subsection (24) is added to section 20.19, Florida Statutes, 1976 Supplement, to read:

20.19 Department of Health and Rehabilitative Services.--There is created a Department of Health and Rehabilitative Services.

(24) FELLOWS PROGRAM.--The Department of Health and Rehabilitative Services is authorized to establish a management fellows program in order to provide highly qualified career candidates for key administrative positions in the department. Such program shall include but not be limited to:

(a) The identification annually by the assistant secretary for administrative services, by the assistant secretary for program planning and development, and by the district administrator in each district of one high-potential, career service employee to be designated a health and rehabilitative services management fellow.

(b) The design and development of a 2-year placement program for each respective fellow in various units of the department.

(c) The participation of each fellow in on-the-job training and inservice training, supplemented by periodic seminars and courses within and outside the department.

Section 3. The Department of Health and Rehabilitative Services shall develop and implement the management fellows program provided by this act within existing resources.

Section 4. This act shall take effect July 1, 1977.

CODING: Words in struck through type are deletions from existing law; words underlined are additions.

****

HOUSE SUMMARY

Authorizes the Department of Health and Rehabilitative Services to establish, within existing resources, a management fellows program to provide highly qualified career candidates for key administrative positions.

CODING: Words in struck through type are deletions from existing law; words underlined are additions.

Florida House of Representatives - 1978　　　　　　HB 562

By Representative McKnight

A bill to be entitled

An act relating to the regional perinatal intensive care center program; amending s. 383.19(1), Florida Statutes, relating to grant disbursements and reimbursements, to provide that grant funds not expended under certain conditions shall be considered appropriated for distribution to other centers, based on a certain formula; providing an effective date.

Be It Enacted by the Legislature of the State of Florida:

Section 1. Subsection (1) of section 383.19, Florida Statutes, is amended to read:

383.19 Grant disbursements and reimbursements; guidelines.--

(1) The department shall use guidelines for development of centers which include, but are not limited to, the need for regional perinatal intensive care program center and affiliate center services and the requirements of the population to be served. One center may be established to serve a geographic area which experiences at least 10,000 live births per year. First priority in the establishment of these centers shall be given to the seven neonatal intensive care centers located in Escambia, Duval, Alachua, Orange, Hillsborough, Pinellas, and Dade counties; and three new centers shall be established, subject to further legislative approval and <u>to appropriations becoming</u> ~~(to appropriations becoming)~~ available specifically for such centers, to be located in Broward, Dade, and Palm Beach counties. From funds appropriated for this program, each established center shall

CODING: Words in ~~struck through~~ type are deletions from existing law; words <u>underlined</u> are additions.

The Golden Years ...　　　　175　　　　*Robert McKnight*

receive an equal minimum support grant. Affiliated centers shall be entitled to funds appropriated for the perinatal intensive care program only after established centers have received minimum support grants as provided above and after agreement, and <u>establishment of</u> [establishment of] a working relationship, between an affiliated center and a center. If the Legislature appropriates funds which are to be distributed to centers on the basis of the proportion of eligible patients served in each center to the total number of eligible patients served statewide during a given fiscal year, such funds shall be distributed according to a formula designed by the department to include the number of patients served, the number of inpatient hospitalization days, the number of outpatient evaluations and services, and the number of infants evaluated serially for developmental anomalies, in both the center and any affiliated center integrated into the program of the center. <u>If funds appropriated by the Legislature for equal minimum support grants to centers are not expended for such grants because a hospital terminates, or does not enter into, a contractual agreement, such funds shall be considered appropriated by the Legislature for distribution to other centers on the basis of the proportion of eligible patients served in each center to the total number served statewide during a given fiscal year, under the formula developed by the department as provided in this subsection.</u>

Section 2. This act shall take effect July 1, 1978.

CODING: Words in struck through type are deletions from existing law; words <u>underlined</u> are additions.

```
****************************************
                HOUSE SUMMARY

With respect to grants and reimbursements made by the
Department of Health and Rehabilitative Services, from
funds appropriated to the department for such purpose, to
hospitals in order to assist them in establishing and
maintaining regional neonatal intensive care centers,
provides that funds not expended for such grants because
a hospital terminates, or does not enter into, a
contractual agreement with the department shall be
considered appropriated by the Legislature for
distribution to other centers, based on the proportion of
eligible patients served, according to a specified
formula.
```

CODING: Words in struck through type are deletions from existing law; words underlined are additions.

Florida House of Representatives - 1978   CS for HB 783

By Committee on Health & Rehabilitative Services and
Representative McKnight and others

A bill to be entitled

An act relating to infancy hygiene; amending s. 383.14, Florida Statutes, relating to screening of infants for certain disorders; including hereditary and congenital disorders among disorders for which infant screening is required; modifying procedure; expanding powers and duties of the Department of Health and Rehabilitative Services; providing that the registry of cases shall be confidential; limiting treatment products which the department may supply in certain cases to dietary treatment products; providing for promotion of public education, genetic studies, and counseling; providing for the establishment of the Infant Screening Advisory Council and matters relative thereto; providing an effective date.

Be It Enacted by the Legislature of the State of Florida:

Section 1. Section 383.14, Florida Statutes, is amended to read:

383.14 <u>Screening of infants</u> ~~Testing~~ for metabolic <u>and other hereditary and congenital</u> disorders ~~of infants~~.--It shall be the duty of the Department of Health and Rehabilitative Services to promote the <u>screening</u> ~~testing~~ of all infants <u>born in Florida</u> for phenylketonuria and other metabolic<u>, hereditary, and congenital</u> disorders known to result in significant impairment of health or intellect<u>, as</u> <u>screening programs accepted by current medical practice become</u>

CODING: Words in ~~struck through~~ type are deletions from existing law; words <u>underlined</u> are additions.

~~using such tests as are~~ available and practical in the judgment of the department ~~and to keep a record of said tests.~~ ~~These~~ Tests shall be performed at such times and in such manner as may be prescribed by the department <u>after consultation with the Infant Screening Advisory Council.</u>

(1) RULES ~~AND REGULATIONS~~.--<u>In consultation with the Infant Screening Advisory Council,</u> the department shall promulgate and enforce rules ~~and regulations~~ requiring that every <u>infant born in Florida shall</u> ~~newborn~~, prior to becoming 2 weeks of age, be subjected to a test for phenylketonuria and<u>, at the appropriate age, be tested for</u> such other metabolic diseases <u>and hereditary or congenital disorders</u> as the department may deem necessary from time to time. The department is empowered to promulgate such additional rules ~~and regulations~~ as are found necessary for the administration of this section, including <u>rules relating to the methods used and time or times for testing as accepted medical practice indicates, and rules requiring</u> mandatory reporting of the results of ~~all~~ tests for these conditions to the department.

(2) DEPARTMENT OF HEALTH AND REHABILITATIVE SERVICES; POWERS AND DUTIES.--The department shall administer<u>, and provide certain services to implement,</u> the provisions of this section and shall:

(a) <u>Furnish the necessary laboratory tests and materials.</u>

<u>(b)</u> ~~(a)~~ Furnish all physicians, public health <u>units</u> ~~nurses~~, and hospitals forms on which the results of tests for phenylketonuria <u>and such other disorders for which testing may be required from time to time</u> shall be reported to the department.

2

CODING: Words in ~~struck through~~ type are deletions from existing law; words <u>underlined</u> are additions.

(c) Promote education of the public about the prevention and management of metabolic, hereditary, and congenital disorders.

(d) ~~(b)~~ Maintain a confidential registry of cases, including information of importance for the purpose of follow-up services to prevent mental retardation, to correct or ameliorate physical handicaps, and for epidemiologic studies, if indicated.

(e) ~~(c)~~ Supply the necessary dietary treatment products ~~product~~ where practicable for diagnosed cases for as long as medically indicated when the products are ~~product is~~ not otherwise available.

(f) Promote the availability of genetic studies and counseling in order that the parents, siblings, and affected infants may benefit from available knowledge of the condition.

(3) OBJECTIONS OF PARENT OR GUARDIAN.-- The provisions of this section shall not apply when the parent or guardian of the child objects thereto. A written statement of such objection shall be presented to the physician or other person whose duty it is to administer and report such tests under the provisions of this section.

(4) ADVISORY COUNCIL.--There is hereby established an Infant Screening Advisory Council made up of 10 members appointed by the Secretary of Health and Rehabilitative Services. The council shall be composed of two consumer members, two practicing pediatricians, one representative from each of the state's three medical schools, and one representative each from the Children's Medical Services Program Office, the Health Program Office, and the Retardation Program Office. One-half of the members of the first council shall be appointed for terms of 2 years and the other half for

3

CODING: Words in ~~struck through~~ type are deletions from existing law; words underlined are additions.

terms of 4 years. Thereafter, all appointments shall be for terms of 4 years. The chairperson of the council shall be elected from the membership of the council and shall serve for a period of 2 years. The council shall meet at least semiannually or upon the call of the chairperson. Council members shall serve without pay. The provisions of ss. 20.05(3) and 112.061 to the contrary notwithstanding, the council members shall not be reimbursed for travel or expenses. It is the purpose of the council to advise the department about:

(a) Conditions for which testing should be included under the screening program.

(b) Procedures for collection and transmission of specimens and recording of results.

(c) Methods whereby screening programs for children now provided or proposed to be offered in the state may be more effectively evaluated, coordinated, and consolidated.

Section 2. This act shall take effect January 1, 1979.

CODING: Words in ~~struck through~~ type are deletions from existing law; words underlined are additions.

****
HOUSE SUMMARY

Provides for screening of infants born in Florida for metabolic and other hereditary and congenital disorders. Provides administrative procedure. (Present law provides for testing for metabolic disorders only.) Pursuant thereto, expands authority of the Department of Health and Rehabilitative Services to include:
   1. Furnishing lab tests and materials.
   2. Furnishing certain additional forms.
   3. Maintaining certain information needed to correct or ameliorate physical handicaps and for epidemiologic studies, if indicated.
   4. Promoting public education, genetic studies, and counseling.

Provides that the registry of cases maintained by the department shall be confidential and limits treatment products which may be supplied by the department, where practicable and medically indicated and when such products are not otherwise available, to dietary treatment products.

Provides for the establishment of a 10-member advisory council appointed by the secretary of the department to advise the department on specified matters related to infant screening and to consult with the department with respect to promulgation and enforcement of rules regulating such screening. Provides that council members shall receive no compensation and shall not be reimbursed for travel expenses or per diem. Provides for terms and organization.

5

CODING: Words in struck through type are deletions from existing law; words underlined are additions.

Florida House of Representatives - 1978　　　　　　　　　HB 784

By Representative McKnight

1　　　　　　　　A bill to be entitled
2　　　　An act relating to the retarded; creating s.
3　　　　393.16, Florida Statutes, relating to
4　　　　intermediate care facilities for the mentally
5　　　　retarded and other developmentally disabled;
6　　　　providing intent; providing a definition;
7　　　　establishing a loan trust fund; authorizing the
8　　　　Department of Health and Rehabilitative
9　　　　Services to grant loans to eligible facilities
10　　　for initial operating costs; providing criteria
11　　　for granting of such loans and for repayment
12　　　thereof; providing an effective date.
13
14　Be It Enacted by the Legislature of the State of Florida:
15
16　　　　Section 1. Section 393.16, Florida Statutes, is
17　created to read:
18　　　　393.16 Intermediate care facilities; intent;
19　definition; trust fund.--
20　　　　(1) The Legislature finds and declares that the
21　establishment of intermediate care facilities for the mentally
22　retarded and other developmentally disabled is financially
23　difficult for private individuals, due to the initial
24　expenditures required before reimbursement can begin for
25　services rendered. Therefore, it is the intent of the
26　Legislature to develop a loan trust fund for the purpose of
27　granting loans to support and encourage the establishment of
28　community-based intermediate care facilities for the mentally
29　retarded and other developmentally disabled.
30　　　　(2) As used in this section, "facility" means any
31　residential intermediate care facility for the mentally

CODING: Words in struck through type are deletions from existing law; words underlined are additions.

retarded and other developmentally disabled which is operated,
approved, or contracted with under the authority of the
Department of Health and Rehabilitative Services, housing not
fewer than 4 or more than 25 mentally retarded or
developmentally disabled persons. A facility may be operated
by a profit or nonprofit corporation, by a partnership, or by
sole proprietorship.

    (3) The Intermediate Care Facilities Trust Fund is hereby established in the State Treasury to be administered by the Department of Health and Rehabilitative Services for the purpose of granting loans to eligible facilities for the initial costs of operating the facilities. Operating costs may not include structural modification, the purchase of equipment or fire and safety devices, or the purchase of insurance, nor shall such costs include the actual construction of a facility.

    (4) The department may grant to an eligible facility a lump sum loan in one payment, not to exceed 75 percent of the operating costs of the facility for up to 6 months' care and maintenance for each mentally retarded or developmentally disabled person to be placed in the facility by the department. Loans granted to facilities shall not be in lieu of payment for maintenance and care provided, but shall stand separate and distinct. Each loan shall be used to provide programs and services as required under 45 CFR 249.13, federal regulations providing standards for intermediate care facility services, and shall be granted to a facility only upon the completion of a facility licensure/certification survey conducted by the department. The department shall promulgate rules, as provided in chapter 120, establishing the minimum

2

CODING: Words in struck through type are deletions from existing law; words underlined are additions.

standards under which a facility shall be eligible to receive a loan as provided in this section.

(5) Any loan granted by the department under this section shall be repaid at no interest by the facility within 6 months of the receipt of the initial facility Medicaid payment.

(6) If any facility which has received such a loan ceases to accept, or to provide care and maintenance to, persons placed in the facility by the department, or if any such facility files papers of bankruptcy, the loan shall become an interest-bearing loan, at the rate of 5 percent per annum on the entire amount of the initial loan, which shall be repaid within a 3-month period from the date on which the facility ceases to provide care or files papers in bankruptcy, and the amount of the loan due, plus interest, shall constitute a lien in favor of the state against all real and personal property of the facility. The lien shall be perfected by the appropriate officer of the department by executing and acknowledging a statement of the name of the facility and the amount due on the loan and a copy of the promissory note, which shall be recorded by the department with the clerk of the circuit court in the county wherein the facility is located. If the facility has filed a petition for bankruptcy, the department shall file and enforce the lien in the bankruptcy proceedings. Otherwise, the lien shall be enforced in the manner provided in s. 85.011. All funds received by the department from the enforcement of the lien shall be deposited in the Intermediate Care Facilities Trust Fund.

Section 2. This act shall take effect July 1, 1978.

CODING: Words in struck through type are deletions from existing law; words underlined are additions.

HOUSE SUMMARY

Establishes a loan trust fund, to be administered by the Department of Health and Rehabilitative Services, from which lump sum loans may be granted to intermediate care facilities for the mentally retarded and other developmentally disabled eligible for federal reimbursement through Medicaid, to assist with initial costs of operating the facilities. Establishes criteria for eligibility. Provides a formula for determining the maximum amount which may be loaned any facility. Authorizes use of loans for certain purposes only.

Provides for repayment at no interest within 6 months of receipt of the first Medicaid payment. Provides for repayment at 5 percent interest within 3 months if the facility ceases to provide care or files papers in bankruptcy, and provides for a lien in favor of the state against all real and personal property of the facility in such an event.

4

CODING: Words in struck through type are deletions from existing law; words underlined are additions.

Florida Senate - 1980

CS for SB 293

By Committee on Health and Rehabilitative Services and Senator McKnight

       A bill to be entitled
    An act relating to death; creating s. 382.085,
    Florida Statutes; providing a nonexclusive
    standard for determining death; providing
    procedures for determination of death;
    exempting specified persons and entities from
    civil or criminal liability for actions in
    accordance with the act; providing an effective
    date.

Be It Enacted by the Legislature of the State of Florida:

    Section 1. Section 382.085, Florida Statutes, is
created to read:
    382.085 Recognition of brain death.--
    (1) For legal and medical purposes, where respiratory
and circulatory functions are maintained by artificial means
of support so as to preclude a determination that these
functions have ceased, the occurrence of death may be
determined where there is the irreversible cessation of the
functioning of the entire brain, including the brain stem,
determined in accordance with this section.
    (2) Determination of death pursuant to this section
shall be made in accordance with currently accepted reasonable
medical standards by two physicians licensed under chapter 458
or chapter 459. One physician shall be the treating
physician, and the other physician shall be a board-eligible
or board-certified neurologist or a board-eligible or board-
certified neurosurgeon. This determination of brain death
shall be evidenced by the signed statement of each of these
two physicians. When determining brain death pursuant to

1

CODING: Words in struck through type are deletions from existing law; words underlined are additions.

300-847-80   CS for SB 293

1 subsection (1), brain death must be determined before
2 artificial means of support of respiratory or circulatory
3 functions are terminated and before any vital organ is removed
4 for purposes of transplantation.
5   (3) If an organ of a donor is to be used for direct
6 organ transplant under chapter 732, and if the donor's death
7 is established by determining that the donor's brain and brain
8 stem have irreversibly ceased to function, the determination
9 shall be made only under this section. Neither physician
10 making the determination of death shall participate in the
11 procedures for removing or transplanting a part of a donor, or
12 in the care of any recipient.
13   (4) No recovery shall be allowed in any court in this
14 state against a physician, medical institution, or medical
15 facility that acts in reliance on a determination of death, or
16 that makes a determination of death in accordance with this
17 section. No individual shall be subject to prosecution in any
18 criminal proceeding for acting in accordance with this
19 section. Nothing in this section shall be deemed to eliminate
20 or modify the accepted standard of care for health care
21 providers as set forth in s. 768.45.
22   (5) The standard set forth in subsection (1) is not
23 the exclusive standard for determining death or for the
24 withdrawal of life support systems.
25   Section 2. This act shall take effect July 1, 1980, or
26 upon becoming a law, whichever occurs later.

2

CODING: Words in struck through type are deletions from existing law; words underlined are additions.

The Golden Years ...   188   Robert McKnight

STATEMENT OF SUBSTANTIAL CHANGES CONTAINED IN
COMMITTEE SUBSTITUTE FOR SENATE BILL 293

1. The bill provides standards for the determination of brain death when respiratory and circulatory functions are maintained by artificial means of support so as to preclude a determination that these functions have ceased.

2. The neurologist or neurosurgeon assisting in making the determination of death may be either board eligible or board-certified.

3. Each of the two physicians making the determination of brain death shall evidence their determinations by a signed statement.

4. The bill eliminates the requirement of good faith on the part of physicians making a determination of brain death in accordance with this section. Physicians acting in accordance with the section will be held to the accepted standard of care for health care providers as set forth in chapter 768.45.

5. The standards set forth for the determination of brain death shall not be the exclusive standards for the withdrawal of life support systems.

6. The advisory board is stricken from the bill.

Florida Senate - 1980

CS for SB 583

By Committee on Natural Resources and Conservation and Senator McKnight-

1   A bill to be entitled
2   An act relating to saltwater fishing; creating
3   the Florida Marine Fisheries Commission;
4   providing for membership and duties; providing
5   for development of a comprehensive saltwater
6   fishery conservation and management policy;
7   providing for public hearings; providing for
8   coordination with federal councils and
9   interstate commissions; providing an
10   appropriation; prohibiting local acts;
11   providing effective and expiration dates.
12
13 Be It Enacted by the Legislature of the State of Florida:
14
15   Section 1. Florida Marine Fisheries Commission.--
16   (1) The Florida Marine Fisheries Commission is created
17 as a part of the Department of Natural Resources. Members of
18 the commission shall be appointed by the Governor and Cabinet.
19 Commission membership shall consist of: two persons
20 representative of Atlantic Ocean commercial fishermen; two
21 persons representative of Atlantic Ocean recreational
22 fishermen; two persons representative of Gulf of Mexico
23 commercial fishermen; two persons representative of Gulf of
24 Mexico recreational fishermen; one person representative of
25 environmental interest groups; one person representative of
26 the marine fisheries industry; and one person representative
27 of consumer interests.
28   (2) Not more than 30 days after the appointment of the
29 commission, the members shall meet to select a chairman and
30 shall establish procedures for the conduct of the commission's
31 business. The commission shall meet not less than once a

1

CODING: Words in struck through type are deletions from existing law; words underlined are additions.

312-1787-80   CS for SB 583

month, and other meetings may be called when necessary by the
chairman at any time.

(3) The commission shall submit an interim report to
the Governor, the President of the Senate, and the Speaker of
the House of Representatives not less than 30 days prior to
the 1981 regular session of the Legislature, and to recommend
to the Legislature, by February 1, 1982, a comprehensive
saltwater fishery conservation and management policy for the
territorial salt waters of the state. The commission shall
study all facets of fisheries conservation and management in
developing recommendations that shall include, but not be
limited to:

(a) State standards to be used in conserving,
managing, and protecting the saltwater fisheries.

(b) Recommendations for new legislation or amendments
to existing law as the commission deems necessary to implement
the policy. Such recommendations shall address existing
general law and special acts relating to saltwater fisheries,
and delegation of rulemaking authority to the Governor and
Cabinet to carry out the policy.

(c) Recommendations as to appropriate administration
of the policy, including appropriate agency or agencies under
the executive branch to be charged with administering the
policy and appropriate funding of the agency or agencies.

(d) Recommendations providing for the appropriate
funding of the policy. Such recommendations shall address
proper permitting of all fishing activity in the state
territorial waters, and proper fees for inspection and
supervision of quality control of saltwater products.

2

CODING: Words in struck through type are deletions from existing law; words underlined are additions.

312-1787-80   CS for SB 583

1   (e) Recommendations for enforcement of the policy,
2 including appropriate penalties for violations and proper
3 funding for enforcement efforts.
4   (f) Recommendations on the seafood promotion and
5 marketing program.
6   (g) Recommendations on marine habitat improvement and
7 fish propagation.
8   (h) Recommendations on marine fisheries research
9 programs.
10   (i) Recommendations on a salt and fresh water boundary
11 for enforcement purposes.
12   (j) Recommendations of procedures for continuing
13 review and update of the policy.
14   (4) The Department of Natural Resources shall provide
15 staff and administrative support to the commission.
16   (5) The commission shall employ the services of
17 persons, both public and private, who are recognized
18 scientists knowledgeable in all aspects of the saltwater
19 fisheries of the state. These scientists shall present to the
20 commission the best scientific and statistical information
21 available to assist the commission in preparation of the
22 policy. To accomplish this purpose all state agencies are
23 hereby authorized to cooperate to the fullest extent possible
24 in assisting the commission.
25   (6) Before making final recommendations to the
26 Legislature, the commission shall hold at least seven public
27 hearings in the state for public input concerning the policy
28 recommendations. At least one of these public hearings shall
29 be held in the interior of the state.
30   (7) The commission shall consult and coordinate with
31 the federal Gulf of Mexico and South Atlantic Fishery

3

CODING: Words in struck through type are deletions from existing law; words underlined are additions.

```
312-1787-80                              CS for SB 583
```

1 Management Councils relative to consistency of state and
2 federal recommendations, and shall consult with and coordinate
3 with the Gulf States Marine Fisheries Commission and the
4 Atlantic States Marine Fisheries Commission relative to
5 interstate fishery management.
6   (8) Commission members shall receive no compensation
7 for their services, but shall be reimbursed for traveling
8 expenses as provided in s. 112.061, Florida Statutes.
9   Section 2. Special acts prohibited.--Pursuant to s.
10 11(a)(21) of Article III of the State Constitution, the
11 Legislature hereby prohibits any special law or general law of
12 local application affecting the management, conservation, and
13 protection of marine crustacean, shell, and anadromous fishery
14 resources within or without the salt waters of the state.
15   Section 3. Nothing in this act shall be construed to
16 repeal any existing special laws, general laws of local
17 application, or rules of the department.
18   Section 4. There is appropriated from the General
19 Revenue Fund to the Department of Natural Resources $100,000
20 for the expenses of the commission and staff.
21   Section 5. This act shall expire and be void and
22 inoperative on June 30, 1982.
23   Section 6. This act shall take effect upon becoming a
24 law except that section 2 shall take effect only if this act
25 is passed by a three-fifths vote of the members of each house
26 of the Legislature.

4

CODING: Words in struck through type are deletions from existing law; words underlined are additions.

STATEMENT OF SUBSTANTIAL CHANGES CONTAINED IN
COMMITTEE SUBSTITUTE FOR SENATE BILL 583

The bill creates an eleven-member Florida Marine Fisheries Commission which is mandated to undertake a two-year review of Florida's saltwater fisheries. The Commission is required to submit an interim report to the Governor and the Legislature prior to the 1981 regular session of the Legislature. Furthermore, by February 1, 1982 the Commission must make recommendations to the Legislature regarding comprehensive policy aspects of fishery conservation and management.

The Commission is required to develop recommendations with regard to: 1) new or amended legislation to implement the policy, 2) appropriate administration, funding, and enforcement of this policy, 3) marine habitat improvement, fish propagation, and fisheries research, 4) seafood promotion and marketing, and 5) procedures for continuing review and update of the policy.

In addition, the Commission is empowered 1) to employ the services of knowledgeable saltwater fisheries scientists, 2) hold at least seven public hearings to take statements concerning the policy recommendations, and 3) consult and coordinate with the two relevant federal management councils.

The Department of Natural Resources is charged with providing the staff and administrative support to the Commission.

The bill also prohibits any special law or general law of local application affecting the management, conservation, or protection of saltwater fishery resources.

The act will expire on June 30, 1982.

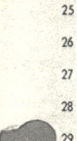

Florida Senate - 1980

CS for SB 584

By Committee on Economic, Community and Consumer Affairs and Senator McKnight-

A bill to be entitled
An act relating to the Local Government
Comprehensive Planning Act of 1975; amending s.
163.3177(6)(f), Florida Statutes; requiring
that the housing element of the comprehensive
plan provide for sites for group home
facilities and foster care facilities;
providing an effective date.

WHEREAS, it is the intent of the Legislature that the elderly, dependent children, physically disabled, developmentally disabled and nondangerous mentally ill persons be entitled to the benefits of living in normal residential communities and that such persons receive treatment, care, rehabilitation, or education in the least restrictive setting possible, and

WHEREAS, the Legislature intends that future planning for housing elements in any comprehensive plan provide adequately for sites for group and foster homes and for other housing modes for those persons, in single family and other residential areas, NOW, THEREFORE,

Be It Enacted by the Legislature of the State of Florida:

Section 1. Paragraph (f) of subsection (6) of section 163.3177, Florida Statutes, is amended to read:

163.3177 Required and optional elements of comprehensive plan; studies and surveys.--

(6) In addition to the general requirements of subsections (1)-(5), the comprehensive plan shall include the following elements:

1

CODING: Words in struck through type are deletions from existing law; words underlined are additions.

311-1844A-80   CS for SB 584

(f) A housing element consisting of standards, plans, and principles to be followed in:

1. The provision of housing for existing residents and the anticipated population growth of the area.
2. The elimination of substandard dwelling conditions.
3. The improvement of existing housing.
4. The provision of adequate sites for future housing, including housing for low-income and moderate-income families, ~~and~~ mobile homes, <u>and group home facilities and foster care facilities,</u> with supporting infrastructure and community facilities as described in paragraphs (6)(c) and (7)(e) and (f).
5. Provision for relocation housing and identification of housing for purposes of conservation, rehabilitation, or replacement.
6. The formulation of housing implementation programs.

Section 2. This act shall take effect October 1, 1980.

STATEMENT OF SUBSTANTIAL CHANGES CONTAINED IN
COMMITTEE SUBSTITUTE FOR SENATE BILL 584

The reference to group home and foster care facilities for the developmentally disabled (s. 393.063, F.S.) is deleted, leaving the general terms, group home facilities and foster care facilities.

A whereas clause is changed to refer to the elderly, dependent children, and physically disabled and nondangerous mentally ill persons, in addition to the developmentally disabled.

CODING: Words in ~~struck through~~ type are deletions from existing law; words <u>underlined</u> are additions.

The Golden Years ...   196   Robert McKnight

ENROLLED
1982 Legislature   SB 425, 2nd Engrossed

An act relating to criminal mischief; adding s.
806.13(3), Florida Statutes; providing
penalties for the desecration of places of
religious worship and certain items located
therein; providing an effective date.

Be It Enacted by the Legislature of the State of Florida:

   Section 1. Subsection (3) is added to section 806.13, Florida Statutes, to read:
   806.13 Criminal mischief.--
   (3) Any person who willfully and maliciously defaces, injures, or damages by any means any church, synagogue, mosque, or other place of worship or any religious article contained therein is guilty of a felony of the third degree, punishable as provided in s. 775.082, s. 775.083, or s. 775.084 if the damage to the property is greater than $200.
   Section 2. This act shall take effect upon becoming a law.

CODING: Words in struck through type are deletions from existing law; words underlined are additions.

Florida Senate - 1982

By Senator McKnight
38-891-82

SB 737

See CS/HB 296

A bill to be entitled
An act relating to the prevention of child
abuse and neglect; creating s. 827.075, Florida
Statutes; providing legislative intent;
requiring a state plan for a comprehensive
approach to the prevention of child abuse and
neglect; providing for state and local
coordination; providing for district plans;
providing that funding for child abuse and
neglect prevention efforts be based upon the
state plan; requiring biennial revisions of the
state plan; providing an effective date.

WHEREAS, in calendar year 1980 there were 71,522 children involved in reported cases of abuse and neglect representing a 192 percent increase of the reported number in fiscal year 1974-1975, and

WHEREAS, of all abuse and neglect cases disposed over the last 2 1/2 calendar years only 18 to 23 percent were required either voluntarily or involuntarily to receive counseling or services and only 9 percent of the cases were judicially handled, and

WHEREAS, in 1979 the number of reported cases of sexual assault on children in Florida increased by 600 percent and national studies indicate that 1 in 10 females will be victims of sexual assault by relatives during childhood, and

WHEREAS, 70 percent or more of all sex offenders have themselves been the victims of a sexual assault or have experienced a sexual trauma during their childhood, and

1

CODING: Words in struck through type are deletions from existing law; words underlined are additions.

38-891-82   See CS/HB 296

1   WHEREAS, some studies on prison populations have
2   indicated that as many as 80 to 90 percent of the inmates had
3   been abused as children, and
4   WHEREAS, almost 65 percent of the dependent children
5   admitted to state hospitals in 1978 had histories of abuse and
6   neglect, and
7   WHEREAS, studies of dependency case files in Florida
8   have indicated that 38 percent of those children who were
9   abused or neglected have later known histories of status
10 offense or delinquent behavior, and
11 WHEREAS, national studies have shown that child abuse
12 is the reason 1,500 children a year develop cerebral palsy as
13 a result of brain damage and that many children become
14 mentally retarded, and
15 WHEREAS, the Legislature recognizes the costs
16 associated with child abuse and neglect not only with regard
17 to the victimized child and the child's family but also the
18 hidden costs of child abuse in later generations, and
19 WHEREAS, the ever increasing number of children who are
20 abused heightens the concern of the Legislature about the need
21 to save lives of children who are abused and neglected, to
22 avoid the physical and emotional suffering caused by the abuse
23 and neglect, and the need to reevaluate the approach the state
24 has heretofore taken with regard to this immensely complex and
25 important family problem, NOW, THEREFORE,

27 Be It Enacted by the Legislature of the State of Florida:

29 Section 1. Section 827.075, Florida Statutes, is
30 created to read:

2

CODING: Words in struck through type are deletions from existing law; words underlined are additions.

The Golden Years ...   199   *Robert McKnight*

38-891-82   See CS/HB 296

827.075 Prevention of abuse and neglect of children.--

(1) LEGISLATIVE INTENT.--The incidence of known child abuse and neglect has increased rapidly over the past 5 years. The impact that abuse and neglect has on the victimized child, siblings, family structure, and inevitably on all citizens of the state has caused the Legislature to determine that the prevention of child abuse and neglect shall be a priority of this state. To further this end, it is the intent of the Legislature that a comprehensive approach for the prevention of child abuse and neglect be developed for the state and that this planned, comprehensive approach be used as a basis for funding.

(2) PLAN FOR COMPREHENSIVE APPROACH.--

(a) The Department of Health and Rehabilitative Services shall develop a state plan on the prevention of child abuse and neglect and shall submit the plan to the Speaker of the House, the President of the Senate, and the Governor no later than January 1, 1983. The Department of Education shall participate and fully cooperate in the development of the state plan at both the state and local level. Furthermore, appropriate local agencies and organizations shall be provided an opportunity to participate in the development of the state plan at the local level. Appropriate local groups and organizations shall include, but not be limited to, community mental health center, guardian ad litem program for children under the circuit court, school board of the local school districts, private or public organization or program with recognized expertise in working with children who are sexually abused, physically abused, emotionally abused, or neglected and with the families of such children, private or public program or organization with expertise in maternal and infant

38-891-82 See CS/HB 296

health care, multidisciplinary child protection team, child daycare center, law enforcement, and circuit court, if a guardian ad litem program is not available in the local area. The state plan to be provided to the Legislature and the Governor shall include, as a minimum, the information required of the various groups in paragraph (b).

(b) The development of the comprehensive state plan shall be accomplished in the following manner:

1. The Department of Health and Rehabilitative Services shall establish an interprogram task force comprised of representatives from the Children, Youth and Families Program Office, the Children's Medical Services Program Office, the Mental Health Program Office, the Developmental Services Program Office, the Health Program Office and the Office of Evaluation. The interprogram task force shall be responsible for the following:

a. Developing a plan of action for better coordination and integration of the goals, activities, and funding pertaining to the prevention of child abuse and neglect conducted by the department in order to maximize staff and resources at the state level. The plan of action shall be included in the state plan.

b. Providing a basic format to be utilized by the districts in the preparation of local plans of action in order to provide for uniformity in the district plans and to provide for greater ease in compiling information for the state plan.

c. Providing the districts with technical assistance in the development of local plans of action, if requested.

d. Examining the local plans to determine if all the requirements of the local plans have been met and if they have

4

CODING: Words in struck through type are deletions from existing law; words underlined are additions.

```
38-891-82                                    See CS/HB 296
```

1 not, the task force shall inform the districts of the
2 deficiency and request the additional information needed.
3   e. Preparing the state plan for submission to the
4 Legislature and the Governor. Such preparation shall include
5 the collapsing of information obtained from the local plans,
6 cooperative plans with the Department of Education, and the
7 plan of action for coordination and integration of
8 departmental activities into one comprehensive plan. The
9 comprehensive plan shall include a section reflecting general
10 conditions and needs, analysis of variations based on
11 population or geographic areas, identified problems, and
12 recommendations for change. In essence, the plan shall
13 provide an analysis and summary of each element of the local
14 plans to provide a statewide perspective. The plan shall also
15 include each separate local plan of action.
16   f. Working with the specified state agency in
17 fulfilling the requirements of subparagraphs 2., 3., 4., and
18 5.
19   2. The Department of Education and the Department of
20 Health and Rehabilitative Services shall work together in
21 developing ways to inform and instruct appropriate district
22 school personnel in all school districts in the detection of
23 child abuse and neglect and the proper action that should be
24 taken in suspected cases of abuse and neglect. The plan for
25 accomplishing this end shall be included in the state plan.
26   3. The Department of Law Enforcement and the
27 Department of Health and Rehabilitative Services shall work
28 together in developing ways to inform and instruct appropriate
29 local law enforcement personnel in the detection of child
30 abuse and neglect and the proper action that should be taken
31 in suspected cases of abuse and neglect.

CODING: Words in struck through type are deletions from existing law; words underlined are additions.

38-891-82   See CS/HB 296

1   4. Within existing appropriations, the Department of
2   Health and Rehabilitative Services shall work with other
3   appropriate public and private agencies to emphasize efforts
4   to educate the general public about the problem of and ways to
5   detect child abuse and neglect and the proper action that
6   should be taken in suspected cases of abuse and neglect. The
7   plan for accomplishing this end shall be included in the state
8   plan.
9   5. The Department of Education and the Department of
10 Health and Rehabilitative Services shall work together on the
11 development of a curriculum on child abuse and neglect
12 identification, intervention, and prevention for a sequential
13 program of instruction at the four progressional levels K-3,
14 4-6, 7-9, and 10-12. Strategies for encouraging all school
15 districts to utilize the curriculum are to be included in the
16 comprehensive state plan on child abuse and neglect
17 prevention. In addition, a report on the strategies to be
18 used in the development of such a curriculum and any barriers
19 to the development or utilization of a curriculum on child
20 abuse and neglect shall be included in the state plan.
21   6. Each district of the Department of Health and
22 Rehabilitative Services shall develop a plan for its specific
23 geographic area. The plan developed at the district level
24 shall be submitted to the interprogram task force for
25 utilization in preparing the state plan. The district local
26 plan of action shall be prepared with the involvement and
27 assistance of the local agencies and organizations listed in
28 paragraph (a) as well as representatives from those
29 departmental district offices participating in child abuse and
30 neglect treatment and prevention. In order to accomplish this
31 the district administrator in each district shall establish a

6

CODING: Words in struck through type are deletions from existing law; words underlined are additions.

The Golden Years ...   203   *Robert McKnight*

38-891-82   See CS/HB 296

1   task force on the prevention of child abuse and neglect. The
2   district administrator shall appoint the members of the task
3   force in accordance with the membership requirements of this
4   act. In addition, the district administrator shall ensure
5   that each subdistrict is represented on the task force and if
6   the district does not have subdistricts the district
7   administrator shall ensure that both urban and rural areas are
8   represented on the task force. The task force shall develop a
9   written statement clearly identifying its operating
10 procedures, purpose, overall responsibilities, and method of
11 meeting responsibilities. The district plan of action to be
12 prepared by the task force shall include, but not be limited
13 to:
14   a. Documentation of the magnitude of the problem of
15 child abuse, including sexual abuse, physical abuse, and
16 emotional abuse, and neglect in its geographical area.
17   b. A description of programs currently serving abused
18 and neglected children and their families and child abuse and
19 neglect prevention programs, including information on impact
20 of programs, cost effectiveness, and sources of funding.
21   c. A continuum of programs and services necessary for
22 a comprehensive approach to all types of child abuse and
23 neglect prevention as well as a brief description of such
24 programs and services.
25   d. A description, documentation, and prioritization of
26 local needs related to child abuse and neglect prevention
27 based upon the continuum.
28   e. A plan for steps to be taken in meeting identified
29 needs, including the coordination and integration of services
30 to avoid unnecessary duplication and cost, and alternative
31 funding strategies for meeting needs through the reallocation

7

CODING: Words in struck through type are deletions from existing law; words underlined are additions.

38-891-82   See CS/HB 296

of existing resources, utilization of volunteers, contracting with local universities for services, and local government or private agency funding.

    f. A description of barriers to accomplishment of a comprehensive approach to child abuse and neglect prevention.

    g. Recommendations for changes that can be accomplished only at the state program level or by legislative action.

The district local plan of action shall be submitted to the interprogram task force by November 1, 1982.

    (3) FUNDING AND SUBSEQUENT PLANS.--

    (a) All budget requests submitted by the Department of Health and Rehabilitative Services, the Department of Education, or any other agency to the Legislature for funding of child abuse and neglect prevention efforts shall be based on the state plan developed pursuant to this section.

    (b) At least biennially, the Department of Health and Rehabilitative Services at the state and district levels and other agencies listed in subsection (2)(a) shall readdress the plan and make necessary revisions. Such revisions shall be submitted to the Speaker of the House of Representatives and the President of the Senate no later than January 1, 1985, and by January 1 of alternate years thereafter.

    Section 2. This act shall take effect upon becoming a law.

****

LEGISLATIVE SUMMARY

Requires the Department of Health and Rehabilitative Services to develop a state plan on the prevention of child abuse and neglect by January 1, 1983. Provides for

8

CODING: Words in struck through type are deletions from existing law; words underlined are additions.

38-891-82 See CS/HB 296

the cooperation of the Department of Education and local agencies and organizations. Creates an interprogram task force to develop the plan and provides duties of the task force.

Requires the Department of Health and Rehabilitative Services and the Department of Education to develop ways to instruct school personnel in the detection of child abuse and neglect and to develop curriculum on child abuse and neglect. Requires the Department of Law Enforcement and the Department of Health and Rehabilitative Services to jointly develop ways of informing and instructing appropriate local law enforcement personnel in the detection of child abuse and neglect and the proper action that should be taken in such suspected cases. Also requires the Department of Health and Rehabilitative Services, in conjunction with appropriate public and private agencies, to endeavor to educate the general public regarding child abuse and neglect.

Requires each district of the Department of Health and Rehabilitative Services to develop a district plan and to establish a district task force. Provides content of the district plan.

Provides that funding for child abuse prevention and neglect efforts be based upon the state plan. Requires biennial revisions of the state plan.

CODING: Words in struck through type are deletions from existing law; words underlined are additions.

Florida Senate - 1982

SB 900

By Senator McKnight-

38-974-82

```
 1              A bill to be entitled
 2         An act relating to public health; creating s.
 3         154.065, Florida Statutes; providing for the
 4         distribution of certain public health funds;
 5         amending s. 402.05, Florida Statutes;
 6         authorizing scholarships and stipends for
 7         individuals entering certain health care
 8         professions; amending s. 402.06, Florida
 9         Statutes; raising the interest on such
10         scholarships; amending s. 402.07, Florida
11         Statutes; providing for interest and repayment;
12         creating s. 402.08, Florida Statutes; providing
13         penalties; providing an effective date.
14
15  Be It Enacted by the Legislature of the State of Florida:
16
17      Section 1.  Section 154.065, Florida Statutes, is
18  created to read:
19      154.065  Distribution of funds.--Funds appropriated by
20  the state for local health units from the General Revenue Fund
21  and federal block grants shall be distributed among the local
22  health units within each county or counties in direct
23  proportion to the respective county's percentage of the state
24  population as defined in the 1980 United States Bureau of
25  Census Report.
26      Section 2.  Section 402.05, Florida Statutes, is
27  amended to read:
28      402.05  Requisites for holding scholarship and
29  stipend.--Scholarships or stipends are to be awarded only to
30  such residents of the state as intend to make psychiatric
31  social work, psychiatry, psychiatric nursing, and clinical
```

1

CODING: Words in struck through type are deletions from existing law; words underlined are additions.

The Golden Years ...   207   *Robert McKnight*

38-974-82

psychology their professions <u>or intend to become health care professionals licensed pursuant to chapters 458, 459, 464, 468, parts III, V, or VI, or 486</u>. Among other essential requisites for holding a scholarship or stipend hereunder are citizenship, residence in Florida for a period of 1 year, good moral character, good health, exceptional scholarship, and the applicant shall have met the entrance requirement at a college or university for their professional specialization.

Section 3. Section 402.06, Florida Statutes, is amended to read:

402.06 Notes required of scholarship holders.--Each person who receives a scholarship or stipend as provided for in this chapter shall execute a promissory note under seal, on forms to be prescribed by the Department of Education, which shall be endorsed by his parent or guardian or, if he is 18 years of age or older, by some responsible citizen and shall deliver said note to the Department of Health and Rehabilitative Services. Each note shall be payable to the state and shall bear interest at the rate of <u>15</u> 5 percent per annum beginning 90 days after completion or termination of the training program. Said note shall provide for all costs of collection to be paid by the maker of the note. Said note shall be delivered by the Department of Health and Rehabilitative Services to said Department of Education for collection and final disposition.

Section 4. Section 402.07, Florida Statutes, is amended to read:

402.07 Payment of notes.--Prior to the award of a scholarship or stipend provided herein for trainees in psychiatric social work, psychiatry, clinical psychology, or psychiatric nursing, <u>or health care professions licensed</u>

2

CODING: Words in struck through type are deletions from existing law; words <u>underlined</u> are additions.

38-974-82

pursuant to chapters 458, 459, 464, 468, parts III, V, and VI, or 486, the recipient thereof must agree in writing to practice his profession in the employ of any one of the following ~~institutions or~~ agencies for 1 month for each month of grant immediately after graduation or, in lieu thereof, to repay the full amount of the scholarship or stipend together with interest at the rate of 15 ~~5~~ percent per annum over a period not to exceed 5 ~~10~~ years:

(1) The Department of Health and Rehabilitative Services. ~~The staff of one of the state hospitals of the Division of Mental Health.~~

(2) The Department of Education.

(3) The Department of Corrections.

(4) ~~(3)~~ A mental health clinic or guidance center.

~~(4) One of the state-operated universities.~~

(5) Such other accredited agency or institution as may be approved by the Department of Health and Rehabilitative Services. ~~A circuit court exercising jurisdiction in connection with juveniles.~~

~~(6) A public school.~~

~~(7) Such other accredited social agencies or state institutions as may be approved by the [Department of Health and Rehabilitative Services.]~~

Section 5. Section 402.08, Florida Statutes, is created to read:

402.08 Penalties for failure to comply.--Failure to comply with the requirements of s. 402.07 shall constitute grounds for disciplinary action by the appropriate licensing agency as follows:

(1) Revocation of the license of the recipient;

3

CODING: Words in ~~struck through~~ type are deletions from existing law; words underlined are additions.

38-974-82

(2) Imposition of an administrative fine not to exceed $1,500.

Section 6. This act shall take effect upon becoming a law.

****

SENATE SUMMARY

Provides for the distribution of certain public health funds based on a ratio of county-to-state population. Authorizes scholarships and stipends for individuals planning a career in certain health care professions. Raises the interest on such scholarships to 15 percent. Provides for interest on notes and repayment. Provides penalties for failing to comply with repayment provisions.

CODING: Words in struck through type are deletions from existing law; words underlined are additions.

Appendix D: Members of the Florida House of Representatives and Senate, 1974-1982

THE JOURNAL OF THE FLORIDA

House of Representatives

ORGANIZATION SESSION

Tuesday, November 19, 1974

Journal of the House of Representatives for the Organization Session of the Fourth Legislature convened under the Constitution of Florida as Revised in 1968, begun and held at the Capitol in the City of Tallahassee, in the State of Florida, on Tuesday, November 19, 1974, being the day fixed by the Constitution for the purpose.

Under Rule 3.1, Allen Morris, Clerk of the preceding Session, delegated the duties of temporary presiding officer to The Honorable Terrell Sessums, former Speaker. Mr. Sessums called the House to order at 2:00 p.m.

The following certified list of Members elected to the House of Representatives was received:

STATE OF FLORIDA } ss
OFFICE OF SECRETARY OF STATE

I, DOROTHY W. GLISSON, Secretary of State of the State of Florida, do hereby certify that the following Members of the House of Representatives were elected at the General Election held on the Fifth day of November, A. D. 1974 as shown by the election returns on file in this office:

HOUSE DISTRICT NUMBER

1—Grover C. Robinson, III, Pensacola
2—R. W. "Smokey" Peaden, Pensacola
3—Clyde H. Hagler, Pensacola
4—Edmond M. Fortune, Pace
5—Jerry G. Melvin, Fort Walton Beach
6—Jere Tolton, Fort Walton Beach
7—Wayne Mixson, Marianna
8—Earl Hutto, Panama City
9—William J. (Billy) Rish, Fort St. Joe
10—James Harold Thompson, Quincy
11—Donald L. Tucker, Tallahassee
12—Herbert F. (Herb) Morgan, Tallahassee
13—Sherrill (Pete) Skinner, Lake City
14—Gene Hodges, Cedar Key
15—George R. Grosse, Jacksonville
16—Mary L. Singleton, Jacksonville
17—John R. Forbes, Jacksonville
18—John W. Lewis, Jacksonville
19—Eric B. Smith, Jacksonville
20—Carl Ogden, Jacksonville
21—Tommy Hazouri, Jacksonville
22—Steve Pajcic, Jacksonville
23—Earl Dixon, Jacksonville
24—Ander Crenshaw, Jacksonville
25—Frank Williams, Starke
26—Sidney Martin, Hawthorne
27—Bill Andrews, Gainesville
28—A. H. (Gus) Craig, St. Augustine
29—William R. Conway, Ormond Beach
30—Samuel P. Bell, III, Ormond Beach
31—Hyatt Brown, Ormond Beach
32—Wayne C. McCall, Ocala
33—Bob Hattaway, Altamonte Springs
34—Vince Fechtel, Jr., Leesburg
35—Richard H. (Dick) Langley, Clermont
36—John R. Culbreath, Brooksville
37—Ronald R. Richmond, New Port Richey
38—William L. Gibson, Orlando
39—Harvey W. Matthews, Orlando
40—Bill Fulford, Orlando
41—Fred B. Hagan, Orlando
42—Bill Gorman, Tangerine
43—Dick J. Batchelor, Orlando

44—David L. Barrett, Indialantic
45—Clark Maxwell, Jr., Melbourne
46—Jane W. Robinson, Merritt Island
47—Bill Nelson, Melbourne
48—Chester Clem, Vero Beach
49—Ray Mattox, Winter Haven
50—John R. Clark, Lakeland
51—Wendell H. Watson, Lakeland
52—C. Fred Jones, Auburndale
53—Mary R. Grizzle, Clearwater
54—S. Curtis Kiser, Palm Harbor
55—Tom R. Moore, Clearwater
56—Betty Easley, Clearwater
57—Dennis McDonald, St. Petersburg
58—George F. Hieber, II, St. Petersburg
59—Richard "Dick" Price, St. Petersburg
60—Roger H. Wilson, Seminole
61—L. W. Larry Belanger, St. Petersburg
62—James L. Redman, Plant City
63—John L. Ryals, Brandon
64—R. Ed Blackburn, Jr., Temple Terrace
65—Jim Foster, Tampa
66—H. Lee Moffitt, Tampa
67—Ray C. Knopke, Tampa
68—Richard S. Hodes, Tampa
69—George H. Sheldon, Tampa
70—Helen Gordon Davis, Tampa
71—Ralph H. Haben, Palmetto
72—Patrick K. (Pat) Neal, Holmes Beach
73—Granville H. Crabtree, Jr., Sarasota
74—Robert M. Johnson, Sarasota
75—Fred Burrall, Port Charlotte
76—Charles "Chuck" Nergard, Port St. Lucie
77—Jack M. Poorbaugh, Jupiter
78—Donald F. Hazelton, West Palm Beach
79—Gene Campbell, West Palm Beach
80—William G. James, Delray Beach
81—Edward J. Healey, West Palm Beach
82—John J. Considine, Mangonia Park
83—Tom Lewis, North Palm Beach
84—Van B. Poole, Fort Lauderdale
85—Arthur H. Rude, Fort Lauderdale
86—Karen Coolman, Fort Lauderdale
87—George A. Williamson, Fort Lauderdale
88—Randy Avon, Fort Lauderdale
89—Mary Ellen Hawkins, Naples
90—Franklin B. (Frank) Mann, Fort Myers
91—Hugh Paul Nuckolls, Fort Myers
92—Tom McPherson, Fort Lauderdale
93—Harold A. Dyer, Hollywood
94—John (Jack) Miller, Hollywood
95—Walter C. "Walt" Young, Pembroke Pines
96—Charles W. Boyd, Hollywood
97—David J. Lehman, Hollywood
98—Elaine Gordon, Miami Beach
99—Barry Kutun, Miami Beach
100—Elaine Bloom, North Miami Beach
101—Paul B. Steinberg, Miami Beach
102—Gwen Margolis, North Miami
103—Alan S. Becker, North Miami
104—William H. Lockward, Miami Lakes
105—Joe Lang Kershaw, Miami

1

The Golden Years ...   211   *Robert McKnight*

JOURNAL OF THE HOUSE OF REPRESENTATIVES — November 19, 1974

HOUSE DISTRICT
NUMBER

- 106—Gwendolyn Cherry, Miami
- 107—A. M. "Tony" Fontana, Miami Lakes
- 108—John A. Hill, Miami Lakes
- 109—Joe Gersten, Miami
- 110—Walter W. Sackett, Jr., Miami
- 111—Tom Gallagher, Coconut Grove
- 112—Barry Richard, Miami
- 113—Nancy O. Harrington, Coral Gables
- 114—Robert C. Hector, Miami
- 115—James F. (Jim) Eckhart, Miami
- 116—Bob McKnight, Miami
- 117—Charles C. Papy, Jr., Coral Gables
- 118—Dick Clark, Miami
- 119—Bill Flynn, Miami
- 120—William A. Freeman, Jr., Key West

GIVEN under my hand and the Great Seal of the State of Florida at Tallahassee, The Capital, this 18th day of November, A. D., 1974.

DOROTHY W. GLISSON
Secretary of State

The names of the Members being called, a quorum was determined to be present.

Prayer

Prayer by Elder Joseph E. Bone, Tallahassee Stake Patriarch Church of Jesus Christ of Latter-day Saints:

O, Father in Heaven: Having thus assembled in this Organizational Session of the Florida Legislative Body, we seek Thy grace, Thy love and continuing mercies. We ask Thy blessings at this hour, and Thy sustaining influence in all the deliberations of this august Body.

We offer up our prayers and supplications on behalf of each member, individually and collectively, that they may reach the highest goals attainable to the human soul. May they each represent their constituency with honesty and integrity; justifying the faith, hope, and trust embodied in their high office. May their collective efforts culminate in resolving the ever-mounting problems of State government.

We pray for the retiring Speaker of the House, that he may find joy in his new endeavors. We pray for the Speaker-elect, that as the mantle of presidency falls upon him, he may accept with a humble and grateful heart, the great trust placed in him and unite this Body in a common effort for the well-being of this great State and its people.

In these troubled times, as the Constitution of this great nation may appear to hang as if by a bare thread, may men and women of good will use the great powers and trust placed in them in a common effort to lift this nation to its great potential.

May we remember the poor and needy of the world; the aged and afflicted, and particularly of this State and nation. May we remember that the fullness of the earth is His who created it. May we consider this land of America to be choice above all other lands, and use its abundance for the good of all mankind.

May charity abound always in our hearts, for it is so written that "Charity is the pure love for Christ which endureth forever, and he who is found with it at the last day, all shall be well with him."

May this Godly ideal permeate our souls and quicken us to action - - - in Jesus Christ's name, we pray. Amen

Pledge

The Members pledged allegiance to the Flag.

Oath taken by Members

The Members, as shown in the certificate from the Secretary of State, came forward and took the Oath of Office prescribed by the Constitution of the State of Florida from Justice B. K. Roberts of the Supreme Court.

Election of the Speaker

The Chairman announced that nominations would now be received for Speaker of the House of Representatives, under Article III, Section 2 of the Constitution, for a term of two years from this date.

Remarks by Mr. Clark

Representative Dick Clark nominated The Honorable Donald L. Tucker for Speaker with the following remarks:

Mr. Chairman and fellow members of the House: I have stood at this well many times to speak for Don Tucker. Today I rise again in his behalf. Don Tucker is a viable leader who can lend his invaluable experience to the many problems this great state must face in the future. He will guide this body as it deals with the grave economic problems we face in the coming months. He is keenly aware of the urban development and growth problems that Florida is encountering today, has the fastest growing state in the Union. He is a man who recognizes that the problems of our environment are all interdependent and cannot be solved in isolation, but should be dealt with in a carefully coordinated program which would insure this state a sound growth policy.

I stood up here during the organizational session of the Democrats to speak for Representative Tucker, and I told everybody in the crowd that I couldn't see. Since then I got bifocals and I'm seeing double right now. So I'm having a problem. I'd like to speak off the cuff for a moment and continue.

It feels like I'm addressing a florist convention, with all the flowers in here today. I welcome all the new members; it's great to have you on board.

This is a very solemn occasion in the history of the State of Florida. Today is our 150th anniversary, and I think it is very fitting that we're here today to nominate a man who I think is going to help Florida grow in the next 150 years through a lot of the legislation we'll pass during the upcoming session. I think Don Tucker is one of the finest, fairest individuals that this House will ever be blessed with, and I deem it a sincere privilege and a complete honor to place in nomination the name of Donald L. Tucker as the next Speaker of the Florida House of Representatives.

Remarks by Mr. Craig

Representative Craig seconded the nomination of Mr. Tucker for Speaker with the following remarks:

Mr. Speaker, members of the House, friends, distinguished guests: It's a pleasure to be here today, to have this privilege that doesn't very often come to a person, to second the nomination of a man whom I've served with since he came to the Florida Legislature.

I believe that probably one of the greatest assets he has is not only the fact that he's a great leader, but one thing that I feel is really important, and should be important to all the new members of the House as well as those of us who have served for a number of years, is the fact that when Don gives you his word, you can count on it and that's the way it's going to be. You won't have to come back the next day and say, "Well, is it a different story, or just where do we really

The Journal of the House of Representatives

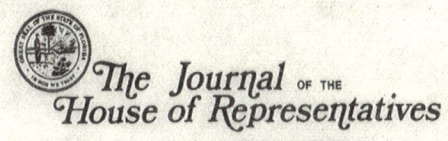

ORGANIZATION SESSION

Tuesday, November 16, 1976

Journal of the House of Representatives for the Organization Session of the Fifth Legislature convened under the Constitution of Florida as Revised in 1968, begun and held at the Capitol in the City of Tallahassee, in the State of Florida, on Tuesday, November 16, 1976, being the day fixed by the Constitution for the purpose.

The House was called to order by The Honorable Donald L. Tucker, Speaker of the 1974-1976 House, at 10:30 a.m.

The following certified list of Members elected to the House of Representatives was received:

STATE OF FLORIDA } ss
OFFICE OF SECRETARY OF STATE

I, BRUCE A. SMATHERS, Secretary of State of the State of Florida, do hereby certify that the following Members of the House of Representatives were elected at the General Election held on the Second day of November, A. D. 1976 as shown by the election returns on file in this office:

HOUSE DISTRICT
NUMBER

1—Grover C. Robinson, III, Pensacola
2—Tom Patterson, Pensacola
3—Clyde H. Hagler, Pensacola
4—Edmond M. Fortune, Pace
5—Jerry G. Melvin, Fort Walton
6—James G. Ward, Fort Walton Beach
7—Wayne Mixson, Marianna
8—Earl Hutto, Panama City
9—William J. (Billy Joe) Rish, Port St. Joe
10—James Harold Thompson, Quincy
11—Donald L. Tucker, Tallahassee
12—Herbert F. (Herb) Morgan, Tallahassee
13—Wayne Hollingsworth, Lake City
14—Gene Hodges, Cedar Key
15—George R. Grosse, Jacksonville
16—Arnett E. Girardeau, Jacksonville
17—John R. Forbes, Jacksonville
18—John W. Lewis, Jacksonville
19—Eric B. Smith, Jacksonville
20—Carl Ogden, Jacksonville
21—Tommy Hazouri, Jacksonville
22—Steve Pajcic, Jacksonville
23—R. Earl Dixon, Jacksonville
24—Ander Crenshaw, Jacksonville
25—Frank Williams, Starke
26—Sidney Martin, Hawthorne
27—Bill Andrews, Gainesville
28—A. H. "Gus" Craig, St. Augustine
29—William R. Conway, Ormond Beach
30—Samuel P. Bell, III, Daytona Beach
31—J. Hyatt Brown, Ormond Beach
32—Wayne C. McCall, Ocala
33—Bob Hattaway, Altamonte Springs
34—Vince Fechtel, Jr., Leesburg
35—Richard H. (Dick) Langley, Clermont
36—John R. Colbreath, Brooksville
37—Ronald R. Richmond, New Port Richey
38—Lawrence R. "Larry" Kirkwood, Winter Park
39—John L. Mica, Winter Park
40—Bill Fulford, Orlando
41—Fran Carlton, Orlando
42—Toni Jennings, Orlando
43—Dick J. Batchelor, Orlando
44—David L. Barrett, Indialantic
45—Clark Maxwell, Jr., Melbourne
46—Marilyn B. Evans, Melbourne
47—Bill Nelson, Melbourne
48—R. Dale Patchett, Vero Beach
49—Bob Crawford, Winter Haven
50—Beverly B. Burnsed, Lakeland
51—Gene Ready, Lakeland
52—C. Fred Jones, Auburndale
53—Mary R. Grizzle, Clearwater
54—S. Curtis Kiser, Palm Harbor
55—Tom R. Moore, Clearwater
56—Betty Easley, Largo
57—Dennis McDonald, St. Petersburg
58—George F. Hieber, II, St. Petersburg
59—Don Poindexter, St. Petersburg
60—T. M. "Tom" Woodruff, St. Petersburg
61—Dorothy Sample, St. Petersburg
62—James L. Redman, Plant City
63—John L. Ryals, Brandon
64—R. Ed Blackburn, Jr., Temple Terrace
65—James S. (Jim) Foster, Tampa
66—H. Lee Moffitt, Tampa
67—Pat Frank, Tampa
68—Richard S. Hodes, Tampa
69—George H. Sheldon, Tampa
70—Helen Gordon Davis, Tampa
71—Ralph H. Haben, Jr., Palmetto
72—Patrick K. Neal, Longboat Key
73—Thomas E. Danson, Jr., Sarasota
74—Ted Ewing, Venice
75—Frederic H. Burrall, Port Charlotte
76—K. Dale Cassens, Fort Pierce
77—William J. Taylor, Tequesta
78—Donald Francis Hazelton, West Palm Beach
79—Reid Moore, Jr., Palm Beach
80—Bill James, Delray Beach
81—Edward J. Healey, West Palm Beach
82—John J. Considine, III, West Palm Beach
83—Tom Lewis, North Palm Beach
84—Van B. Poole, Fort Lauderdale
85—Terry O'Malley, Hallandale
86—Linda Cox, Lauderhill
87—Stephen James "Steve" Warner, Pompano Beach
88—Tom Gustafson, Fort Lauderdale
89—Mary Ellen Hawkins, Naples
90—Franklin B. (Frank) Mann, Fort Myers
91—Hugh Paul Nuckolls, Fort Myers
92—Tom McPherson, Fort Lauderdale
93—Harold J. Dyer, Hollywood
94—John Adams, Hollywood
95—Walter C. Young, Pembroke Pines
96—Charles W. Boyd, Hollywood
97—David J. Lehman, Hollywood
98—Elaine Gordon, Miami
99—Barry Kutun, Miami Beach
100—Elaine Bloom, North Miami Beach
101—Paul B. Steinberg, Miami Beach
102—Gwen Margolis, North Miami

1

JOURNAL OF THE HOUSE OF REPRESENTATIVES   November 16, 1976

103—Alan S. Becker, North Miami Beach
104—William H. Lockward, Miami Lakes
105—Joe Lang Kershaw, Miami
106—Gwendolyn S. Cherry, Miami
107—A. M. "Tony" Fontana, Miami Lakes
108—John A. Hill, Miami Lakes
109—Joe Gersten, Miami
110—Roberta Fox, Miami
111—Tom Gallagher, Coconut Grove
112—Barry Richard, Miami
113—William E. "Bill" Sadowski, Miami
114—Robert C. Hector, Miami
115—James F. Eckhart, Miami
116—Bob McKnight, Miami
117—Charles C. Papy, Jr., Miami
118—John Cyril Malloy, Miami
119—Hugo Black, III, Miami
120—Joe Allen, Key West

GIVEN under my hand and the Great Seal of the State of Florida at Tallahassee, the Capital, this 12th day of November, A. D. 1976.

Bruce A. Smathers
Secretary of State

The following Members were recorded present:

The Chair	Eckhart	Hollingsworth	Neal
Adams	Evans	Hutto	Nelson
Allen	Ewing	James	Nuckolls
Andrews	Fechtel	Jennings	Ogden
Barrett	Fontana	Jones	O'Malley
Batchelor	Fortune	Kershaw	Pajcic
Becker	Foster	Kirkwood	Papy
Bell	Fox	Kiser	Patchett
Black	Frank	Kutun	Patterson
Blackburn	Pulford	Langley	Poindexter
Bloom	Gallagher	Lehman	Poole
Boyd	Gersten	Lewis, J. W.	Ready
Brown	Girardeau	Lewis, T.	Redman
Burnsed	Gordon	Lockward	Richard
Burrall	Grizzle	Malloy	Richmond
Carlton	Grosse	Mann	Rish
Cassens	Gustafson	Margolis	Robinson
Cherry	Haben	Martin	Ryals
Considine	Hagler	Maxwell	Sadowski
Conway	Hattaway	McCall	Sample
Cox	Hawkins	McDonald	Sheldon
Craig	Hazelton	McKnight	Smith
Crawford	Hanouri	McPherson	Taylor
Crenshaw	Healey	Melvin	Thompson
Culbreath	Hector	Mica	Ward
Danson	Hieber	Moffitt	Warner
Davis	Hill	Moore, R.	Williams
Dixon	Hodes	Moore, T.	Woodruff
Easley	Hodges	Morgan	Yeung

Excused: Representatives Dyer, Forbes, Mixson, and Steinberg.

A quorum was present.

Prayer

Prayer by Bishop Stephen Campora, Church of Jesus Christ of Latter-day Saints:

Our Father in Heaven, we're grateful for this opportunity as we gather here in the capacity of this Organizational Session for the Florida House of Representatives. We're grateful for a free form of government that makes this type of representation possible. We truly know that it is a government inspired of Thee. Father, we ask that those elected officials might be truly blessed as they go forth and serve in their capacity in this two-year tenure of their elected offices. We pray that they might be blessed for safety as they come and go in their capacities in these two years in transportation to and from the capital and their various meetings, that they might do so in total safety and well-being. We pray that their families might be blessed in their absence, that they might be safe. And Father, we pray at all times that the elected officials and Members of this House might be truly cognizant of their responsibilities and aware of the needs of the people of Florida. We ask that they might be blessed with the power of discernment, that they might truly be able to discern the right and good things for the people of Florida and so accordingly vote. We ask that Thy Spirit be present here with us during this session, and we do it in the name of our Lord and Saviour, Jesus Christ. Amen.

Pledge

The Members pledged allegiance to the Flag.

Oath taken by Members

The Members together took the Oath of Office prescribed by the Constitution of the State of Florida from Justice B. K. Roberts of the Supreme Court.

Representative Mixson, on November 9, 1976, and Representative Dyer, on November 10, 1976, took the Oath of Office from Mr. Allen Morris, Clerk of the House, because they were necessarily prevented from being present today.

The Speaker requested the Senior Member of the House, Representative Craig, to preside.

MR. CRAIG IN THE CHAIR

Election of the Speaker

The Chair announced that nominations would now be received for Speaker of the House of Representatives for a term of two years from this date.

Remarks by Mr. Fortune

Representative Fortune nominated The Honorable Donald L. Tucker for Speaker with the following remarks:

It's good for each of us to be here in Tallahassee, our home away from home, and of course it's always a great honor for each of us to participate in such a historical occasion as that of selecting the Speaker of our House, one who will lead us for two years. I've told many of you many times how proud I am of my state and the district that I represent, and I am confident that you are just as proud of being a Member of this House and to be able to represent the people from your district and the people of our Florida.

A few weeks ago the citizens of our state expressed confidence in our ability to work as a team for all the people of our state, and I'm here again to participate in this process of nominating the Speaker of the Florida House. Each of these occasions has been very significant for me, for it charts the government of our state for the coming two years, and the vote that you register here today will be one of the most important votes that you will make as a Member of the Florida House of Representatives as you represent the people of our state.

I rise today to place in nomination an individual whom I have worked with during many legislative sessions and who has demonstrated his great attributes as a concerned American, loyal citizen to his party and to his country, a native Floridian, and most of all a dedicated legislator. Mr. Chairman, I'm honored to place in nomination as Speaker of the House of Representatives, the name of Donald L. Tucker.

When we look and search for a leader for the Florida House, we look for a person who has outstanding ability. The ability should be evidenced by many ingredients: He must be able to lead us, to guide us. He must possess the authority and ability

The Golden Years ...   214   *Robert McKnight*

The Journal OF THE House of Representatives

ORGANIZATION SESSION

Tuesday, November 18, 1980

Journal of the House of Representatives for the Organization Session of the Seventh Legislature convened under the Constitution of Florida as Revised in 1968, begun and held at the Capitol in the City of Tallahassee, in the State of Florida, on Tuesday, November 18, 1980, being the day fixed by the Constitution for the purpose.

Under Rule 3.1, Dr. Allen Morris, Clerk of the preceding Session, delegated the duties of temporary presiding officer to the Honorable J. Hyatt Brown, former Speaker. Mr. Brown called the House to order at 10:30 a.m.

The following certified list of Members elected to the House of Representatives was received:

STATE OF FLORIDA
OFFICE OF SECRETARY OF STATE

I, GEORGE FIRESTONE, Secretary of State of the State of Florida, do hereby certify that the following Members of the House of Representatives were elected at the General Election held on the Fourth day of November, A. D., 1980, as shown by the election returns on file in this office:

HOUSE DISTRICT
NUMBER

1—Grover C. Robinson, III, Pensacola
2—Tom Patterson, Pensacola
3—Clyde H. (Jack) Hagler, Pensacola
4—Bolley "Bo" Johnson, Gulf Breeze
5—Kenneth E. Beles, Ft. Walton Beach
6—James G. Ward, Ft. Walton Beach
7—Sam Mitchell, Vernon
8—Ron Johnson, Panama City
9—Leonard J. Hall, Panama City
10—James Harold Thompson, Quincy
11—Don C. Price, Tallahassee
12—Herbert F. (Herb) Morgan, Tallahassee
13—Wayne Hollingsworth, Lake City
14—Gene Hodges, Cedar Key
15—George Crady, Yulee
16—Arnett E. Girardeau, Jacksonville
17—John Thomas, Jacksonville
18—John W. Lewis, Jacksonville
19—Andrew E. (Andy) Johnson, Jacksonville
20—Carl Ogden, Jacksonville
21—Tommy Hazouri, Jacksonville
22—Steve Pajcic, Jacksonville
23—Fred Tygart, Jacksonville
24—William G. (Bill) Bankhead, Jacksonville
25—Frank Williams, Starke
26—Sidney Martin, Hawthorne
27—Jon Mills, Gainesville
28—Hamilton D. Upchurch, Elkton
29—Tom Brown, Port Orange
30—Samuel P. Bell III, Daytona Beach
31—T. K. Wetherell, Altamonte
32—Christian (Chris) Meffert, Ocala
33—Bob Hattaway, Altamonte Springs
34—Bobby Brantley, Longwood
35—Everett A. Kelly, Tavares
36—Charles E. "Chuck" Smith, Brooksville
37—Ron Richmond, New Port Richey
38—Bruce McEwan, Orlando
39—Daniel Webster, Orlando
40—Richard Crotty, Orlando
41—Fran Carlton, Orlando
42—Tom Drage, Jr., Orlando
43—Dick J. Batchelor, Orlando
44—Jason Steele, Indialantic
45—W. W. "Bud" Gardner, Titusville
46—Marilyn B. Evans, Melbourne
47—Tim Deratany, Indian Harbour Beach
48—R. Dale Patchett, Vero Beach
49—Bob Crawford, Winter Haven
50—Beverly B. Burnsed, Lakeland
51—Gene Ready, Lakeland
52—C. Fred Jones, Auburndale
53—Peter M. Dunbar, Dunedin
54—S. Curtis "Curt" Kiser, Clearwater
55—Jim Smith, Clearwater
56—Betty Easley, Largo
57—Dennis L. Jones, St. Petersburg
58—George F. Hieber II, St. Petersburg
59—Bob Melby, St. Petersburg
60—F. M. "Tom" Woodruff, St. Petersburg
61—Dorothy Eaton Sample, St. Petersburg
62—Carl Carpenter, Jr., Plant City
63—S. L. (Spud) Clements, Brandon
64—John Grant, Tampa
65—"Trooper Jim" Jim Foster, Odessa
66—H. Lee Moffitt, Tampa
67—Elvin L. Martinez, Tampa
68—Richard S. Hodes, Tampa
69—George H. Sheldon, Tampa
70—Helen Gordon Davis, Tampa
71—Ralph H. Haben, Jr., Palmetto
72—Lawrence F. Shackelford, Palmetto
73—Thomas E. Danson, Jr., Sarasota
74—Ted Ewing, Venice
75—Fred H. Burrall, Port Charlotte
76—Charles (Chuck) Nergard, Port St. Lucie
77—William G. "Doc" Myers, Hobe Sound
78—Ray Liberti, West Palm Beach
79—Eleanor Weinstock, West Palm Beach
80—Jim Watt, Lake Park
81—Reid Moore, Jr., Palm Beach
82—Bernard Kimmel, West Palm Beach
83—Frank S. Messersmith, Lake Worth
84—Tom Bush, Ft. Lauderdale
85—Terry O'Malley, Lauderhill
86—Linda Cox, Ft. Lauderdale
87—Robert M. Woodburn, Ft. Lauderdale
88—Tom Gustafson, Ft. Lauderdale
89—Mary Ellen Hawkins, Naples
90—Franklin B. (Frank) Mann, Ft. Myers
91—Hugh Paul Nuckolls, Ft. Myers
92—Tom McPherson, Ft. Lauderdale
93—Harold Dyer, Hollywood
94—Fred Lippman, Hollywood
95—Walter C. "Walt" Young, Pembroke Pines
96—Lawrence J. "Larry" Smith, Hollywood
97—David J. Lehman, Hollywood
98—Elaine Gordon, Miami

1

The Golden Years ...   215   Robert McKnight

JOURNAL OF THE HOUSE OF REPRESENTATIVES
November 18, 1980

99—Barry Kutun, Miami Beach
100—Virginia L. Rosen, N. Miami
101—Harold (Hal) W. Spaet, Miami Beach
102—Michael Friedman, Miami Beach
103—Ronald (Ron) A. Silver, N. Miami Beach
104—William "Ray" Hodges, Hialeah
105—Joe Lang Kershaw, Miami
106—Carrie P. Meek, Miami
107—A. M. "Tony" Fontana, Miami Lakes
108—Bob Reynolds, Miami Lakes
109—Joe Gersten, S. Miami
110—Roberta Fox, Coral Gables
111—Tom Gallagher, Coconut Grove
112—Lawrence H. "Larry" Plummer, Miami
113—William E. "Bill" Sadowski, Miami
114—John Plummer, Miami
115—James K. "Jim" Brodie, Miami
116—Dexter Lehtinen, Miami
117—Scott McPherson, Miami
118—Charlie Hall, Miami
119—Larry Hawkins, Miami
120—Joe Allen, Key West

GIVEN under my hand and the Great Seal of the State of Florida at Tallahassee, the Capitol, this 17th day of November, A.D. 1980

GEORGE FIRESTONE
Secretary of State

The following Members were recorded present:

Allen	Friedman	Kutun	Plummer, L. H.
Bankhead	Gallagher	Lehman	Price
Batchelor	Gardner	Lehtinen	Ready
Bell	Gersten	Lewis	Reynolds
Boles	Girardeau	Liberti	Richmond
Brantley	Gordon	Lippman	Robinson
Brodie	Grant	Mann	Rosen
Brown	Gustafson	Martin	Sadowski
Burnsed	Haben	Martinez	Sample
Burrall	Hagler	McEwan	Shackelford
Bush	Hall, C. A.	McPherson, S.	Sheldon
Carlton	Hall, L. J.	McPherson, T.	Silver
Carpenter	Hattaway	Meek	Smith, C. R.
Clements	Hawkins, L. R.	Meffert	Smith, J. H.
Cox	Hawkins, M. E.	Melby	Smith, I. J.
Crady	Hazouri	Messersmith	Spaet
Crawford	Hieber	Mills	Steele
Crotty	Hodes	Mitchell	Thomas
Danson	Hodges, G.	Moffitt	Thompson
Davis	Hodges, W. R.	Moore	Tygart
Deratany	Hollingsworth	Morgan	Upchurch
Drage	Johnson, A. S.	Myers	Ward
Dunbar	Johnson, D. L.	Nergard	Watt
Dyer	Johnson, R. C.	Nuckolls	Webster
Easley	Jones, C. F.	Ogden	Weinstock
Evans	Jones, D. L.	O'Malley	Wetherell
Ewing	Kelly	Pajcic	Williams
Fontana	Kershaw	Patchett	Woodburn
Foster	Kimmel	Patterson	Woodruff
Fox	Kiser	Plummer, J.	Young

A quorum was present.

Prayer

Prayer was offered by Rep. Fran Carlton.

Pledge

The Members pledged allegiance to the Flag, led by the following representatives of veterans organizations: State Commander Ray Mattox, American Legion; Legislative Chairman Bob Clark, AMVETS; State Commander Roland Oakley, Past State Commander Lester Pittman, Chapter 13 Commander Carl Shoudel, Disabled American Veterans; Legislative Counsel Bill Byerts, Florida Council of The Retired Officers Association; Commander Alton Zucker, Jewish War Veterans; Northwest Florida Vice Commandant Pete Peterson, Marine Corps League; State Commander Carl A. Brown, Military Order of the Purple Heart; Commander John Burns, Veterans of Foreign Wars; and Curt Craig, The Retired Officers Association.

House Physician

The Chair presented Rep. David J. Lehman, who is serving as House Physician today.

Oath Taken by Members

The Members together took the Oath of Office prescribed by the Constitution of the State of Florida from the Honorable Robert E. Hensley, Judge in the 12th Judicial Circuit.

Election of the Speaker

The Chair announced that nominations would now be received for Speaker of the House of Representatives for a term of two years from this date.

Remarks by Rep. Moffitt

Rep. Moffitt nominated the Honorable Ralph H. Haben, Jr. for Speaker with the following remarks:

Mr. Speaker, Members of the House, distinguished guests, ladies and gentlemen: Let me first speak to the new Members who were sworn in today. You may not realize it yet, but you are now a part of the best legislature in this country, and as such you will have the rare opportunity to work with, and form friendships with, some of the finest people I have met in my life. Congratulations and welcome. In the years ahead when you look back on your legislative careers, each of you will be able to point to moments that had special significance to you.

I have today the opportunity to share with you a moment in my life that has special significance to me, and that is to have the honor of nominating Ralph Haben to be Speaker of the Florida House. My friendship with Ralph, as many of you know, started 16 years ago when we met in law school. Since that time I've had the opportunity to know the man better than most anyone. I struggled with him through our law school days when neither of us had two nickels to rub together. I worked with him when he served as a legislative aide and got his first taste of the legislative process. I watched him prosecute criminals as Assistant State Attorney, and I saw him dispense fair justice as a Judge in Manatee County. I probably have shared more moments in his life than most any friend he has. Because of this, I am firmly convinced that Ralph Haben has the strength, the sensitivity, and the ability to lead this body.

Throughout his service in the Legislature, he has been honored time and time again for his legislative skills. I won't tick them all off but you are well aware of them. He has received the Allen Morris Award as Most Effective in Debate, and earlier this year he was chosen by his colleagues to receive the award as the Most Effective Member of this House. Ralph Haben loves this House. He's demonstrated his ability to thrive in its processes. He has given of himself; he's proven his worth; he has earned our trust.

Without a doubt, the most valuable contribution to Ralph's character and development is the love and devotion given to him by his parents. His father, before he passed away, knew that one day his son might become Speaker and he had the opportunity to savor that pride. His mother, Mrs. Jonnie Haben, who is here with us today, who has devoted her life to her son, has given us a man instilled with basic old-time values that are too often forgotten in these modern times. Those of you who have not yet grown to know her have a real treat in store for you.

Ralph grew up in the small town of Palmetto which, in my opinion, is "All America USA". The people in Palmetto are warm, they're real, and they, too, deserve the credit for the man before you today. As you drive in to Palmetto, those of you who have had the occasion to be there, you'll notice on the

1978 House

The Org Session and 1979 Regular Session Journals were missing but this picks up the members from the 1980 Regular Session who were elected in 1978.

JOURNAL OF THE HOUSE OF REPRESENTATIVES — INDEX

Members of the House, Bills Sponsored, and Committee Assignments

[Source: Information Division, Joint Legislative Management Committee]

ALLEN, JOE—120th District
Sponsored: 398, 676, 675, 824, 1003, 1106, 1230, 1233, 1334
Co-sponsored: 24, 102, 121, 122, 140, 142, 179, 212, 306, 324, 350, 387, 731, 773, 1433, 1743, 1869, 1870, 1871, 1872, 1873, 1874, 1875, 1876, 1878
Local Bills: 452, 758, 790, 1107, 1229, 1231, 1232, 1580
Committees: Natural Resources (Vice Chairman); Community Affairs; Finance & Taxation

BANKHEAD, WILLIAM G.—24th District
Sponsored: 497, 638, 745, 1252, 1253, 1254, 1388
Co-sponsored: 17, 306, 350, 387, 389, 677, 735, 1433, 1544, 1572, 1743
Local Bills: 610, 611, 612, 613, 614, 615, 666
Committees: Commerce; Governmental Operations; Tourism & Economic Development

BARRETT, DAVID L.—44th District
Sponsored: 122, 248, 305, 557, 558, 559, 561, 562, 592, 593, 672, 674, 675, 708, 709, 821, 825, 837, 940, 1075, 1076, 1079, 1108
Co-sponsored: 24, 68, 201, 212, 306, 324, 383, 443, 773, 973, 1004, 1116, 1117, 1404, 1427, 1433, 1525, 1743
Local Bills: 660, 759, 814, 932
Committees: Ethics & Elections (Vice Chairman); Commerce; Finance & Taxation

BATCHELOR, DICK J.—43rd District
Sponsored: 117, 118, 335, 556, 1009, 1025, 1101, 1236, 1298, 1307, 1308, 1309, 1310, 1311, 1312, 1313, 1314, 1345, 1449, 1519, 1617
Co-sponsored: 121, 179, 217, 306, 307, 310, 337, 431, 465, 511, 541, 798, 1224, 1236, 1432, 1513, 1743, 1841
Local Bills: 948, 1218, 1219, 1220, 1221, 1222, 1228, 1352
Committees: Health & Rehabilitative Services (Chairperson); Appropriations; Governmental Operations; Regulatory Reform; Rules & Calendar

BELL, SAMUEL P., III—30th District
Sponsored: 159, 392, 705, 976, 977, 978, 979, 1412, 1702, 1863
Co-sponsored: 26, 134, 179, 183, 212, 349, 604, 665, 1379, 1577, 1743
Local Bills: 706, 1036
Committees: Appropriations; Education, Higher; Regulatory Reform

BOLES, KENNETH E.—5th District
Sponsored: 2, 141, 142, 189, 200, 241, 242, 337, 727, 1105, 1385, 1577, 1804, 1864
Co-sponsored: 1, 6, 16, 101, 102, 121, 122, 140, 152, 188, 252, 262, 306, 311, 350, 377, 387, 389, 397, 525, 535, 724, 725, 731, 764, 765, 854, 937, 1025, 1212, 1291, 1317, 1552, 1553, 1603, 1616, 1651, 1743
Local Bills: 1190, 1213, 1478, 1479, 1480, 1481, 1484, 1485, 1486, 1487, 1488, 1489, 1490, 1492, 1496, 1497, 1500
Committees: Education, K-12; Natural Resources; Veterans Affairs

BRANTLEY, BOBBY—34th District
Sponsored: 29, 90, 145, 163, 255, 334, 1297, 1238, 1239, 1240, 1241, 1672

BRANTLEY, BOBBY (Cont.)
Co-sponsored: 122, 158, 179, 212, 306, 350, 537, 1004, 1037, 1116, 1117, 1572, 1743
Local Bills: 908, 1279, 1280
Committees: Agriculture & General Legislation; Ethics & Elections; Tourism & Economic Development

BROWN, J. HYATT—31st District
Sponsored: 906, 1611
Co-sponsored: 231, 1577, 1743, 1864
Local Bills: 706

BURNSED, BEVERLY B.—50th District
Sponsored: 264, 521, 779, 818, 1176, 1206, 1207, 1208, 1209, 1716
Co-sponsored: 306, 1379, 1433, 1442, 1743, 1769
Local Bills: 1554
Committees: Education, Higher (Chairman); Appropriations; Health & Rehabilitative Services; Rules & Calendar

BURRALL, FREDERIC R.—75th District
Sponsored: 106, 143, 537, 728, 815
Co-sponsored: 121, 122, 158, 179, 306, 540, 773, 1027, 1157, 1743, 1834, 1835
Local Bills: 501, 1514, 1554
Committees: Agriculture & General Legislation; Judiciary; Natural Resources; Regulatory Reform; Rules & Calendar

BUSH, THOMAS J.—84th District
Sponsored: 86, 107, 108, 109, 230, 876, 1249, 1342
Co-sponsored: 122, 158, 179, 212, 306, 537, 590, 973, 1433, 1743
Local Bills: 1793
Committees: Corrections, Probation & Parole; Judiciary; Regulatory Reform

CAMPBELL, GENE—82nd District
Sponsored: 371, 372, 589, 623, 711, 875, 1286
Co-sponsored: 12, 24, 57, 74, 121, 212, 306, 326, 973, 1182, 1286, 1295, 1346, 1371, 1375, 1376, 1427, 1433, 1573, 1743
Local Bills: 883, 884, 885, 886, 887, 888, 889, 890, 891, 892, 982, 990, 1083, 1248
Committees: Corrections, Probation & Parole (Vice Chairman); Health & Rehabilitative Services; Regulatory Reform

CARLTON, FRAN—41st District
Sponsored: 129, 130, 151, 152, 179, 540, 1265
Co-sponsored: 6, 17, 122, 306, 1377, 1433, 1519, 1526, 1529, 1530, 1572, 1698, 1743
Local Bills: 948, 1218, 1219, 1220, 1221, 1222, 1228, 1352
Committees: Tourism & Economic Development (Vice Chairperson); Appropriations; Corrections, Probation & Parole

CARPENTER, CARL, JR.—62nd District
Sponsored: 321, 896, 1056, 1501, 1502, 1714
Co-sponsored: 24, 155, 179, 212, 295, 306, 430, 973, 1294, 1433, 1537, 1538, 1743

INDEX — JOURNAL OF THE HOUSE OF REPRESENTATIVES 1361

CARPENTER, CARL JR. (Cont.)
Local Bills: 1160, 1161, 1162, 1163, 1164
Committees: Agriculture & General Legislation; Tourism & Economic Development; Transportation

CONWAY, WILLIAM R.—29th District
Sponsored: 134, 407, 514, 517, 526, 753, 778, 805, 806, 808, 822, 823, 827, 838, 949, 1089, 1250, 1277, 1278
Co-sponsored: 121, 179, 201, 212, 259, 306, 307, 389, 973, 1025, 1295, 1433, 1519, 1601, 1743
Local Bills: 706
Committees: Appropriations (Vice Chairman); Education, Higher; Governmental Operations; Insurance

COX, LINDA C.—86th District
Sponsored: 43, 116, 172, 181, 326, 631, 1057, 1244, 1245, 1246, 1581
Co-sponsored: 12, 24, 121, 183, 212, 215, 287, 297, 298, 299, 324, 369, 484, 773, 973, 1121, 1179, 1180, 1181, 1236, 1242, 1266, 1295, 1375, 1376, 1377, 1433, 1519, 1678, 1743
Local Bills: 384, 1793
Committees: Regulated Industries & Licensing (Vice Chairperson); Finance & Taxation; Regulatory Reform; Retirement, Personnel & Collective Bargaining

CRADY, GEORGE A.—15th District
Sponsored: 503, 730, 731, 732, 733
Co-sponsored: 1, 47, 57, 306, 326, 377, 389, 397, 525, 535, 598, 724, 726, 764, 765, 804, 973, 1087, 1433, 1603, 1651, 1680, 1743, 1794
Local Bills: 610, 611, 612, 613, 614, 615, 632, 666, 1493
Committees: Governmental Operations (Vice Chairman); Agriculture & General Legislation; Energy (Select); Natural Resources; Veterans Affairs

CRAWFORD, ROBERT B.—49th District
Sponsored: 365, 369, 457, 584, 1023, 1290, 1378, 1387, 1410, 1455
Co-sponsored: 212, 349, 532, 1433, 1520
Local Bills: 704, 1482, 1554
Committees: Criminal Justice (Chairman); Governmental Operations; Judiciary; Regulated Industries & Licensing; Rules & Calendar

CROTTY, RICHARD—40th District
Sponsored: 152, 228, 239, 481, 482, 532, 555, 556, 630, 722, 1111, 1146, 1267, 1442
Co-sponsored: 24, 120, 145, 158, 165, 185, 201, 209, 221, 226, 306, 324, 350, 590, 1157, 1290, 1433, 1743, 1845
Local Bills: 948, 1218, 1219, 1220, 1221, 1222, 1223
Committees: Corrections, Probation & Parole; Education, Higher

DANSON, THOMAS E. JR.—73rd District
Sponsored: 167, 272, 273, 324, 351, 408, 416, 417, 609, 633, 662, 663, 665, 816, 817, 996, 1005, 1006, 1368, 1390
Co-sponsored: 6, 122, 179, 188, 212, 260, 306, 350, 378, 622, 702, 916, 1025, 1252, 1254, 1743
Local Bills: 1494, 1495
Committees: Regulatory Reform; Retirement, Personnel & Collective Bargaining

DAVIS, HELEN GORDON—70th District
Sponsored: 22, 222, 226, 261, 331, 394, 395, 489, 553, 918, 1056, 1227, 1294, 1714

DAVIS, HELEN GORDON (Cont.)
Co-sponsored: 57, 121, 183, 212, 229, 354, 731, 973, 1066, 1121, 1236, 1266, 1295, 1377, 1427, 1433, 1513, 1519, 1567, 1568, 1641, 1642, 1644, 1647, 1648
Local Bills: 1160, 1161, 1162, 1163, 1164
Committees: Education, K-12 (Vice Chairperson); Health & Rehabilitative Services; Natural Resources

DERATANY, TIMOTHY D.—47th District
Sponsored: 221, 461, 590
Co-sponsored: 102, 158, 188, 212, 973, 1157, 1252, 1254, 1525, 1743, 1794
Local Bills: 814, 1135, 1491
Committees: Community Affairs; Governmental Operations

DUNBAR, PETER M.—52nd District
Sponsored: 50, 145, 239, 250, 307, 338, 502, 703, 855, 924, 989, 1395, 1597
Co-sponsored: 6, 68, 101, 158, 188, 203, 306, 310, 387, 472, 590, 773, 836, 1025, 1336, 1433, 1440, 1583, 1591, 1635, 1659, 1743, 1848, 1866
Local Bills: 564, 831, 878, 1216, 1217, 1476, 1477, 1499, 1516
Committees: Judiciary; Regulatory Reform; Transportation

DYER, HAROLD J.—93rd District
Sponsored: 149, 150, 212, 213, 214, 249, 278, 282, 296, 322, 323, 324, 332, 347, 348, 1072, 1177, 1189, 1191, 1227, 1396, 1397, 1418, 1445, 1446, 1447, 1450
Co-sponsored: 68, 179, 306, 338, 329, 830, 973, 1179, 1180, 1181, 1182, 1345, 1433, 1743, 1869, 1870, 1871, 1872, 1873, 1874, 1875, 1876, 1878
Local Bills: 384, 1627, 1628, 1629, 1630, 1793
Committees: Community Affairs (Vice Chairman); Energy (Select); Finance & Taxation; Natural Resources

EASLEY, BETTY—56th District
Sponsored: 99, 184, 185, 198, 255, 352, 378, 528, 1425, 1450, 1519, 1583
Co-sponsored: 6, 24, 68, 85, 158, 212, 306, 307, 342, 387, 479, 1025, 1157, 1224, 1379, 1433, 1743
Local Bills: 564, 831, 878, 995, 1159, 1476, 1477, 1499, 1516
Committees: Appropriations; Criminal Justice; Finance & Taxation

ECKHART, JAMES F.—115th District
Sponsored: 21, 22, 91, 92, 93, 193, 224, 290, 455, 492, 540, 1032, 1033, 1035, 1110, 1357, 1390
Co-sponsored: 212, 389, 590, 1067, 1182, 1299, 1433, 1625, 1743, 1841, 1869, 1870, 1871, 1872, 1873, 1874, 1875, 1876, 1878
Committees: Finance & Taxation (Vice Chairman); Agriculture & General Legislation; Governmental Operations

EVANS, MARILYN BAILEY—46th District
Sponsored: 68, 147, 170, 260, 274, 429, 443, 462, 664, 721, 798, 1255, 1256, 1257, 1366, 1879
Co-sponsored: 6, 14, 17, 18, 20, 24, 49, 62, 90, 95, 120, 158, 169, 205, 256, 257, 287, 306, 311, 324, 395, 469, 540, 541, 552, 590, 773, 973, 1157, 1252, 1254, 1433, 1525, 1743
Local Bills: 814, 1491
Committees: Education, K-12; Health & Rehabilitative Services; Natural Resources

EWING, TED—74th District
Sponsored: 25, 49, 95, 235, 236, 237, 256, 257, 260, 272, 273, 480, 622, 702, 1369

The Golden Years ... 219 *Robert McKnight*

EWING, TED (Cont.)
Co-sponsored: 6, 12, 24, 102, 122, 158, 201, 212, 306, 324, 350, 427, 773, 1005, 1008, 1009, 1025, 1133, 1254, 1743

Committees: Commerce; Ethics & Elections

FLINN, GENE—116th District
Sponsored: 8, 26, 111, 112, 223, 376, 428, 586, 964, 1010, 1299, 1304, 1305

Co-sponsored: 12, 107, 108, 121, 193, 212, 306, 340, 341, 353, 383, 496, 585, 648, 697, 751, 973, 1025, 1048, 1815, 1427, 1433, 1743, 1805, 1848, 1870, 1871, 1872, 1873, 1874, 1875, 1876, 1878

Committees: Commerce; Insurance; Natural Resources

FLYNN, BILL—117th District
Sponsored: 41, 245, 980, 981

Co-sponsored: 1, 6, 12, 22, 24, 34, 42, 53, 54, 55, 57, 63, 68, 87, 91, 93, 114, 119, 121, 127, 131, 137, 141, 179, 190, 193, 198, 205, 212, 242, 244, 259, 266, 287, 306, 353, 340, 377, 389, 397, 402, 414, 419, 427, 525, 535, 540, 725, 731, 764, 765, 829, 830, 864, 973, 1004, 1025, 1116, 1117, 1182, 1212, 1266, 1268, 1299, 1366, 1427, 1433, 1562, 1553, 1680, 1743, 1794, 1805, 1841, 1869, 1870, 1871, 1872, 1873, 1874, 1875, 1876, 1878

Committees: Community Affairs; Ethics & Elections; Veterans Affairs

FONTANA, A. M.—107th District
Sponsored: 154, 329, 707, 739, 960, 1333

Co-sponsored: 11, 17, 18, 19, 108, 121, 158, 174, 181, 250, 326, 349, 773, 973, 1299, 1427, 1433, 1519, 1628, 1678, 1743, 1794, 1805, 1869, 1870, 1871, 1872, 1873, 1874, 1875, 1876, 1878

Committees: Rules & Calendar (Vice Chairman); Criminal Justice; Regulated Industries & Licensing

FOSTER, JAMES S.—85th District
Sponsored: 357, 358, 359, 360, 361, 362, 363, 364, 390, 658, 1056, 1074, 1714, 1862

Co-sponsored: 1, 192, 281, 306, 377, 397, 489, 535, 764, 765, 864, 973, 1097, 1294, 1433, 1534, 1680, 1743

Local Bills: 1160, 1161, 1162, 1163, 1164

Committees: Veterans Affairs (Vice Chairman); Agriculture & General Legislation; Transportation

FOX, ROBERTA—110th District
Sponsored: 23, 248, 249, 251, 271, 344, 468, 545, 587, 768, 773, 868, 926, 927, 950, 951, 968, 1048, 1125, 1126, 1295, 1375, 1376, 1377, 1467

Co-sponsored: 121, 145, 174, 184, 212, 315, 324, 470, 546, 960, 973, 1121, 1242, 1269, 1299, 1433, 1519, 1601, 1678, 1704, 1743, 1805, 1869, 1870, 1871, 1872, 1873, 1874, 1875, 1876, 1878

Committees: Retirement, Personnel & Collective Bargaining (Vice Chairperson); Commerce; Energy (Select); Finance & Taxation; Regulated Industries & Licensing

GALLAGHER, C. THOMAS, III—111th District
Sponsored: 184, 495, 496, 694, 744, 768, 809, 810, 811, 812, 900, 1065, 1094, 1104, 1175, 1178, 1296

Co-sponsored: 251, 310, 1157, 1299, 1467, 1677, 1743, 1805, 1869, 1870, 1871, 1872, 1873, 1874, 1875, 1876, 1878

Committees: Appropriations; Commerce; Insurance

GARDNER, WINSTON W., JR.—45th District
Sponsored: 70, 71, 72, 73, 229, 467, 637, 746, 938, 1070, 1127, 1139, 1346, 1412, 1526, 1553, 1845

Co-sponsored: 17, 158, 287, 306, 380, 489, 590, 973, 1294, 1519, 1526, 1527, 1534, 1572, 1678, 1743, 1804

Local Bills: 673, 814, 1491

Committees: Education, K-12; Regulated Industries & Licensing; Tourism & Economic Development

GERSTEN, JOSEPH, M.—109th District
Sponsored: 211, 251, 358, 447, 667, 751, 796, 959, 960, 965, 1048, 1092, 1299, 1330, 1331, 1335, 1467

Co-sponsored: 24, 81, 121, 152, 182, 306, 387, 397, 525, 535, 596, 724, 731, 973, 1018, 1242, 1266, 1295, 1375, 1376, 1377, 1453, 1519, 1634, 1697, 1743, 1805, 1847, 1869, 1870, 1871, 1872, 1873, 1874, 1875, 1876, 1878

Committees: Governmental Operations (Chairman); Finance & Taxation; Regulatory Reform; Rules & Calendar

GIRARDEAU, ARNETT E.—16th District
Sponsored: 121, 215, 225, 262, 310, 553, 554, 1068

Co-sponsored: 12, 24, 183, 212, 306, 798, 973, 1266, 1433, 1519, 1743

Committees: Corrections, Probation & Parole (Chairman); Health & Rehabilitative Services; Regulatory Reform; Rules & Calendar

GORDON, ELAINE—98th District
Sponsored: 14, 215, 310, 473, 521, 588, 679, 680, 681, 1136, 1253, 1259, 1290, 1291, 1292, 1295, 1360, 1375, 1376, 1377, 1414, 1415, 1436, 1427, 1438, 1439, 1440, 1441, 1443, 1838

Co-sponsored: 12, 24, 118, 121, 176, 181, 183, 212, 222, 331, 386, 395, 773, 1025, 1061, 1096, 1121, 1342, 1433, 1704, 1743, 1805, 1869, 1870, 1871, 1872, 1873, 1874, 1875, 1876, 1878

Committees: House Administration (Chairperson); Appropriations; Corrections, Probation & Parole; Health & Rehabilitative Services; Regulatory Reform; Rules & Calendar

GRANT, JOHN A., JR.—64th District
Sponsored: 1533, 1534, 1535, 1536, 1537, 1538, 1539, 1540, 1543, 1544, 1545, 1549, 1550, 1557, 1558, 1714

Co-sponsored: 6, 78, 84, 91, 93, 105, 107, 108, 122, 130, 135, 144, 158, 179, 193, 205, 212, 219, 221, 230, 306, 350, 389, 517, 539, 540, 590, 658, 821, 973, 1074, 1263, 1433, 1519, 1743

Local Bills: 1160, 1161, 1162, 1163, 1164, 1554

Committees: Community Affairs; Retirement, Personnel & Collective Bargaining; Tourism & Economic Development

GUSTAFSON, TOM—88th District
Sponsored: 79, 97, 297, 298, 299, 338, 369, 395, 406, 422, 444, 454, 464, 483, 484, 513, 546, 591, 617, 635, 839, 1069, 1150, 1373, 1880

Co-sponsored: 24, 89, 179, 212, 217, 973, 1453, 1519, 1577, 1591, 1601, 1743

Local Bills: 1774, 1793

Committees: Appropriations; Education, K-12; Judiciary; Transportation

HABEN, RALPH H., JR.—71st District
Sponsored: 1343, 1466, 1743, 1881

Co-sponsored: 389, 1577, 1804, 1811, 1848, 1864

Committees: Rules & Calendar (Chairman); Commerce; Finance & Taxation; Tourism & Economic Development; Transportation

HAGLER, CLYDE H.—3rd District
Sponsored: 252, 253, 254, 283, 284, 303, 544, 738, 1419, 1420, 1421

Co-sponsored: 18, 22, 73, 140, 141, 212, 306, 389, 1133, 1201, 1433, 1616, 1743

Local Bills: 1480, 1481, 1483, 1484, 1485, 1486, 1487

Committees: Community Affairs; Health & Rehabilitative Services; Transportation

HALL, LEONARD J.—9th District
Sponsored: 61, 276, 430, 1358, 1704

JOHNSON, BOLLEY L. (Cont.)
Committees: Education, K-1; Ethics & Elections; Tourism & Economic Development

JOHNSON, RONALD CLYDE—8th District
Sponsored: 377, 382, 533, 506, 684, 800, 801, 1149, 1351, 1704

Co-sponsored: 1, 24, 107, 121, 127, 158, 262, 306, 337, 350, 387, 389, 397, 525, 535, 540, 724, 725, 731, 764, 765, 864, 928, 973, 1121, 1152, 1291, 1383, 1433, 1680, 1742, 1804

Committees: Regulatory Reform; Transportation; Veterans Affairs

JONES, C. FRED—52nd District
Sponsored: 1866

Co-sponsored: 1743

Committees: Transportation (Chairman); Appropriations; Community Affairs; Energy (Select); Insurance; Regulatory Reform; Rules & Calendar

JONES, DENNIS L.—57th District
Sponsored: 529, 530, 565, 566, 568, 569, 570, 798, 969, 1026, 1361, 1404

Co-sponsored: 12, 24, 158, 201, 306, 307, 500, 1004, 1116, 1117, 1336, 1433, 1553, 1743

Local Bills: 564, 831, 878, 995, 1008, 1159, 1216, 1217, 1476, 1477, 1499, 1516

Committees: Education, Higher; Ethics & Elections; Health & Rehabilitative Services

KELLY EVERETT A.—55th District
Sponsored: 335, 511, 532, 538, 775, 970, 983, 1009, 1025

Co-sponsored: 24, 101, 121, 122, 158, 179, 193, 201, 213, 306, 349, 505, 537, 731, 795, 855, 1016, 1020, 1087, 1254, 1438, 1743

Local Bills: 1280

Committees: Agriculture & General Legislation; Health & Rehabilitative Services; Natural Resources

KERSHAW, JOE LANG—105th District
Sponsored: 11, 250, 550, 1293, 1333, 1731, 1794

Co-sponsored: 121, 349, 377, 1433, 1678, 1743, 1805, 1869, 1870, 1871, 1872, 1873, 1874, 1875, 1876, 1878

Committees: Health & Rehabilitative Services (Vice Chairperson); Criminal Justice; Regulated Industries & Licensing

KIRKWOOD, LAWRENCE R.—38th District
Sponsored: 16, 135, 144, 145, 308, 314, 343, 418, 539, 607, 748, 773

Co-sponsored: 24, 57, 117, 121, 152, 201, 212, 213, 214, 324, 392, 1254, 1433, 1591, 1601, 1743

Local Bills: 948, 1218, 1219, 1220, 1221, 1222, 1223

Committees: Commerce; Judiciary

KISER, S. CURTIS—54th District
Sponsored: 15, 143, 145, 387, 499, 527, 853, 854, 855, 1009, 1025, 1045, 1157, 1192, 1225, 1367, 1398, 1433, 1597, 1796, 1811

Co-sponsored: 27, 121, 158, 188, 202, 212, 306, 307, 333, 350, 773, 836, 1268, 1440, 1528, 1577, 1583, 1738, 1743

Local Bills: 564, 831, 878, 995, 1008, 1159, 1216, 1217, 1476, 1477, 1499

Committees: Energy (Select); House Administration; Rules & Calendar

KUTUN, BARRY—99th District
Sponsored: 17, 18, 19, 20, 46, 162, 338, 339, 340, 436, 522, 523, 757, 820, 919, 1018, 1088, 1095, 1123, 1140, 1301, 1302, 1303, 1531, 1869, 1870, 1871, 1872, 1873, 1874, 1875, 1876, 1878

KUTUN, BARRY (Cont.)
Co-sponsored: 117, 212, 310, 324, 388, 1121, 1166, 1252, 1254, 1295, 1299, 1375, 1376, 1377, 1433, 1536, 1527, 1528, 1872, 1577, 1578, 1591, 1743, 1781, 1782, 1794, 1805

Committees: Tourism & Economic Development (Chairman); Appropriations; Community Affairs; Rules & Calendar

LEHMAN, DAVID J.—97th District
Sponsored: 37, 46, 85, 279, 349, 426, 1251

Co-sponsored: 188, 212, 221, 259, 324, 350, 773, 973, 1026, 1183, 1266, 1295, 1343, 1375, 1376, 1377, 1427, 1433, 1445, 1446, 1447, 1743, 1869, 1870, 1871, 1872, 1873, 1874, 1875, 1876, 1878

Local Bills: 1627, 1628, 1630, 1793

Committees: Criminal Justice; Health & Rehabilitative Services

LEWIS, JOHN W.—18th District
Sponsored: 218, 219, 311, 471, 802, 803, 1391, 1392, 1422, 1423, 1434, 1451, 1452

Co-sponsored: 17, 121, 122, 158, 179, 554, 598, 736, 874, 1109, 1433, 1519, 1531, 1572, 1615, 1691, 1743, 1752, 1797, 1801, 1833, 1834, 1835

Local Bills: 610, 611, 612, 613, 615, 632, 666

Committees: Natural Resources (Chairman); Energy (Select) (Vice Chairman); Appropriations; Rules & Calendar; Tourism & Economic Development

LEWIS, THOMAS F.—83rd District
Sponsored: 13, 143, 232, 233, 234, 265, 272, 273, 377, 399, 400, 653, 669, 1133, 1151, 1152, 1156

Co-sponsored: 24, 62, 68, 101, 121, 153, 179, 188, 201, 212, 306, 349, 350, 540, 559, 755, 800, 822, 973, 1027, 1157, 1253, 1371, 1377, 1433, 1519, 1534, 1591, 1743

Local Bills: 883, 884, 885, 886, 887, 888, 889, 890, 891, 892, 962, 990, 1052, 1248, 1554

Committees: Agriculture & General Legislation; Appropriations; Energy (Select); Rules & Calendar; Transportation

LIBERTI, RAY—78th District
Sponsored: 74, 266, 442, 551, 552, 563, 626, 627, 628, 629, 711, 822, 894, 895, 1171, 1300

Co-sponsored: 17, 24, 57, 62, 121, 158, 179, 183, 186, 212, 214, 259, 265, 306, 322, 323, 324, 347, 348, 350, 387, 451, 590, 669, 676, 671, 836, 973, 1025, 1121, 1242, 1271, 1427, 1433, 1572, 1573, 1743

Local Bills: 883, 884, 885, 886, 887, 888, 889, 890, 891, 892, 962, 990, 1052, 1248

Committees: Corrections, Probation & Parole; Education, K-12; Energy (Select); Tourism & Economic Development

LIPPMAN, FREDERICK—94th District
Sponsored: 24, 30, 54, 175, 332, 356, 359, 460, 836, 904, 1025, 1055, 1179, 1206, 1449, 1617

Co-sponsored: 121, 179, 212, 220, 324, 333, 333, 349, 773, 849, 973, 1004, 1116, 1117, 1180, 1181, 1242, 1268, 1347, 1348, 1349, 1375, 1376, 1433, 1743, 1794, 1869, 1870, 1871, 1872, 1873, 1874, 1875, 1876, 1878

Local Bills: 1793

Committees: Education, Higher; Ethics & Elections; Health & Rehabilitative Services

LOCKWARD, WILLIAM H.—104th District
Sponsored: 171

Co-sponsored: 1, 24, 121, 158, 179, 186, 212, 259, 287, 397, 525, 535, 724, 725, 764, 765, 773, 864, 973, 1212, 1299, 1377, 1433, 1552, 1553, 1603, 1651, 1680, 1743, 1794, 1805, 1869, 1870, 1871, 1872, 1873, 1874, 1875, 1876, 1878

Committees: Veterans Affairs (Chairman); Rules & Calendar; Transportation

INDEX JOURNAL OF THE HOUSE OF REPRESENTATIVES 1363

HALL, LEONARD J. (Cont.)
Co-sponsored: 17, 153, 179, 193, 306, 307, 350, 389, 1182, 1253, 1254, 1291, 1433, 1572, 1743, 1804
Committees: Education, K-12; Ethics & Elections; Tourism & Economic Development

HATTAWAY, BOB—33rd District
Sponsored: 7, 63, 64, 65, 246, 413, 595, 717, 718, 719, 752, 989, 1148, 1185, 1275, 1328, 1341, 1756
Co-sponsored: 57, 193, 212, 306, 537, 781, 773, 898, 1087, 1433, 1678, 1743
Local Bills: 908, 1279
Committees: Agriculture & General Legislation (Vice Chairman); Appropriations; Insurance; Regulated Industries & Licensing; Transportation

HAWKINS, LAWRENCE R.—119th District
Sponsored: 269, 289, 332, 342, 410, 431, 491, 581, 596, 597, 603, 870, 1268, 1502
Co-sponsored: 12, 24, 68, 121, 170, 179, 251, 259, 306, 324, 701, 773, 973, 1121, 1166, 1254, 1266, 1320, 1376, 1377, 1427, 1433, 1743, 1805, 1869, 1870, 1871, 1872, 1873, 1874, 1875, 1876, 1878
Committees: Governmental Operations; Health & Rehabilitative Services; Regulatory Reform

HAWKINS, MARY ELLEN—89th District
Sponsored: 5, 6, 180, 260, 285, 286, 787, 997, 998, 999, 1000, 1001, 1021, 1093, 1289, 1399, 1400, 1457
Co-sponsored: 17, 122, 168, 306, 350, 532, 973, 1157, 1182, 1433, 1572, 1743
Local Bills: 509, 760, 761, 762, 763, 774, 910, 993, 994, 1198, 1199, 1200, 1201, 1202, 1203, 1204, 1205, 1274, 1458, 1514, 1626
Committees: Education, K-12; Natural Resources; Tourism & Economic Development

HAZOURI, THOMAS L.—21st District
Sponsored: 40, 139, 210, 598, 723, 736, 1077, 1228, 1434, 1519, 1683
Co-sponsored: 28, 57, 73, 121, 179, 212, 306, 549, 554, 589, 590, 773, 973, 1068, 1084, 1242, 1266, 1345, 1423, 1424, 1433, 1451, 1743
Local Bills: 610, 611, 612, 613, 614, 615, 632, 666
Committees: Retirement, Personnel & Collective Bargaining (Chairman); Appropriations; Community Affairs; Insurance; Rules & Calendar

HEALEY, EDWARD, J.—81st District
Sponsored: 45, 55, 60, 123, 124, 125, 137, 166, 183, 232, 243, 433, 434, 478, 479, 525, 879, 1077, 1250, 1785
Co-sponsored: 14, 24, 40, 50, 51, 66, 217, 287, 295, 306, 424, 611, 604, 973, 1004, 1025, 1116, 1117, 1266, 1371, 1377, 1427, 1433, 1519, 1743, 1794
Local Bills: 883, 884, 885, 886, 887, 888, 889, 890, 891, 892, 982, 990, 1083, 1248
Committees: Ethics & Elections (Chairman); Commerce; Finance & Taxation; Rules & Calendar

HECTOR, ROBERT C.—114th District
Sponsored: 145, 212, 287, 903, 1064
Co-sponsored: 148, 156, 193, 251, 447, 596, 973, 1096, 1266, 1295, 1299, 1375, 1376, 1427, 1433, 1497, 1591, 1678, 1743, 1794, 1805, 1869, 1870, 1871, 1872, 1873, 1874, 1876, 1878
Committees: Insurance; Regulated Industries & Licensing; Regulatory Reform; Transportation

HIEBER, GEORGE F., II—58th District
Sponsored: 66, 88, 110, 300, 401, 405, 446, 741, 1034, 1073, 1465
Co-sponsored: 1, 24, 158, 179, 188, 307, 326, 535, 535, 724, 725, 765, 773, 1004, 1212, 1236, 1433, 1552, 1553, 1683, 1603, 1651, 1680, 1743
Local Bills: 504, 831, 878, 995, 1008, 1159, 1216, 1476, 1477, 1499
Committees: Education, K-12; Ethics & Elections; Veterans Affairs

HODES, RICHARD S.—68th District
Sponsored: 10, 53, 24, 81, 636, 1056, 1112, 1153, 1215, 1325, 1332, 1413, 1442, 1519, 1714, 1796
Co-sponsored: 121, 179, 201, 1207, 1433, 1577, 1743
Local Bills: 1160, 1161, 1162, 1163, 1164
Committees: Appropriations (Chairman, Education); Education, Higher; Finance & Taxation; Retirement, Personnel & Collective Bargaining; Rules & Calendar

HODGES, GENE—14th District
Sponsored: 123, 220, 221, 304, 377, 537, 652, 716, 731, 901, 902, 1087, 1795, 1827
Co-sponsored: 168, 193, 212, 295, 389, 472, 505, 540, 1362, 1743
Local Bills: 645, 650, 651, 1128, 1129, 1515, 1532
Committees: Agriculture & General Legislation (Chairman); Appropriations; Energy (Select); Judiciary; Natural Resources; Rules & Calendar

HOLLINGSWORTH, WAYNE—13th District
Sponsored: 47, 130, 131, 220, 455, 502, 516, 519, 540, 541, 789, 1343, 1351, 1324, 1472, 1607, 1865
Co-sponsored: 107, 158, 179, 193, 306, 350, 389, 973, 1087, 1254, 1678, 1743
Committees: Agriculture & General Legislation; Regulated Industries & Licensing; Transportation

JENNINGS, TONI—42nd District
Sponsored: 35, 119, 120, 151, 201, 306, 445, 1184, 1250
Co-sponsored: 24, 122, 164, 165, 190, 212, 221, 237, 350, 724, 725, 1254, 1433, 1743
Local Bills: 32, 948, 1218, 1219, 1220, 1221, 1222, 1223
Committees: Commerce; Finance & Taxation; Rules & Calendar

JOHNSON, ANDREW E.—19th District
Sponsored: 56, 57, 58, 59, 60, 76, 77, 78, 89, 317, 677, 735, 1002, 1014, 1015, 1017, 1067, 1068, 1145, 1177, 1297, 1354
Co-sponsored: 2, 14, 24, 28, 35, 49, 74, 121, 126, 150, 152, 183, 201, 212, 214, 253, 239, 248, 264, 265, 306, 322, 323, 324, 345, 347, 348, 432, 489, 533, 554, 598, 604, 641, 646, 660, 672, 680, 681, 683, 700, 729, 731, 736, 773, 797, 940, 957, 973, 1040, 1087, 1121, 1133, 1252, 1295, 1375, 1376, 1377, 1381, 1433, 1434, 1440, 1743, 1809, 1870, 1871, 1872, 1873, 1876
Local Bills: 610, 611, 612, 613, 614, 615, 632, 666
Committees: Agriculture & General Legislation; Corrections, Probation & Parole; Energy (Select); Finance & Taxation

JOHNSON, BOLLEY L.—4th District
Sponsored: 382, 389, 458, 459, 533, 547, 1141, 1142, 1235, 1535
Co-sponsored: 17, 18, 20, 24, 31, 120, 131, 141, 193, 306, 330, 337, 540, 588, 973, 1087, 1433, 1526, 1527, 1572, 1616, 1743, 1804
Local Bills: 1190, 1213, 1478, 1479, 1480, 1484, 1485, 1486, 1487, 1488, 1489, 1490, 1492, 1496, 1497, 1500

MALLOY, JOHN CYRIL—118th District
Co-sponsored: 121, 212, 251, 1182, 1242, 1528, 1743, 1805, 1869, 1870, 1871, 1872, 1873, 1874, 1875, 1876, 1878

Committees: Commerce (Vice Chairman); Appropriations; Tourism & Economic Development; Transportation

MANN, FRANKLIN B.—50th District
Sponsored: 145, 268, 849, 874, 909, 928, 930, 931, 1133, 1177, 1239, 1442

Co-sponsored: 306, 590, 624, 731, 1743, 1794

Local Bills: 304, 501, 599, 609, 760, 761, 762, 763, 774, 910, 1453, 1514, 1518, 1594, 1626

Committees: Appropriations (Chairman, HRS/Criminal Justice); Energy (Select) (Chairman); Education, Higher; Insurance; Natural Resources; Rules & Calendar

MARGOLIS, GWEN—102nd District
Sponsored: 38, 39, 67, 114, 153, 169, 258, 336, 414, 1011, 1082, 1096, 1299, 1365, 1408, 1433, 1606

Co-sponsored: 87, 121, 212, 259, 310, 332, 338, 340, 353, 406, 520, 521, 549, 670, 671, 773, 829, 830, 996, 1037, 1038, 1039, 1061, 1242, 1266, 1296, 1375, 1376, 1377, 1572, 1591, 1743, 1805, 1823, 1869, 1870, 1871, 1872, 1873, 1874, 1875, 1876, 1878

Committees: Appropriations; Finance & Taxation; Regulatory Reform

MARTIN, SIDNEY—26th District
Sponsored: 28, 1168, 1169, 1195, 1636

Co-sponsored: 57, 121, 193, 212, 973, 1211, 1327, 1375, 1376, 1433, 1519, 1572, 1601, 1743, 1794

Local Bills: 1193, 1194, 1267

Committees: Community Affairs (Chairman); Appropriations; Retirement, Personnel & Collective Bargaining; Rules & Calendar

MARTINEZ, ELVIN L.—67th District
Sponsored: 113, 220, 474, 536, 578, 579, 699, 1056, 1461, 1467, 1474, 1475, 1714

Co-sponsored: 24, 122, 179, 212, 349, 472, 489, 973, 1294, 1433, 1520, 1743, 1848, 1866

Local Bills: 1161, 1163

Committees: Criminal Justice (Vice Chairman); Ethics & Elections; Judiciary

McCALL, WAYNE C.—32nd District (Deceased April 11, 1980)
Co-sponsored: 121, 179, 212, 537, 540

Committees: Judiciary (Vice Chairman); Agriculture & General Legislation; Regulated Industries & Licensing

McPHERSON, TOM—92nd District
Sponsored: 51, 84, 160, 161, 181, 212, 294, 402, 403, 513, 767, 791, 815, 829, 830, 874, 915, 929, 973, 1037, 1038, 1039, 1158, 1409, 1678

Co-sponsored: 24, 121, 306, 406, 844, 1182, 1266, 1348, 1390, 1433, 1542, 1572, 1676, 1743, 1869, 1870, 1871, 1872, 1873, 1874, 1875, 1876, 1878

Local Bills: 1793

Committees: Natural Resources; Regulated Industries & Licensing; Tourism & Economic Development

MEEK, CARRIE P.—106th District
Sponsored: 259, 344, 393, 435, 756, 943, 983, 1012, 1046, 1120, 1121, 1122, 1123, 1226, 1272, 1598, 1673, 1905

Co-sponsored: 24, 121, 179, 306, 590, 739, 775, 798, 985, 1266, 1377, 1432, 1743, 1869, 1870, 1871, 1872, 1873, 1874, 1875, 1876, 1878

Committees: Corrections, Probation & Parole; Education, Higher; Health & Rehabilitative Services

MEFFERT, CHRISTIAN—32nd District
Committees: Commerce; Community Affairs; Finance & Taxation

Sponsored: 164, 165, 724, 725, 735, 797, 925, 1047

MELBY, ROBERT E.—59th District

Co-sponsored: 1, 6, 121, 122, 145, 158, 179, 201, 212, 306, 307, 389, 397, 525, 535, 764, 765, 773, 864, 1157, 1212, 1290, 1433, 1519, 1562, 1653, 1683, 1980, 1743

Local Bills: 564, 831, 878, 995, 1008, 1150, 1215, 1476, 1477, 1499

Committees: Education, K-12; Retirement, Personnel & Collective Bargaining; Veterans Affairs

MICA, JOHN L.—39th District
Sponsored: 201, 216, 655, 657, 712, 799

Co-sponsored: 122, 158, 179, 306, 481, 1004, 1116, 1117, 1252, 1254, 1743

Local Bills: 943, 1218, 1219, 1220, 1221, 1222, 1223

Committees: Appropriations; Community Affairs; Energy (Select); Ethics & Elections

MILLS, JON L.—27th District
Sponsored: 184, 366, 367, 373, 381, 382, 387, 421, 533, 893, 897, 908, 896, 939, 956, 974, 975, 1210, 1211, 1212, 1236, 1267, 1389, 1416, 1601

Co-sponsored: 150, 221, 724, 725, 731, 773, 849, 973, 1195, 1206, 1327, 1433, 1519, 1552, 1636, 1743, 1856

Committees: Education, Higher; Energy (Select); Governmental Operations; Insurance

MITCHELL, SAM—7th District
Sponsored: 301, 549, 776, 777, 1016, 1019, 1020, 1054, 1234, 1606

Co-sponsored: 87, 101, 121, 140, 141, 142, 143, 158, 212, 262, 306, 350, 377, 389, 537, 731, 859, 973, 1087, 1187, 1291, 1433, 1673, 1704, 1743, 1794, 1804

Local Bills: 1742

Committees: Agriculture & General Legislation; Finance & Taxation; Natural Resources

MOFFITT, H. LEE—66th District
Sponsored: 104, 105, 115, 144, 202, 292, 387, 504, 587, 701, 952, 1024, 1056, 1080, 1188, 1224, 1317, 1350, 1405, 1417, 1433, 1714

Co-sponsored: 121, 973, 1267, 1566, 1572, 1577, 1743, 1811

Local Bills: 1160, 1161, 1162, 1163, 1164, 1476

Committees: Commerce (Chairman); Appropriations; Governmental Operations; House Administration; Insurance; Rules & Calendar

MORGAN, HERBERT F.—12th District
Sponsored: 767, 815, 1170, 1286, 1291, 1327, 1362, 1379, 1600, 1667, 1721, 1796, 1868

Co-sponsored: 6, 179, 306, 505, 731, 1519, 1743

Local Bills: 1783

Committees: Appropriations (Chairman); Education, Higher; Natural Resources; Rules & Calendar

MYERS, WILLIAM G.—77th District
Sponsored: 99, 100, 101, 102, 103, 293, 388, 682, 866, 1007, 1306, 1374, 1406, 1522

Co-sponsored: 24, 33, 47, 107, 121, 122, 158, 179, 186, 201, 212, 306, 350, 773, 973, 1025, 1157, 1254, 1571, 1433, 1519, 1743

Local Bills: 883, 884, 885, 886, 887, 888, 889, 890, 892, 917, 982, 990, 1053, 1248, 1707

Committees: Community Affairs; Health & Rehabilitative Services; Retirement, Personnel & Collective Bargaining

NERGARD, CHARLES L.—76th District
Sponsored: 383, 494, 531, 1337
Co-sponsored: 1, 24, 47, 99, 121, 158, 179, 193, 212, 306, 329, 272, 377, 397, 525, 535, 541, 725, 764, 765, 973, 1025, 1433, 1680, 1712, 1743

Local Bills: 934, 1124

Committees: Education, K-12; Governmental Operations; Veterans Affairs

NUKOLLS, HUGH PAUL—91st District
Sponsored: 143, 304, 328, 377, 427, 441, 476, 488, 489, 490, 537, 543, 624, 625, 961, 1015, 1143, 1144
Co-sponsored: 1, 24, 122, 121, 158, 287, 306, 324, 338, 350, 378, 389, 397, 502, 525, 535, 540, 724, 725, 731, 764, 765, 864, 1025, 1040, 1087, 1182, 1212, 1254, 1433, 1545, 1552, 1553, 1603, 1651, 1678, 1680, 1743, 1841

Local Bills: 204, 501, 599, 605, 760, 761, 762, 763, 774, 910, 1458, 1514, 1518, 1594, 1626

Committees: Agriculture & General Legislation; Regulated Industries & Licensing; Rules & Calendar; Transportation; Veterans Affairs

OGDEN, CARL—20th District
Sponsored: 549, 1040, 1041, 1042, 1043, 1044, 1084, 1405, 1606
Co-sponsored: 306, 554, 736, 1027, 1038, 1039, 1277, 1433, 1678, 1743

Local Bills: 610, 612, 613, 614, 615

Committees: Regulatory Reform (Vice Chairman); Finance & Taxation; Regulated Industries & Licensing

O'MALLEY, TERENCE T.—85th District
Sponsored: 184, 244, 245, 331, 409, 413, 548, 600, 601, 686, 734, 826, 880, 881, 882, 1315, 1317, 1318, 1319, 1323, 1393, 1394, 1401, 1402, 1403, 1429, 1430, 1431, 1432, 1435, 1444, 1460
Co-sponsored: 24, 28, 51, 97, 121, 179, 212, 324, 391, 511, 540, 636, 973, 1025, 1261, 1433, 1435, 1439, 1743

Local Bills: 1793

Committees: Commerce; Corrections, Probation & Parole; Insurance

PAJCIC, STEVE—22nd District
Sponsored: 146, 176, 177, 205, 206, 207, 438, 1109, 1250, 1282, 1283, 1284, 1285, 1433, 1868
Co-sponsored: 57, 121, 598, 604, 646, 668, 736, 1236, 1242, 1276, 1379, 1519, 1577, 1743

Local Bills: 610, 611, 612, 613, 614, 615, 632, 666

Committees: Finance & Taxation (Chairman); Appropriations; Education, Higher; Retirement, Personnel & Collective Bargaining; Rules & Calendar

PATCHETT, R. DALE—48th District
Sponsored: 186, 199, 318, 661, 695, 743, 834, 835, 935, 955, 1022, 1085, 1353, 1712
Co-sponsored: 96, 101, 158, 212, 306, 406, 590, 1026, 1182, 1254, 1525, 1680, 1743

Local Bills: 814, 917

Committees: Community Affairs; Finance & Taxation; Natural Resources

PATTERSON, THOMAS R.—2nd District
Sponsored: 31, 191, 315, 988, 1337, 1848
Co-sponsored: 18, 20, 121, 158, 183, 252, 306, 377, 389, 540, 590, 731, 919, 1182, 1291, 1317, 1433, 1519, 1527, 1616, 1743

Local Bills: 1480, 1484, 1485, 1486, 1487

Committees: Education, Higher (Vice Chairman); Finance & Taxation; Retirement, Personnel & Collective Bargaining

PLUMMER, LAWRENCE H.—112th District
Sponsored: 53, 126, 127, 128, 174, 182, 251, 751, 828, 1299, 1367
Co-sponsored: 24, 121, 158, 193, 212, 226, 287, 489, 798, 973, 1290, 1433, 1743, 1869, 1870, 1871, 1872, 1873, 1874, 1875, 1876, 1878

Committees: Community Affairs; Health & Rehabilitative Services; Transportation

PRICE, DON C.—11th District
Sponsored: 247, 700, 872, 1170, 1291, 1317, 1326, 1327, 1600, 1607, 1721, 1868
Co-sponsored: 6, 158, 179, 193, 306, 505, 773, 973, 1519, 1743, 1804

Local Bills: 453, 1783

Committees: Community Affairs; Insurance; Retirement, Personnel & Collective Bargaining

READY, GENE—51st District
Sponsored: 178, 325, 377, 415, 1214, 1292, 1386, 1444
Co-sponsored: 24, 188, 212, 306, 540, 1004, 1116, 1117, 1433, 1678, 1743

Local Bills: 1554

Committees: Commerce; Ethics & Elections; Regulated Industries & Licensing

REYNOLDS, ROBERT—108th District
Sponsored: 42, 355, 356, 385, 386, 424, 486, 487, 515, 648, 649, 707, 911, 912, 1183, 1299, 1427
Co-sponsored: 24, 105, 121, 162, 201, 212, 259, 306, 340, 349, 435, 476, 477, 520, 532, 773, 758, 973, 1121, 1166, 1266, 1383, 1433, 1519, 1743, 1805, 1869, 1870, 1871, 1872, 1873, 1874, 1875, 1876, 1878

Committees: Criminal Justice; Health & Rehabilitative Services; Retirement, Personnel & Collective Bargaining

RICHMOND, RONALD R.—37th District
Sponsored: 227, 618, 793, 795, 1138, 1382, 1453, 1454, 1468, 1469, 1470, 1471, 1751
Co-sponsored: 158, 212, 973, 1377, 1433, 1583, 1591, 1618, 1678, 1743, 1811

Local Bills: 794, 878, 1217, 1476, 1477, 1516

Committees: Governmental Operations; Judiciary; Regulated Industries & Licensing; Rules & Calendar

ROBINSON, GROVER C. III—1st District
Sponsored: 31, 163, 231, 1090, 1102, 1196, 1197, 1287, 1356, 1519, 1616, 1868
Co-sponsored: 17, 18, 20, 24, 97, 141, 179, 252, 306, 324, 389, 1088, 1235, 1317, 1433, 1526, 1527, 1534, 1572, 1743

Local Bills: 1480, 1481, 1484, 1485, 1486, 1487

Committees: Appropriations (Chairman, General Government); Rules & Calendar; Tourism & Economic Development

ROSEN, VIRGINIA L.—100th District
Sponsored: 463, 545, 582, 583, 751, 769, 770, 771, 865, 1024, 1027, 1028, 1029, 1030, 1031, 1091, 1154, 1155, 1273, 1276, 1299, 1344, 1421
Co-sponsored: 97, 226, 340, 1743, 1805, 1869, 1870, 1871, 1872, 1873, 1874, 1875, 1876, 1878

Committees: Corrections, Probation & Parole; Education, Higher; Health & Rehabilitative Services

RYALS, JOHN L.—63rd District
Sponsored: 731, 851, 1056, 1714
Co-sponsored: 306, 973, 1676, 1678

RYALS, JOHN L. (Cont.)
Local Bills: 1160, 1161, 1162, 1163, 1164
Committees: Regulated Industries & Licensing (Chairman); Finance & Taxation; Rules & Calendar

SADOWSKI, WILLIAM E.—113th District
Sponsored: 145, 251, 341, 391, 437, 468, 469, 542, 545, 580, 604, 646, 668, 729, 773, 1080, 1118, 1119, 1136, 1299, 1364, 1428, 1462
Co-sponsored: 51, 74, 310, 387, 1376, 1377, 1433, 1467, 1566, 1601, 1743, 1869, 1870, 1871, 1872, 1873, 1874, 1875, 1876, 1878
Committees: Insurance (Chairman); Appropriations; Education, K-12; Rules & Calendar

SAMPLE, DOROTHY EATON—61st District
Sponsored: 1, 267, 277, 313, 571, 616, 737, 749, 750, 833, 905, 923, 942, 957, 967, 1134, 1372, 1407, 1436, 1463
Co-sponsored: 6, 158, 179, 296, 306, 349, 693, 773, 874, 1066, 1254, 1343, 1433, 1517, 1584, 1540, 1583, 1591, 1743
Local Bills: 564, 831, 1008, 1477
Committees: Criminal Justice; Natural Resources

SHACKELFORD, LAWRENCE F.—72nd District
Sponsored: 295, 540, 842, 844, 916, 1389, 1390
Co-sponsored: 17, 122, 158, 179, 306, 389, 537, 731, 973, 1087, 1133, 1572, 1625, 1743, 1866
Local Bills: 840, 841, 843, 1498, 1819, 1820
Committees: Agriculture & General Legislation; Natural Resources; Tourism & Economic Development

SHELDON, GEORGE H.—49th District
Sponsored: 288, 396, 475, 742, 1056, 1066, 1097, 1113, 1121, 1262, 1263, 1264, 1350, 1355, 1411, 1597, 1714, 1867
Co-sponsored: 121, 212, 310, 439, 773, 973, 1294, 1427, 1433, 1519, 1743
Local Bills: 1160, 1161, 1162, 1163, 1164
Committees: Regulatory Reform (Chairman); Appropriations; Corrections, Probation & Parole; Energy (Select); Health & Rehabilitative Services; Rules & Calendar

SILVER, RONALD A.—103rd District
Sponsored: 12, 55, 87, 148, 173, 174, 190, 327, 353, 374, 375, 386, 419, 420, 439, 449, 493, 520, 521, 524, 585, 605, 698, 707, 751, 768, 773, 929, 921, 1137, 1167, 1464
Co-sponsored: 24, 212, 217, 246, 353, 338, 340, 395, 486, 829, 830, 973, 1268, 1299, 1384, 1427, 1433, 1449, 1591, 1743, 1805, 1869, 1870, 1871, 1873, 1874, 1875, 1876, 1878
Committees: Commerce; Ethics & Elections; Judiciary

SMITH, CHARLES R.—30th District
Sponsored: 540, 587, 688, 941, 1186, 1187
Co-sponsored: 17, 24, 158, 179, 193, 306, 350, 389, 537, 731, 773, 1025, 1087, 1182, 1433, 1572, 1743, 1794
Local Bills: 813, 933
Committees: Agriculture & General Legislation; Judiciary; Natural Resources; Tourism & Economic Development

SMITH, JAMES HARRISON, JR.—55th District
Sponsored: 6, 155, 156, 163, 185, 346, 1130, 1131, 1132, 1336, 1338, 1340
Co-sponsored: 17, 121, 150, 179, 212, 214, 306, 307, 323, 349, 350, 372, 589, 731, 1025, 1254, 1433, 1440, 1572, 1583, 1743
Local Bills: 564, 831, 878, 995, 1159, 1216, 1217, 1477, 1499, 1516
Committees: Criminal Justice; Energy (Select); Natural Resources; Tourism & Economic Development

SMITH, LAWRENCE J.—96th District
Sponsored: 27, 30, 48, 54, 94, 276, 332, 395, 425, 1179, 1180, 1181, 1182
Co-sponsored: 12, 24, 121, 179, 212, 217, 324, 338, 349, 350, 773, 973, 1004, 1025, 1116, 1117, 1266, 1347, 1348, 1349, 1433, 1445, 1446, 1447, 1520, 1591, 1717, 1743, 1843, 1869, 1870, 1871, 1872, 1873, 1874, 1875, 1876, 1878
Local Bills: 1628, 1630, 2793
Committees: Criminal Justice; Ethics & Elections; Judiciary

SPAET, HAROLD W.—101st District
Sponsored: 42, 53, 87, 123, 148, 174, 190, 248, 302, 353, 354, 355, 356, 379, 383, 385, 500, 520, 521, 585, 656, 660, 697, 751, 773, 788, 798, 804, 1045, 1049, 1050, 1061, 1114, 1166, 1299, 1339, 1383, 1384, 1427, 1660
Co-sponsored: 14, 24, 38, 46, 65, 68, 96, 135, 141, 144, 150, 152, 194, 212, 214, 222, 226, 266, 322, 323, 324, 338, 340, 347, 348, 546, 973, 1025, 1133, 1182, 1183, 1242, 1252, 1254, 1266, 1295, 1375, 1376, 1377, 1433, 1591, 1743, 1805, 1869, 1870, 1871, 1872, 1873, 1874, 1875, 1876, 1878
Local Bills: 1248
Committees: Community Affairs; Energy (Select); Health & Rehabilitative Services

THOMAS, JOHN—17th District
Sponsored: 132, 1147, 1381
Co-sponsored: 57, 121, 179, 201, 212, 217, 259, 306, 350, 472, 554, 598, 731, 773, 973, 1025, 1121, 1266, 1433, 1519, 1743, 1794
Local Bills: 610, 611, 614, 632
Committees: Commerce; Judiciary; Retirement, Personnel & Collective Bargaining

THOMPSON, JAMES HAROLD—10th District
Sponsored: 47, 261, 364, 472, 571, 587, 720, 1087, 1250, 1291, 1329, 1362, 1363, 1597, 1607, 1721, 1880
Co-sponsored: 121, 179, 193, 311, 587, 505, 731, 773, 1327, 1519, 1572, 1577, 1591, 1743
Local Bills: 945, 1783
Committees: Judiciary (Chairman); Appropriations; Commerce; Natural Resources; Regulatory Reform; Rules & Calendar

TYGART, FREDERICK B.—23rd District
Sponsored: 186, 240, 265, 476, 477, 710, 939, 944, 945, 946, 947, 1002, 1053, 1269, 1270, 1271
Co-sponsored: 158, 179, 188, 212, 350, 540, 541, 596, 1157, 1295, 1359, 1433, 1601, 1743, 1848
Local Bills: 610, 611, 614, 632
Committees: Criminal Justice; Ethics & Elections; Insurance

UPCHURCH, HAMILTON D.—28th District
Sponsored: 306, 587, 634, 695, 997, 1268
Co-sponsored: 24, 47, 57, 121, 158, 179, 212, 350, 540, 541, 731, 773, 1295, 1375, 1433, 1601, 1743
Local Bills: 512, 991, 992, 1281
Committees: Commerce; Judiciary; Natural Resources

WARD, JAMES G.—6th District
Sponsored: 140, 197, 306, 658, 659, 830, 936, 937, 1051, 1052, 1053, 1184
Co-sponsored: 18, 141, 158, 179, 188, 212, 252, 295, 311, 337, 389, 540, 973, 1291, 1433, 1616, 1743
Local Bills: 1190, 1213, 1478, 1479, 1480, 1481, 1484, 1485, 1486, 1487, 1488, 1489, 1490, 1492, 1496, 1497, 1500
Committees: Insurance (Vice Chairman); Appropriations; Commerce; Energy (Select); Natural Resources

WARNER, STEPHEN JAMES—57th District
Sponsored: 9, 96, 194, 195, 326, 338, 642, 647, 670, 671, 683, 697, 807, 983, 984, 985, 1071, 1072, 1114, 1115, 1442, 1456

Co-sponsored: 128, 212, 250, 599, 859, 973, 1025, 1097, 1179, 1180, 1181, 1182, 1242, 1295, 1376, 1377, 1427, 1433, 1743

Local Bills: 384

Committees: Transportation (Vice Chairman); Education, Higher; Finance & Taxation

WATT, JAMES L.—80th District
Sponsored: 62, 192, 203, 312, 313, 567, 594, 692, 923, 972, 1103, 1177, 1370, 1571

Co-sponsored: 24, 121, 122, 158, 212, 306, 731, 973, 1025, 1032, 1039, 1254, 1433, 1534, 1544, 1601, 1743

Local Bills: 883, 884, 885, 886, 887, 888, 889, 890, 891, 892, 982, 990, 1083, 1248

Committees: Community Affairs; Finance & Taxation; Governmental Operations

WEINSTOCK, ELEANOR—79th District
Sponsored: 589, 590, 591, 682, 968, 1078, 1247

Co-sponsored: 57, 121, 183, 306, 973, 1121, 1295, 1375, 1376, 1377, 1433, 1743

Local Bills: 883, 884, 885, 886, 887, 888, 890, 891, 892, 982, 990, 1083, 1248

Committees: Education, K-12; Governmental Operations; Health & Rehabilitative Services

WILLIAMS, FRANK—25th District
Sponsored: 287, 307, 534, 540, 685, 852, 907, 987, 1058, 1059, 1060

WILLIAMS, FRANK (Cont.)
Co-sponsored: 179, 201, 306, 349, 389, 590, 773, 973, 1433, 1534, 1678, 1743

Local Bills: 432, 1564, 1582, 1595, 1599

Committees: Criminal Justice; Finance & Taxation; Regulated Industries & Licensing

WOODRUFF, T. M.—60th District
Sponsored: 208, 209, 221, 330, 350, 415, 466, 641, 747, 751, 1088

Co-sponsored: 24, 108, 148, 158, 190, 198, 201, 215, 226, 302, 307, 349, 354, 385, 427, 500, 537, 636, 798, 1114, 1157, 1166, 1377, 1384, 1433, 1558, 1583, 1591, 1743

Local Bills: 831, 878, 1008, 1159, 1216, 1217, 1476, 1516

Committees: Corrections, Probation & Parole; Education, Higher; Insurance

YOUNG, WALTER C.—95th District
Sponsored: 97, 146, 217, 222, 309, 456, 451, 572, 573, 574, 575, 576, 577, 639, 640, 644, 647, 772, 845, 846, 847, 848, 953, 954, 963, 970, 1098, 1009, 1158, 1172, 1173, 1174, 1316, 1320, 1321, 1322, 1347, 1348, 1349, 1433, 1448, 1668, 1796, 1806, 1845

Co-sponsored: 57, 148, 179, 212, 306, 338, 340, 382, 642, 648, 949, 973, 1179, 1180, 1181, 1242, 1384, 1519, 1736, 1743, 1869, 1870, 1871, 1872, 1873, 1874, 1875, 1876, 1878

Local Bills: 384, 1793

Committees: Education, K-12 (Chairman); Appropriations; Corrections, Probation & Parole; Energy (Select); Rules & Calendar

1974 Senate

MEMBERS OF THE SENATE
District 1-W.D. Childers (D), Pensacola*
District 2 Tom Tobiassen (R), Pensacola**
District 3-Dempsey J. Barron (D), Panama City*
District 4 Pat Thomas (D), Quincy**
District 5-Bob Saunders (D), Gainesville*
District 6- Kenneth H. MacKay, Jr. (D), Ocala**
District 7-Dan I. Scarborough (D), Jacksonville*
District 8- Lew Brantley (D), Jacksonville**
District 9-Mattox Hair (D), Jacksonville***
District 10-Edgar M. Dunn, Jr. (D), Daytona Beach**
District 11-Jim Glisson (R), Eustis*
District 12 Curtis Peterson (D), Lakeland**
District 13-Alan Trask (D), Fort Meade*
District 14 Ken Plante (R), Winter Park**
District 15-Walter Sims (R), Orlando*
District 16-Lori Wilson (I), Merritt Island**
District 17-John W. Vogt (D), Cocoa Beach*
District 18- John T. Ware (R), St. Petersburg**
District 19-Richard J. Deeb (R), St. Petersburg*
District 20-Henry B. Sayler (R), St. Petersburg**
District 21-David H. McClain (R), Tampa*
District 22 -Guy Spicola (D), Odessa**
District 23-Julian B. Lane (D), Tampa*
District 24- Tom Gallen (D), Bradenton**
District 25-Warren S. Henderson (R), Venice*
District 26-Harry A. Johnston, II (D), West Palm Beach**
District 27-Philip D. Lewis (D), West Palm Beach*
District 28- Don C. Childers (D), West Palm Beach**
District 29-Chester W. (Chet) Stolzenburg (R), Fort Lauderdale*
District 30-Jon C. Thomas (R), Fort Lauderdale**
District 31-David C. Lane (R), Fort Lauderdale*
District 32- William G. Zinkil, Sr. (D), Hollywood**
District 33-D. Robert Graham (D), Miami Lakes*
District 34-Sherman S. Winn (D), Miami**
District 35-Jack D. Gordon (D), Miami Beach*
District 36-George Firestone (D), Miami**
District 37-Kenneth M. Myers (D), Miami*
District 38-Ralph R. Poston, Sr. (D), Miami**
District 39-Vernon C. Holloway (D), Miami***
District 40-Richard (Dick) Renick (D), Coral Gables**
* Holdovers

** Elected General Election, November 5, 1974, for a four-year term
** Elected General Election, November 5, 1974, for a two-year term

1976 Senate

MEMBERS OF THE SENATE
District 1-W. D. Childers (D), Pensacola**
District 2-Tom Tobiassen (R), Pensacola*
District 3-Dempsey J. Barron (D), Panama City**
District 4-Pat Thomas (D), Quincy*
District 5-Sherrill (Pete) Skinner (D), Lake City**
District 6-Kenneth H. MacKay, Jr. (D), Ocala*
District 7-Dan I. Scarborough (D), Jacksonville**
District 8-Lew Brantley (D), Jacksonville*
District 9-Mattox Hair (D), Jacksonville**
District 10-Edgar M. Dunn, Jr. (D), Daytona Beach*
District 11-Jim Glisson (D), Eustis**
District 12-Curtis Peterson (D), Eaton Park*
District 13-Alan Trask (D), Fort Meade**
District 14-Kenneth A. Plante (R), Winter Park*
District 15-Bill Gorman (R), Tangerine**
District 16-Lori Wilson (I), Cocoa Beach*
District 17-John W. Vogt (D), Cocoa Beach**
District 18-John T. Ware (R), St. Petersburg*
District 19-Don Chamberlin (D), Clearwater**
District 20-Henry B. Sayler (R), St. Petersburg*
District 21-David H. McClain (R), Tampa**
District 22-Guy Spicola (D), Odessa*
District 23-Betty Castor (D), Tampa**
District 24-Tom Gallen (D), Bradenton*
District 25-Warren S. Henderson (R), Venice**
District 26-Harry A. Johnston, II (D), West Palm Beach*
District 27-Philip D. Lewis (D), West Palm Beach**
District 28-Don C. Childers (D), West Palm Beach*
District 29-George A. Williamson (R), Ft. Lauderdale**
District 30-Jon C. Thomas (D), Ft. Lauderdale*
District 31-Jim Scott (R), Ft. Lauderdale**
District 32-William G. Zinkil, Sr. (D), Hollywood*
District 33-D. Robert Graham (D), Miami Lakes**

District 34-Sherman S. Winn (D), Miami*
District 35-Jack D. Gordon (D), Miami Beach**
District 36-George Firestone (D), Miami*
District 37-Kenneth M. Myers (D), Miami**
District 38-Ralph R. Poston, Sr. (D), Miami*
District 39-Vernon C. Holloway (D), Miami**
District 40-Richard (Dick) Renick (D), Coral Gables*
* Holdovers
** Elected General Election November 2, 1976

1978 Senate

MEMBERS OF THE SENATE

District 1-W. D. Childers (D), Pensacola*
District 2-Tom Tobiassen (R), Pensacola**
District 3-Dempsey J. Barron (D), Panama City*
District 4-Pat Thomas (D), Quincy**
District 5-Sherrill (Pete) Skinner (D), Lake City*
District 6-K. H. "Buddy" MacKay (D), Ocala**
District 7-Dan I. Scarborough (D), Jacksonville*
District 8-Joe Carlucci (D), Jacksonville**
District 9-Mattox Hair (D), Jacksonville*
District 10-Edgar M. (Ed) Dunn, Jr. (D), Daytona Beach**
District 11-Vince Fechtel, Jr. (R), Leesburg***
District 12 Curtis Peterson (D), Eaton Park**
District 13 Alan Trask (D), Fort Meade*
District 14-George Stuart, Jr. (D), Orlando**
District 15-Bill Gorman (R), Tangerine*
District 16-Clark Maxwell, Jr. (R), Melbourne**
District 17-John W. Vogt (D), Cocoa Beach*
District 18-John T. Ware (R), St. Petersburg**
District 19-Don Chamberlin (D), Clearwater*
District 20 -Mary R. Grizzle (R), Indian Rocks Beach**
District 21-David H. McClain (R), Tampa*
District 22-Malcolm E. Beard (D), Seffner****
District 23-Pat Frank (D), Tampa***
District 24-Patrick K. "Pat" Neal (D), Bradenton**
District 25-Warren S. Henderson (R), Venice*
District 26-Harry A. Johnston, II (D), West Palm Beach**
District 27-Philip D. Lewis (D), West Palm Beach*
District 28-Don C. Childers (D), West Palm Beach**
District 29-George A. Williamson (R), Ft. Lauderdale*
District 30-Van B. Poole (R), Ft. Lauderdale**
District 31-Jim Scott (R), Ft. Lauderdale*
District 32-Ken Jenne (D), Hollywood**
District 33-John A. Hill (D), Miami Lakes***
District 34-Sherman Winn (D), Miami**
District 35-Jack D. Gordon (D), Miami Beach*

District 36-Paul B. Steinberg (D), Miami Beach**
District 37-Kenneth M. Myers (D), Miami*
District 38-Bob McKnight (D), Miami**
District 39-Vernon C. Holloway (D), Miami*
District 40-Dick Anderson (D), Miami**
*Holdovers
**Elected General Election November 7, 1978 for term of 4 years
***Elected General Election November 7, 1978 for term of 2 years
****Elected Special General Election March 25, 1980

1980 Senate

MEMBERS OF THE SENATE
District 1-W. D. Childers (D), Pensacola**
District 2-Tom Tobiassen (R), Pensacola*
District 3-Dempsey J. Barron (D), Panama City**
District 4-Pat Thomas (D), Quincy*
District 5-Sherrill "Pete" Skinner (D), Lake City**
District 6-George Kirkpatrick (D), Gainesville**
District 7-Dan Jenkins (D), Jacksonville**
District 8-Joe Carlucci (D), Jacksonville*
District 9-Mattox Hair (D), Jacksonville**
District 10-Edgar M. (Ed) Dunn, Jr. (D), Daytona Beach*
District 11-Richard H. (Dick) Langley (R), Clermont**
District 12-Curtis Peterson (D), Eaton Park*
District 13-Alan Trask (D), Winter Haven**
District 14-George Stuart, Jr. (D), Orlando*
District 15-Toni Jennings (R), Orlando**
District 16-Clark Maxwell, Jr. (R), Melbourne*
District 17-John W. Vogt (D), Cocoa Beach**
District 18-John T. Ware (R), St. Petersburg*
District 19-Gerald S. (Jerry) Rehm (R), Dunedin**
District 20-Mary R. Grizzle (R), Indian Rocks Beach*
District 21-David H. McClain (R), Tampa**
District 22-Malcolm E. Beard (D), Seffner***
District 23-Pat Frank (D), Tampa**
District 24-Patrick K. "Pat" Neal (D), Bradenton*
District 25-Warren S. Henderson (R), Venice**
District 26-Harry A. Johnston, II (D), West Palm Beach*
District 27-Tom Lewis (R), Palm Beach**
District 28-Don C. Childers (D), West Palm Beach*
District 29-J. W. "Bill" Stevens (R), Parkland**
District 30-Van B. Poole (R), Fort Lauderdale*
District 31-Jim Scott (R), Ft. Lauderdale**
District 32-Ken Jenne (D), Hollywood*
District 33-John A. Hill (D), Miami**
District 34-Sherman Winn (D), Miami*
District 35-Jack D. Gordon (D), Miami Beach**

District 36-Paul B. Steinberg (D), Miami Beach*
District 37-Gwen Margolis (D), Miami Beach**
District 38-Bob McKnight (D), Miami*
District 39-Richard (Dick) Renick (D), Miami**
District 40-Dick Anderson (D), Miami*
*Holdovers
**Elected General Election November 4, 1980
***Elected Special General Election March 25, 1980

Index

Symbols

1960 Cuban Air Lift 104
1980 Speaker's race 68
38th parallel 19
48 Hours 107
60 Minutes 107
60 Minutes TV magazine 64
60 Oaks 138

A

Abberger, Lester 134
ABC TV 85
Abrams, Mike 39
Adams, Sam
Administrative Procedures Act 3
African Americans 103, 110, voters 18
Air Force 13
Alaska 105
Alda, Alan 84
All-American 7
All-Pro Safety 92
Allen, Dr. Morris 69
Allen, Ellen 85
Allen, Joe 85, 93, 103
Althea, Mamma Range 135
Amaryllis 14, 15, 16
America 22, 101, 137
American 19, 21
American prisoners of war 20
Americans 19, 101
amicus curiae briefs 54
Adkins, Billy 90
Adkins, Dianne 90
Anderson, Dick 92, 93, 103
Anderson, Joy 93
Andrew's 103
Andrews, Andy 2, 93, 103
Andrews, Bill 108

Angor Watt 22
anti-ERA crowd 84
Appropriations Committee 64
Appropriations Conference Committee 64, 105
Appropriations Subcommittee 104
Apthorp, Jim 28, 48
ARCOM 22
Areas of Critical State Concern 93
Arkansas 104
Army 5, 18, Commendation Medal 22
Artificial Reef program 97, 98
Arvida 135
Ashler, Phil 108, 109
Askew, Donna Lou 106
Askew, Reubin 3, 4, 28, 41, 48-9, 91, 100, 106, 109
Assistant Secretary of the Treasury 4
Associated Press 85
"Attack on Entebbe" 67
Auburn University 27
Avon, Randy 38, 99

B

Babcock Companies 135
baby boomers 98
Bahamas 32
Baker, Connie 39
Baker, Maxine 39
Baker-Hamilton Commission on U.S. National Security 101
Bank of America 3
Banty Rooster 96
Baptist Hospital in Kendall 38
Barnett Bank 3
Barron, Dempsey 2, 17, 89, 91-2, 96-8, 101, 104, 109, 156
Barron, Territo 92
Batchelor, Dick 108

The Golden Years ...

Becker, Representative Alan 38
Bell, Sam 48, 55, 67, 134
Bendixen, Sergio 140
Bergida, Hal 83
Bermello, Willy 135
Bermont, Peter 39
Bermont, Ronnie 39
Beta Gamma Sigma 17
bible-toting Baptist 65
Big Apple 17
Bill, Fulford 48
billet 21
Bishop, Ann 107
Blaik, Red 19
Blair, Curt 94, 95
Blank, Phil 53
Blumberg, David 63, 69, 71, 135
Blumberg, Lee 63
Bob, Senator McKnight 55
Boca Raton 14, 27
Boecklen, Connie 39
Boecklen, Larry 7, 39
Bonifay 92
Book, Ronnie 133
Boston 86
Bradenton 90, 99
Brandon 68
Brantley, Lew 70, 71, 91
Brodie, Jim 108
Brooklyn 17
Broward 100
Brown, Hyatt 64, 66, 67, 68, 100
Brown, Jo 90
Brown, Tom 90
Brown, Tony 90
Bryant, Farris 3, 6
bubba 93
Bucher, Lloyd 20
Bue, Vern 29
Bundy, Theodore 54
Burger King 135
Burkholtz, Yvonne 55
Burnsed, Bev 137
Bush, George H.W., President 100
Bush, Jeb 52, 109

BusinessWeek 140
Butterworth, Bob 108, 109
Byrd, Harry, Jr. 9, 18
Byrd, Robert 18

C

Cabinet 66, 93, 103
Caddell, Pat 140
Cadman, George 39
Cadley, William 19
Caldwell, Bill 138
Calley, Lt. William 19
Cambodia 21
Camp Red Cloud 20, 21
Capitol 28, 29, 103
Capitol bureau reporters 101
Carlucci, Joe 99
Carter Administration 68, supporters 68
Carter, Jimmy, President 38, 68, 100, 102, 104, 139, 140
Cassidy, Patrick 20, 22
Castor, Betty 68
Castro, Fidel 103-104
Cedar Key 40
Central Park 19
Central Virginia 9
Chaplain School 18
Chapman, Alvah 135
Cherry, Gwen 67
Chief Justice of the Florida Supreme Court 7, 90
Childers, W.D. 2, 92, 95, 96, 97, 104
Children's Home Society 106
Chiles, Lawton 2, 28, 140, 141
civil rights 110
Civil Rights Act 18
Claiborne, Caroline 5
Clark, Dick 38, 47, 48, 51, 53
Class of 1978 91
Clayton, Ralph 16
Clayton, Wiley 7
Clerk of the House of Representatives Emeritus 69

Clerk's Manual 108
Clermont 95
Cleveland Indians 2
Clinton Administration 31
Clinton, Bill 104
CNN 21, 54
Cobb, Chuck 135
Coburn, David 64
Coca-Cola Corporation 68
Coconut Grove 40, 71
Codina, Armando 135
Coffman, Dick 4
Colson, Bill 135
Columbia 18
Commerce Committee 93
Committee on Health and Rehabilitative Services 90
Community Affairs 90
Community Care for the Elderly 102, Act 64
Congress 18, 83, 100
Cooper, George 39
Coral Gables 7, 31, 54, 96, Jaycees 39, 99
Coral Reef Hospital 93, 94
Corrections Subcommittee 54, meeting 48
Costello, Michael V. 54
Costello v. Wainwright 54
Council of State Legislatures 108
Courtney radio show 54
Cox, Linda 108
Craig, Gus 50, 65
Crawford, Bob 108
Crenshaw, Ander 16
Crist, Charlie 109
Croft, Steve 107
Cuba 103, 104
Cuban 55, missile crisis 15, 156, prisoners 104
Culbreath, John 108
Cullom, Bill 135
Cusick, Mike 64

D

Dade County 21, 51, senators 89, Legislative Delegation 29, 51, 89, 99-100, 102, legislators 100, Young Democratic ticket 37
Dade senators 89
Daily, Steve 54
Dallas 27
Dartmouth 48
David and Goliath fight 94
Daytona Beach 64, 90
Dean of the Senate 91
"Death with Dignity" 52
Deland 7, 16
de la Parte, Louis 17, 156
Delray Beach Inlet Board 2
Delta Sigma Pi Business Fraternity 8
Democrat 22, 28, 90, 100, 109
Democratic Caucus 67, Convention 103, nomination 29, nominee 85, Party 33, 40, 141, primary 6, 28
Democrats 6, 41, 97, 104
Department of Education 102
Department of Highway Safety and Motor Vehicles 56
DePontis, George 28, 69
Devane, Rhett 5
Dickinson, Fred 3, 6
Disney 14
Distinguished Service Cross 20
District 116 47, 63
District 119 29, 31, 32, 33
District 38 71, 83, campaign 83, race 84, Senate seat 85
districts 115-119 47
DMZ 19, 20
Doak Campbell stadium 138
Dobson, Jack 9
Douglass, Dexter 140
Dubbin, Murray 30
Duck's Nest 15

Duke 48
Dunbar, David 97
Dunbar, Pete 108
Dunn, Ed 108
Dupont Plaza Hotel 83
Dyckman, Martin 98

E

Easley, Betty 108
Eastern United States 29
Eaton Park 97
Eccles, Patsy 105
Eckerd, Jack 22, 28, 68
Eckhart, Jim 47
Ed, Dr. Massey 135
Election Day 32, 33
Electoral College votes 112
Elkton, Virginia 9
Elliott Key 16
environmental community 51
Epiphany Lutheran School 141
Equal Rights Amendment (ERA) 83-84
Erhman, Max 10
Ervin, Sam 18
Executive Branch 7

F

Fair, Tal 135
Faircloth, Earl 28
Fascell, Dante 18, 103
FBMC 141
Federal Reserve Board 139
Federal Systems Division 13
Fellows Program 96
Fenner, Lane 138
Ferre, Maurice 39
Fine, Marty 135
Firestone, George 54
First Friday 39
First Marine Banks 3
Fisher, Lou 135
Fisher, Steve 28

Fitzgerald, Lynn 39
Fitzgerald, Mike 39
Five Outstanding Young Men In Florida 99
Florida 138
Florida Bar 106, *Journal* 54
Florida Catholic Conference 65
Florida Chamber of Commerce 52, 134, 140
Florida Constitution 29, 47
Florida Constitutional Revision Commission 109
Florida Department of Transportation 135
Florida Government 7, 8
Florida Handbook 69
Florida House 111
Florida House Chamber 40
Florida House of Representatives 3, 16, 30, 32, 33, 47, 63, 71
Florida Jaycees 38, 99
Florida Keys 29, 47, 93, 94
Florida Keys Community College 135
Florida legislature 65
Florida Management Fellows 96
Florida Medical Association 133
Florida politics 7-8, 69
Florida Senate 4, 71, 92
Florida Southern College 1, 5, 7-8, 13, 17, 19, 39, 67, 97, 101
Florida Speaker of the House of Representatives 13
Florida State University 3, 7, 137
Florida Supreme Court 106
Florida Times Union 57
Florida Trend magazine 56
Floridians 40, 69, 98, 104, 109, 112, 133
Flynn, Bill 47
Foote, Tad 135
Forbes, John 64
Ford, Gerald, President 4
Ford-Coates, Barbara 108, 109
Fort Hamilton 17, 18, 19
Fort Myers 16, 139

Fortune, Ed 64, 66-67
Fox, Lanny 1
Fox, Roberta 96
Frank, Pat 90
Frazier, Scotty 133
Freeman, Lester 135
French, John 133
Friday, Elmer 16
Fringe Benefits Management Company 141
FSC 5, 6, 7, 8, 9, 13
FSU 7, 8, 9, 13, 16, 17
FSU's School of Business 7
Ft. Lauderdale 38
Fulford, Bill 48

G

Gainesville 102
Gallagher, Tom 31, 38, 40
Gardner, Bud 108
Gautier, Jeff 29, 31, 32, 33, 39
General Appropriations Bill 7
Georgia 68, 100
GMAC 134, 135
GMCC 134, 135
Golden Age 98
Golden Years, The
    98, 110, 111, 112, of the Florida Legislature 108, 112
Gong, Eddie 86
Gonzalez, Larry 13
Goode, Ray 135
Gordon, Elaine 38
Gordon, Jack 55, 65, 92, 101, 106, 110, 111
Gordon, Seth 69
Gore, Albert 18
governor's mansion 49
Graham, Adele 64, 93, 102
Graham, Bob 64, 67, 68, 89, 90, 93, 97, 101, 102, 103, 109, 134, 140
Greater Miami Chamber of Commerce 134
Greater Miami Citizens Against Crime 134

Greene, Raleigh 67
Gregory, Gary 32, 39
Gregory, Lee 7
Gregory, Shelia 39
Grizzle, Mary 108
Gruber, Don 71, 86
Gulf Stream 104
Gunter, Bill 134, 139
Gustafson, Tom 108

H

Haben, Ralph 68
Haben, Representative 68
Hair, Mattox 70, 92, 106, 107
Hall, Don 7
Halstead, Sherry 63
Hamilton, Lee 101
Harper, Valerie 84
Harris, Marshall 39, 49
Hartnett, Bob 39
Harvard 63, 86, 109, law school graduate 138
Harvester, James 17
Hazelton, Representative Don 48
Head Start Program 27
Hector, Bob 51, 54
Henderson, Warren 17, 95, 156
Hialeah 96, Race Track 96
High, Robert King 14
Hispanics 110
Hobe Sound 14
Hodes, Dick 66
Hollahan 91
Hollahan, George 37, 91
Holland, Spessard 18
Holloway, Vernon 38, 92, 93, 103
Hollywood 89, 90
Homestead 7
Hong Kong 21, 22
hooch 21
Hoover, J. Edgar 108
Horkan, Tom 65
Horne, Mallory 90

The Golden Years ...   239   Robert McKnight

House 30, 41, 47, 48, 50, 51, 53, 56, 65, 66, 67, 68, 69, 70, 71, 90, 101, 102, 103, 108, 110, 111
House Appropriations Committee 47
House Appropriations Subcommittee 102
House Bill 804 49
House Chamber 40, 71
House Democratic caucus 40
House District 116 63
House Governmental Operations Committee 54
House Health and Mental Health Subcommittee 65
House members 69
House of Representative conferees 105
House of Representatives 18, 31, 41, 47, 49, 51, 69, 71, 84, 93, 101
House on the Appropriations Conference Report 137
House Subcommittee on Corrections 41
Howard, Ray 48
HRS department 97
Hugli, Bob 53
Humphrey, Hubert 21
Huntsville, Alabama 13, 17, 27
Hurwitz, Bob 28

I

I Corps Headquarters 20
IBM 13, 14, 17, 21, 22, 27, 28, 29, 37, 96
IBMer 28, 97
Indian River Community College 135
Indiana 101
Iran 104
IRCC faculty 136, 137
Israeli 67
Ivy League school 4

J

Jack, Senator Gordon 65
Jackson, Henry "Scoop" 101
Jacksonville 6, 55, 64, 70, 89, 98, 106, 138, 139
James, Bill 108
James, Chappy 103
Japan 22
Jaycee "Speak Up" program 29
Jaycees 38
Jenne, Ken 89, 90, 92, 134
Jennings, Toni 108
Johnson, Lyndon, President 18, 94, 95
Johnston, Harry 71, 89, 100, 101, 105, 106, 107, 134, 139
Johnston, Mary 107
Joint Legislative Committee 3
Jones, Dennis 108
Jones, Fred 108
Jones, Tom 7

K

Kahn, Larry 63, 138
Kelly, Scott 6
Kendale Lakes 30
Kendall 93
Kennedy, John F., President 15, 95, 98, 100, 104, 156
Kennedy, Robert 15, 156
Kennedy, Ted 100
Kershaw, Joe Lang 108
Key West 85, 93, 94, 103, 135
Keys 85, 97, 103, 104
Kiddy Fair 3
Kim, Sergeant 22
Kim-shi 22
kimchi 22
Kimpo Airport 22
King, Larry 21, 54
King, Robert High 14
Kirk, Claude 7, 13, 14, 15, 16, 22, 28, 49

The Golden Years ... 240 *Robert McKnight*

Kirkpatrick, George 99
Kiser, Curt 108
Korea 19, 21, 22, 27
Korean War 20
Koufax, Sandy 3
Krog, Jim 28, 141
Kutun, Barry 38, 41, 51, 53

L

Labor unions 31
Lake City 90
Lake Okeechobee 50, 51, cleanup legislation 50
Lake Worth 1, 2, 3, 9, 14, 21, High School 2, 3, 89, Trojan football team 41
Lakeland 6, 137
Lam, Bill 9
Langley, Dick 95
Leadership Florida Program 134
Leech, Les 52, 141
Letts, Gavin 106
Levan, Alan 37
Leverentz, Carl 2
Levitt, Ron 28-29, 33
Lewis, Catherine 2
Lewis, Fred 7
Lewis, Gerald 63
Lewis, Harold 2
Lewis, Phil 89, 90, 92, 105
Liberty City 135
Lieberman, Ron 37
Limbaugh, Andrew 4
Limbaugh, Bailey, 4
Limbaugh, Michell 4
Limbaugh, Riley 4
Limbaugh, Von 4
Lippman, Fred 134
Lithohaus Printers 5
Littlejohn, Chuck 50
lobbyists 7, 41, 47, 50, 52, 53, 105, 106, 107, 111, 135, 157
Long, Russell 18
Los Angeles Dodgers 3

Lowell 54
Lugar, Richard 101
Lytal, Lake 2

M

M*A*S*H 20
Mabe, Susan 47
McCarthy, Eugene 19
MacKay, Buddy 89, 99, 140
MacMillan, Hugh 41
Majority Leader of the House 48
Management Fellows 97
Manhattan 19
Mann, Frank 139
Mansfield, Mike 101
Margolis, Gwen 90, 108
Mariel Boat Lift 103, 133
Marine Corps 4, 19
Marks, John 141
Marlin, Bob 40
Martinez, Bob 55, 109, 139, 140
Massachusetts 100
Massey, Ed 135
Masters of Business Administration degree 7
Matthews, Jack 6
Maxwell, Clark 101
Maxwell, Russ 22
Mayfair Church of Christ 27
MBA 13, 63
McArthur, John 3
McCaffery, Pat 50, 150
McCarthy, Eugene 19
McClain, David 108
McCoy, Don 2
McDermott, John 56, 64
McGovern, George 138
McKnight, Bob 8, 10, 14, 22, 32, 40, 55, 85, 142, 157
McKnight, Elizabeth Michelle 4, 38, 40, 57, 93, 94, 138
McKnight, Heather 4
McKnight, Lisa 4
McKnight, Miles 4

McKnight, Norah 4
McKnight, Robert Joel "Bobby" 64, 71, 93, 138
McKnight, Susan 2, 4, 13, 16, 27, 31, 33, 37, 38, 40, 47, 49, 57, 63, 64, 66, 67, 69, 71, 83, 84, 85, 86, 90, 92, 93, 95, 97, 102, 103, 105, 106, 107, 135, 137, 139, 141, 155
McKnight campaign 33, Commission 133, 134, Financial Corporation 141
McLemore, Jim 135
McMullen, Andy 97
Medicaid program 106
Meek, Carrie 108
Mental Health Association 29, 37
Merrill, Clark 31, 32
Merritt Island 51, 101
Meyer, Hank 135
Miami 2, 13, 16, 27, 28, 29, 30, 37, 38, 39, 40, 47, 49, 51, 54, 66, 67, 69, 70, 71, 86, 89, 91, 92, 97, 98, 99, 104, 138
Miami Airport Sheraton Hotel 89
Miami Beach 65, 90, 110
Miami Dolphins 39, 92
Miami Herald 21, 22, 32, 56, 135
Miami *Herald* article 64
Miami Marriott Hotel 63
Miami *News* 32, 137
Miami Springs Villas 16
Miami Urban League 135
Miami's Cuban community 104
Miami's Young Democrats 28
Mica, John 108
Michigan 28
Mills, Jon 102
Mills, Wilbur 18
Minnesota 19
Mitchell, Peter 47
Mixson, Wayne 103
Moffitt, Lee 41
Mondale, Walter 100

Monroe County 93, 94, 95, 103
Montana 101
Moore, Mary Tyler 84
Morgan, Herb 56
Morgenstern, Rhoda 84
Morris Award 57, 101
Morris, Dr. Allen 69
Most Outstanding First-Term Member of the Senate 101
Most Valuable Member of the Senate 101
Mother's Day 100
Mott, Stuart 84
Mount Fuji 22
Mr. Speaker 65
My Lai 19
Myers, Ken 89, 99, 104

N

Nagle, Dianne 5
Natural Resources Committee 48, 50
NBC-TV 21
Neal, Pat 90, 99
Nelson, Bill 38, 47, 99
Neonatal Intensive Care Program 57
New Jersey 7
New York 15, 18, City 17, 18, 19, Yankees 3
Newman, Bud 47
Nixon, Richard, President 19, 20, 96
Noonan, Karl 39
North Florida 16, 91
North Florida politicos 16
North Korea 20
North Koreans 20
North Miami 7, 13
North Vietnam 20
Nunn, Sam 100

O

Ocala 6, 89
O'Connor, Bill 1
Old Capitol 49
Old Constitution 7

Omicron Delta Kappa 8
On Wings of Eagles 21
Orange Bowl 135
Orlando 14, 16, 48, 70, 90, *Sentinel* 137
Ormond Beach 48
Outstanding Alumni Award 8
Outstanding First Term Member of the House 57
Oviedo 16, 86

P

Pace 64
Pajcic Campaign for Governor 64
Pajcic, Steve 55, 138
Pajcic-Mann campaign staff 140
Pajcic-Mann ticket 139
Palm Beach 2, 100, County 2, 3, 4, 14, 21, 41, 106, Legislative Delegation 3, School Board 41, High 41, *Post* 47
Palmer, Patsy 134
Palmetto 68
Panama City 17, 89, 156
Pankowski, Joe 97
Pankowski, Mary 97
Pantin, Leslie 135
Papy, Charlie 31, 38, 40, 47
pari-mutuel gaming industry 65
Parole and Probation Commission 48
Patchett, Dale 108
PDC 69, 138, development activities 138
Pearson, Drew 21
Pensacola 3, 28, 95, 103, 109
Pentagon 18, 20
Pentagon policy 19
Pepper, Claude 2, 18, 155
Perot, Ross 20
Peterson, Curtis 92, 97, 98
Pettigrew, Dick 13, 37, 38, 91, 100
Phelps, John 47, 58
Philadelphia 18
Pi Kappa Alpha 5, 8

Pier House 135
ping-pong diplomacy 96
Pingree, David 97
Planned Development Corporation 69
Plant City 53
Plante, Ken 16, 86
Poole, Van 108
Pork Choppers 16, 67, 91, 98
Poston, Ralph 69, 70, 71, 83, 84, 85, campaign brochure 83
POWs 20
Prado, Marta 109
President of the Florida Senate 6
Princeton University 4, 41, 138
pro-ERA crowd 84
professional lobbyist 106
Public Counsel 51
Public Service Commission 51
Pueblo 20
Putney, Michael 107

Q

quorum of the House 50

R

Rayborn, Sam 18
Reagan International Airport 102
Reagan, Ronald, President 100
Recycling Business Ventures 140
Red China 96
Redford, Robert 86
Redlands 52
Redman, Jim 53
Reed, Charlie 133-134
Reed, Nat 14
Reigle, Don 28
Renick, Ralph 107
Reno, Janet 31
Rent a Supporter 30, 156
"report card" 63
Republic of Korea 22
Republican 13, 15, 19, 22, 39, 71, 90, 95, 97, 104, 109, candidates

31, 67, colleagues 31, opponent 33, Party 4, 6, 90, primary 28, Senate leader 86
Rest and Recuperation 21, 22
Reuschling, Dr. Tom 8
Revell, Walter 135
Richard, Barry 108
Richmond, Ron 108
Rish, Billy Joe 108
Rivers, Mendall 18
Riviera Beach 3
Roberts, John 89
Roberts, B.K. 47
Roberts Rules of Order 1
Robertson, Pat 9
Robertson, Willis A. 9
Robinson, Jane 108
Rockefeller, Nelson 15
Rodgers, Paul 2
Rogers, William 5
Rookie of the Year 29
Roosevelt, Theodore 142
Rose, Stu 28, 69
Ross, Steve 28
ROTC 5, Distinguished Military Graduate 8, 17
Ruben, Bill 133, 135
Run-off elections 33
Russell, Richard 18
Russians 15, 156
Ryalls, Bob 28
Ryals, John 68
Ryll, Frank 140

S

Sachs, Ron 69
Sackett, Dr. Walter 51, 52
Sadowski, Bill 67
Sailors, Ree 134
SALT II 100
Sarasota 95, League of Woman Voters 109
Saunders, Bob 91
Save Our Rivers 138

Saving Private Ryan 19
Scarborough, Dan 89, 92
Schiavo, Terri 65
Schlesinger, Richard 107
Score, Herb 2
Scott, Jim 108
Scott, Kelly 6
Secretary of Children and Families 109
Seeker, Dr. Bill 135
Selmon Brothers 99
Seminoles 13
Senate 41, 56, 66, 68, 69, 70, 71, 86, 89, 90, 91, 92, 93, 95, 96, 97, 98, 99, 101, 102, 108, 109, 110, 111, campaign 85, Chamber 70, 107, colleagues 71, Committee on Health and Rehabilitative Serv 94, 104, District 38 70, floor 109, Health and Rehabilitative Services Committe 64, 133, 134, office building 71, president 91, rules of ethics 70, staff 108
Sentry Press 5
Seoul 20, 22
Sessums, Terrell 8
Shapiro, Ellison 47
Sheldon, George 55, 56, 67
Shell Chemical 13
Shenandoah Valley 9
Sheridan, Mike 31, 141
Sheriff of Broward County 89
Sherman, Winn 13, 89
Shevin, Bob 67, 68, 70
Shreve, Jack 51
Shultz, Fred 139
Siegendorff, Arden 28
Silver, Ron 108
Simon and Garfunkel 136
Simons, Colonel Bull 20
Singer Island 14, 15
Sixty Oaks 138, 153
Skinner, Pete 90
"Sleepy Hollow," 51

Smith, Eric 38
Smith, Jim 28, 139
"Son Tay Raid," 20
South 7, 18
South Dade 38, 39, 48, 52, 69,
    County district 29, District 119
    32
South Florida
    50, 63, 104, 107, 109, HRS
    97, members 50, news outlets
    84, senators 91
South Grade 9
South Korea 20
South Miami 38, 40
South Miami Hospital 71
South Vietnam 18
Southeast Asia 22
Sparkman, John 17, 18
Speaker 48, 50, 51, 52, 53, 55, 56,
    57, 64, 65, 67, 68
Speaker, Florida of the House of
    Representatives 37, 52, 67
Speaker Pro-Tempore of the Florida
    House of Representatives 66, 68,
    71
Speaker's race 53, 66
Speakership 53, 66
Spearman, Guy 28
Spelios, George 141
Spurrier, Steve 138
St. Augustine 50, 65
St. Petersburg *Times* 67, 98, 101
Stack, Bud 39
Standing Room Only (SRO) 30, 156
State Comptroller 3, Constitution 7
Government 7, of the State Address
    134, Senate 41
Stearns, Gene 13
Steinberg, Paul 38, 90
Steinem, Gloria 84
Sternstein, Gerry 53
Steven, Ted 105
Strategic Arms Limitation Agreement
    100
Strickland, Lorraine 141

Stuart, George 90
Student Union 9
Subcommittee on Health and Mental
    Health 64
Sundberg, Alan 106
Sunrise 52, Community 52, 141,
    School 57
Sunset Act 99, Road 40
Sutton, Bill 108
Sykes, Bob 18

T

Taiwan 21
Tallahassee 9, 15, 29, 39, 40, 50,
    56, 63, 64, 84, 90, 93, 105,
    107, 140
Tallman, Ben 1
Tamiami Trail 47
Tampa 8, 17, 41, 54, 66, 68, 90,
    98, 156
Tampa Bay Buccaneers 99
Tate, Dr. Rob 8
Taylor, Rick 138
teacher's union 31
Thailand 21, 22
the 38th 86, 89
The Bull 21
The Candidate 86
The Redneck Party 67
The Robert W. McKnight Administra-
    tion Building 52
Thomas, Jerry 3, 4, 7, 37, 55, 90
Thomas, Jon 108
Thomas, Pat 108
Thomas, Stu 135
Thompson, James Harold 108
Thrasher, John 133
Thurmond, Strom 18
Tiger Bay Club 85, 107, Debate 83
Timberlane Church of Christ 141
Time magazine 64
Tokyo 21
Tolton, Jere 108
Tornillo, Pat 31

Traurig, Bob 135
trophies 105
Troxel, Dick 28
Tucker, Don 40, 41, 53, 64, 68, 102
TV evangelist 9

U

U.S. Army 7, 17, Chaplain School 17, 18, post 17, Attorney General 31, Capitol 9, Constitution 83, House Foreign Relations Committee 103, Senate 16, 28, 37, 38, space program 13
UCLA 22
Uganda 67
Uijongbu, South Korea 13, 19, 20
United States 22, 95, 108, Senate 21
United Teachers of Dade County 55
United Way 134
University of Florida 1, 2, Kentucky 7, Miami 7, 135, Texas 9, West Florida 96
Upchurch, Hamilton 108

V

Vasalinda, Mike 84
Venice 17, 156
Vero Beach 138
Viet Cong 22
Vietnam 6, 7, 19, 20, 22, 27, protests 19, War 5, 18, 21, army chaplains 18, guests 18
Villella, Ron 103
VIP guests 18
Virginia 9, 18
Visiting Committee for the University of Miami School of Business 134
Vogt, John 92, 108
Voich, Dan 17

W

Wainwright, Louie 54
Walking Lawton 28
Wall Street Journal 140
Walton, Howard 108
Ware, John 108
Washington 6, 47, 68, 100, 101, 102, 107, *Post* 9, State 22
Watergate Scandal 7
Water Resources Act 51
Webb, Carroll 3
Webster, Dan 108
Weissenborn, Lee 16
Werner and Wollack 39
Werner, Seth 37
West Palm Beach 2, 3, 6, 41, 48, 71, 89, 100, 106
West Point 18
West Virginia 7, 18, 95
Westinghouse Corporations 13
Wetherell, T.K. 108
White House 68, 100
Whitman, Charlie 9
Whitman Plumbing 9
Who's Who in American Colleges and Universities 8
Wildcat 41
Williams, Elizabeth 90
Williams, Herb 90
Williams, Jim 67, 68
Williams, Susan 27
Winn, Steve 13
WIOD 54
Wollack, Dick 37
WPLG 85, 107
WPLG/ABC 107
WQAM 54
Wren, Daniel 17
Wright, Frank Lloyd 5
WSVN/NBC 107
WTVJ 107
WTVJ/CBS 107
WVCG 54

The Golden Years ...   246   Robert McKnight

Y

YD's 28
Yordon, Gary 84
Young Democrats 29
Young, Roy 140

Z

Zinkell, Bill 89